HIERARCHICAL HYPERCUBE MULTICOMPUTER INTERCONNECTION NETWORKS

ELLIS HORWOOD SERIES IN COMPUTERS AND THEIR APPLICATIONS

Series Editor: IAN CHIVERS, Senior Analyst, The Computer Centre, King's College, London, and formerly Senior Programmer and Analyst, Imperial College of Science and Technology, University of London

Abramsky, S. & Hankin, C.J.	ABSTRACT INTERPRETATION OF DECLARATIVE LANGUAGES
Alexander, H.	FORMALLY-BASED TOOLS AND TECHNIQUES FOR HUMAN–COMPUTER DIALOGUES
Atherton, R.	STRUCTURED PROGRAMMING WITH BBC BASIC
Atherton, R.	STRUCTURED PROGRAMMING WITH COMAL
Baeza-Yates, R.A.	TEXT SEARCHING ALGORITHMS
Bailey, R.	FUNCTIONAL PROGRAMMING WITH HOPE
Barrett, R., Ramsay, A. & Sloman, A.	POP-11
Berztiss, A.	PROGRAMMING WITH GENERATORS
Bharath, R.	COMPUTERS AND GRAPH THEORY
Bishop, P.	FIFTH GENERATION COMPUTERS
Bullinger, H.-J. & Gunzenhauser, H.	SOFTWARE ERGONOMICS
Burns, A.	NEW INFORMATION TECHNOLOGY
Carberry, J.C.	COBOL
Carlini, U. & Villano, U.	TRANSPUTERS AND PARALLEL ARCHITECTURES
Chivers, I.D.	AN INTRODUCTION TO STANDARD PASCAL
Chivers, I.D.	MODULA 2
Chivers, I.D. & Sleighthome, J.	INTERACTIVE FORTRAN 77
Clark, M.W.	PC-PORTABLE FORTRAN
Clark, M.W.	TEX
Cockshott, W. P.	A COMPILER WRITER'S TOOLBOX: How to Implement Interactive Compilers for PCs with Turbo Pascal
Cockshott, W. P.	PS-ALGOL IMPLEMENTATIONS: Applications in Persistent Object-Oriented Programming
Colomb, R.	IMPLEMENTING PERSISTENT PROLOG
Cope, T.	COMPUTING USING BASIC
Curth, M.A. & Edelmann, H.	APL
Dahlstrand, I.	SOFTWARE PORTABILITY AND STANDARDS
Dandamudi, S. P.	HIERARCHICAL HYPERCUBE MULTICOMPUTER INTERCONNECTION NETWORKS
Dongarra, J., Duff, I., Gaffney, P., & McKee, S.	VECTOR AND PARALLEL COMPUTING
Dunne, P.E.	COMPUTABILITY THEORY
Eastlake, J.J.	A STRUCTURED APPROACH TO COMPUTER STRATEGY
Eisenbach, S.	FUNCTIONAL PROGRAMMING
Ellis, D.	MEDICAL COMPUTING AND APPLICATIONS
Ennals, J.R.	ARTIFICIAL INTELLIGENCE
Ennals, J.R.	BEGINNING MICRO-PROLOG
Ennals, J.R., *et al.*	INFORMATION TECHNOLOGY AND EDUCATION
Filipič, B.	PROLOG USER'S HANDBOOK
Ford, N.	COMPUTER PROGRAMMING LANGUAGES
Ford, N.J., Ford, J.M., Holman, D.F. & Woodroffe, M.R.	COMPUTERS AND COMPUTER APPLICATIONS: An Introduction for the 1990s
Grill, E.	RELATIONAL DATABASES
Grune, D. & Jacobs, C.J.H.	PARSING TECHNIQUES: A Practical Guide
Guariso, G. & Werthner, H.	ENVIRONMENTAL DECISION SUPPORT SYSTEMS
Harland, D.M.	CONCURRENCY AND PROGRAMMING LANGUAGES
Harland, D.M.	POLYMORPHIC PROGRAMMING LANGUAGES
Harland, D.M.	REKURSIV
Harris, D.J.	DEVELOPING DEDICATED DBASE SYSTEMS
Henshall, J. & Shaw, S.	OSI EXPLAINED, 2nd Edition
Hepburn, P.H.	FURTHER PROGRAMMING IN PROLOG
Hepburn, P.H.	PROGRAMMING IN MICRO-PROLOG MADE SIMPLE
Hill, I.D. & Meek, B.L.	PROGRAMMING LANGUAGE STANDARDISATION
Hirschheim, R., Smithson, S. & Whitehouse, D.	MICROCOMPUTERS AND THE HUMANITIES: Survey and Recommendations
Hutchins, W.J.	MACHINE TRANSLATION
Hutchison, D.	FUNDAMENTALS OF COMPUTER LOGIC
Hutchison, D. & Silvester, P.	COMPUTER LOGIC
Koopman, P.	STACK COMPUTERS
Koops, A. & J. Dreijklufft	WORKING WITH COREL DRAW!
Kenning, M.-M. & Kenning, M.J.	COMPUTERS AND LANGUAGE LEARNING: Current Theory and Practice
Koskimies, K. & Paaki, J.	AUTOMATING LANGUAGE IMPLEMENTATION
Koster, C.H.A.	TOP-DOWN PROGRAMMING WITH ELAN
Last, R.	ARTIFICIAL INTELLIGENCE TECHNIQUES IN LANGUAGE LEARNING
Lester, C.	A PRACTICAL APPROACH TO DATA STRUCTURES

Series continued at back of book

HIERARCHICAL HYPERCUBE MULTICOMPUTER INTERCONNECTION NETWORKS

SIVARAMA P. DANDAMUDI

School of Computer Science
Carleton University, Ottawa, Canada

ELLIS HORWOOD

NEW YORK LONDON TORONTO SYDNEY TOKYO SINGAPORE

First published in 1991 by
ELLIS HORWOOD LIMITED
Market Cross House, Cooper Street,
Chichester, West Sussex, PO19 1EB, England
A division of
Simon & Schuster International Group
A Paramount Communications Company

Printed and bound in Great Britain
by Bookcraft Limited, Midsomer Norton, Avon

British Library Cataloguing in Publication Data

Dandamudi, S.P.
Hierarchical hypercube multicomputer interconnection networks
CIP catalogue record for this book is available from the British Library
ISBN 0–13–447798–7

Library of Congress Cataloging-in-Publication Data available

Contents

To

my parents

Subba Rao and **Prameela Rani**

and

my wife and best friend

Sobha

Preface

There is an increasing interest in parallel systems. With the advent of VLSI technology, multiple processor systems are considered economically viable. A wide variety of parallel system architectures have been proposed. These include shared-memory multiprocessor systems and distributed-memory multicomputer systems. This monograph considers general purpose multicomputer systems. These systems communicate by explicitly passing messages.

These types of systems are best suited for applications with "natural" parallelism. That is, the problems permit easy decomposition into several sub-problems that can be executed in parallel. When a collection of processors are executing a parallel solution to a problem, there is a need for the processors to exchange the results of their computations. Thus it is necessary for the processors to communicate efficiently. Much of the power may be wasted if the processors spend a considerable amount of time in communication. The interconnection network is the means to connect the various processors. In a uniprocessor environment, a single interconnection network like the time-shared bus is sufficient. In parallel systems, as the number of processors increases, the interconnection network becomes the dominant component of the system, in terms of both cost and performance. Therefore, it is important to design an interconnection network that is both efficient and cost-effective.

Efficiency is often measured by the network latency. Ideally, we can minimize latency for a particular application if we know the exact communication requirements of the application program that is generating the message exchanges. Then we can minimize communication delay by providing a direct communication connection between the communicating nodes on which the tasks reside. That is, what is required is a match between the structure of the problem and the communication structure of the system (i.e., network topology). Such a close match can only be achieved for special purpose systems which have a narrow application domain.

With general purpose systems, achieving such a match is difficult, if not impossible. So in order to design an efficient and cost-effective interconnection network for general purpose systems, we have to exploit some fundamental phenomena underlying most (at least, a wide class of) applications. The chief characteristic that we exploit to derive an interconnection network is the locality in communication. Locality in memory referencing behaviour has been very successfully utilized in memory management schemes. In this monograph, we show that communication locality can also be effectively utilized in interconnection network design. We use a hierarchical design to exploit locality in communication.

Chapter 2 presents necessary background material on interconnection networks. Hierarchical interconnection networks (HINs), which use a cluster-based organization, are introduced in Chapter 3. Chapter 4 studies the issue of how big "clusters" in HINs should be to achieve optimal performance. Chapter 5 discusses the impact of hot-spot contention in hypercube-based static interconnection networks. Fault-tolerance and reliability issues of binary hypercube-based HINs are considered in Chapter 6. Routing algorithms for binary hypercube-based HINs are considered in Chapter 7. Finally, Chapter 8 concludes the monograph with some general observations on the efficacy of HINs.

Acknowledgements

This monograph is partly based on my Ph.D. thesis, which was supervised by Prof. Derek Eager of the Department of Computational Science, University of Saskatchewan, Saskatoon, Canada. I am indebted to Derek for supervising this thesis. His supervision has significantly contributed to the quality of the research.

My graduate study years have been greatly influenced by Professors Derek Eager, Paul Sorenson, Rick Bunt, and

Udaya Shankar (of the University of Maryland, College Park, U.S.A.). I thank them all for their influence and help during my graduate studies.

The research for the thesis was done between 1986 and 1988. During this period I was generously supported by a scholarship and teaching assistantship from the College of Graduate Studies and Research and the Department of Computational Science, University of Saskatchewan. Without this financial support I could not have undertaken the research reported here. I also gratefully acknowledge the financial support provided in the form of a Post-Graduate scholarship while I was a student at the Indian Institute of Technology, Madras, India.

I would like to thank Sue Horwood for initiating the project and the House and Series editors for making numerous suggestions to improve the monograph.

I have been very fortunate to receive encouragement and support from my parents and my wife. More than anyone else it is these three people who have made everything possible for me. Finally, a special thanks to my wife for her help during the preparation of this monograph.

S. Dandamudi
Ottawa, Canada

1

Introduction

There is an increasing interest in parallel systems. One reason for this interest is the need to increase execution speed and fault-tolerance in today's computer systems. The other, and perhaps more important, reason is to broaden the realm of solvable problems by bringing more complex problems into solvable range.

Traditionally, improved performance was obtained by incorporating improvements in component technology (e.g., faster CPUs) and modifications to the von Neumann architecture. For over a period of three decades the component technology as measured by the delay time has improved 1000-fold, while the computer performance as measured by the number of operations executed per second has improved by a factor of 10^5 [HOCK 81]. The extra improvement, over that provided by gate delay times, is attributable to the improvements in system architectures. It is, however, becoming increasingly difficult to obtain order of magnitude performance improvements by such techniques alone. Recent advances in VLSI technology have made it feasible to construct a computer system utilizing a large number of small processors.

Flynn [FLYN 72] characterized computer system architectures into four categories based on the number of instruction streams and the number of data streams. Single (SI) or multiple (MI) instruction streams may be combined with single (SD) or multiple (MD) data streams to form an architectural category. By this classification, the von Neumann model belongs to the SISD category. Of the four possible architectural categories, SIMD and MIMD are considered generally useful for parallel processing applications. The MIMD category can further be divided into shared-memory MIMD systems and distributed-memory MIMD systems. These three types of systems are described briefly in Section 1.1.

These types of systems are best suited for applications with "natural" parallelism. That is, the problems permit easy decomposition into several sub-problems that can be executed in parallel. When a collection of processors are executing a parallel solution to a problem, there is a need for the processors to exchange the results of their computations. Thus it is necessary for the processors to communicate efficiently. Much of the power may be wasted if the processors spend a considerable amount of time in communication. The interconnection network is the means to connect the various entities (processors, memory modules, etc.). In a uniprocessor environment, a single interconnection network like the time-shared bus is sufficient. In parallel systems, as the number of processors increases, the interconnection network becomes the dominant component of the system, in terms of both cost and performance.

The suitability of an interconnection network for a target system depends on the kind of applications that the system is going to support. Parallel systems can be broadly divided into two classes depending on the type of applications that run on them: special purpose systems and general purpose systems. There are advantages and disadvantages associated with each type of system. These are discussed in Section 1.2. Section 1.3 gives an overview of the monograph.

1.1. A Taxonomy of Parallel Systems

There are several classifications of parallel systems. For the purposes of our discussion, Flynn's taxonomy of computer systems, which is simple and popular, is sufficient. The Further Reading section at the end of this chapter contains references that provide details on other classifications. This section discusses SIMD and MIMD architectural categories of Flynn's taxonomy.

1.1.1. SIMD Systems

In SIMD systems, which are sometimes called array processors, multiple processing elements (PEs) operate in lock-step performing the same operation on different data. Figure 1.1 shows the architecture of a typical SIMD system. Typically, these processing elements receive the same broadcast instruction. The results computed by one PE can be transmitted to another PE in synchronous fashion. An interconnection network is used for such data routing. SIMD systems are faster than the von Neumann model in two ways:

- they avoid a separate instruction fetch for each data item, and
- the execution of the data items can be done in parallel.

The Illiac IV [BOUK 72] and Goodyear Aerospace's massively parallel processor (MPP) [BATC 80] are examples of this type of architecture. The Illiac IV has one central control unit and 64 mesh-connected processing elements (PEs). The control unit broadcasts an instruction to be executed on local data by all PEs. Such array processors are suitable to a class of very structured problems that usually involve a large proportion of array data types.

The MPP contains 16,384 bit-serial processing elements connected in a square array with strictly nearest-neighbour connections. The MPP can input or output data from either side of the 128×128 square array. The MPP was built for NASA primarily to process satellite imagery at high speed. Preliminary studies indicate that MPP can also support general image processing, weather simulation, and aerodynamic studies [HAYN 82].

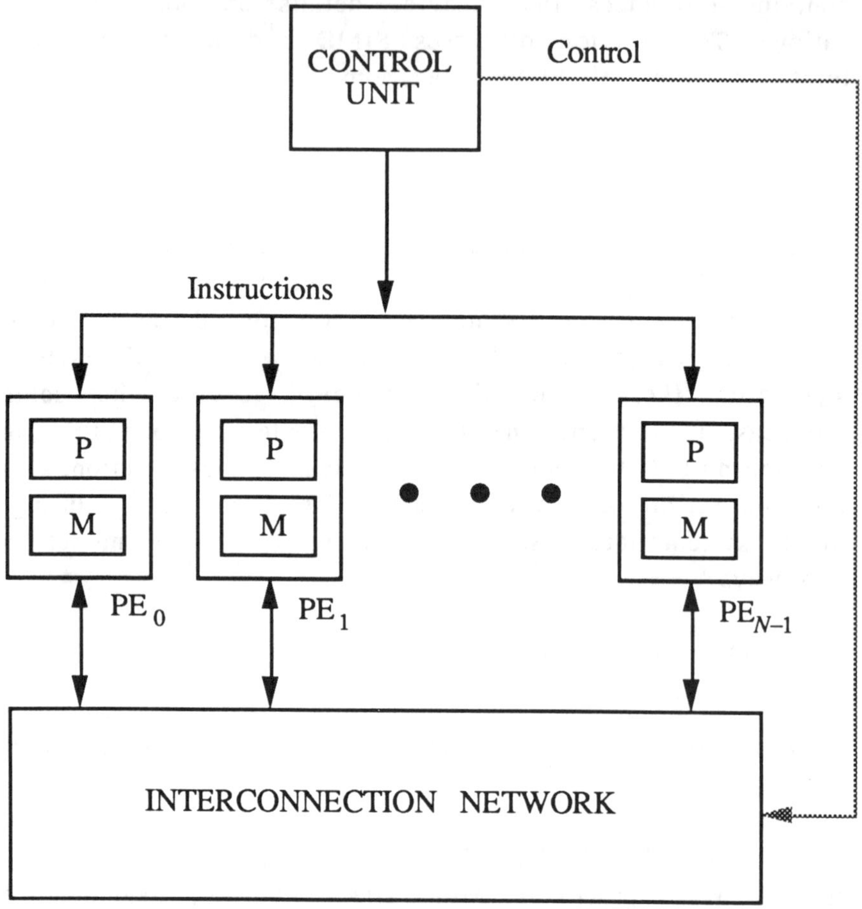

Figure 1.1 A typical SIMD system organization

The Connection Machine [HILL 85] can also be included in this class. As stated earlier, SIMD architecture limits their applicability and they are not as widely accepted commercially as MIMD systems. The next section discusses MIMD systems.

1.1.2. MIMD Systems

With the advent of VLSI technology, multiple processor systems are considered economically viable. In these systems, each processor is fully programmable and can execute its own program. These types of systems are general purpose, asynchronous machines and are more widely accepted commercially than the SIMD systems. The price for this generality in highly parallel systems is decreased speed, decreased efficiency of hardware utilization, and increased software requirements [HAYN 82].

MIMD machines can be divided into two groups: shared-memory systems and distributed-memory systems. Shared-memory systems are also called tightly coupled MIMD systems or multiprocessor systems whereas distributed-memory systems are known as loosely coupled MIMD systems or multicomputer systems. (The distributed-memory systems are also referred to as multi-microcomputer systems [REED 83] or network computers [FRAN 85, BADR 86].) Shared-memory systems can use the memory as a communication medium; distributed-memory systems must communicate by explicitly passing messages.

Both architectural classes are subjects of ongoing research. Bell Labs' S/Net [AHUJ 83], the Cosmic Cube [SEIT 85], the Intel iPSC [RATT 85], and the NCUBE/ten [HAYE 86] are examples of distributed-memory systems. The Butterfly Parallel Processor [CROW 85], the IBM RP3 [PFIS 85a, BRAN 85], the Sequent Symmetry [LOVE 88], the NYU Ultracomputer [GOTT 83] and CEDAR [GAJS 83] are examples of shared-memory systems. Each architecture has its advantages and disadvantages. The shared-memory systems are able to support code and data sharing; but they are architecturally (relatively) complex. The distributed-memory systems are architecturally simple and economical.

There are two important issues that should be considered in the context of parallel systems. These are granularity of tasks and system scalability. The granularity refers to the average size of the interacting tasks that constitute the original problem. It may be defined as the average amount of computation between task interactions.

Since task interactions are typically considered an overhead, the granularity is very much dependent on the amount of overhead incurred for these interactions (either by inter-processor synchronization in shared-memory systems or by message exchange in distributed-memory systems). Ideally, we would like to decompose the program into many small tasks so that we can exploit the inherent parallelism existing within the program to the maximum extent allowed by the problem. If a system can support such fine grain parallelism, then it can support a wide range of applications. The data flow architecture is an example system that exploits parallelism at the instruction level. However, in practice, we need to consider the interaction overhead associated with each system. To execute efficiently the granularity of tasks should dominate task interaction overheads. Thus, among the three systems that we are considering here, the SIMD systems support fine grain parallelism while the distributed-memory MIMD systems support medium grain parallelism with shared-memory systems supporting intermediate grain parallelism.

Scalability refers to the ability of a parallel system to provide speedup that is in direct proportion to the number of processors (i.e., linear speedup), assuming that there are no limitations inherent in the program. One of the factors affecting the scalability of a parallel system is the task interaction overhead. If this overhead scales up super-linearly with the number of processors in the system, then it is impossible to obtain linear speedup. In general, shared-memory organizations are suitable for systems with tens of processors while the distributed-memory organizations are preferred for systems with hundreds or thousands of processors. Hybrid forms may be attractive for systems having intermediate numbers of processors [SEIT 85]. There is a trade-off between scalability and granularity. Typically, increased scalability is obtained at the cost of increased granularity. Shared-memory systems generally have a smaller granularity and scalability than the distributed-memory systems.

1.1.2.1. Multiprocessor Systems

Conceptually, a shared-memory MIMD system can be viewed as shown in Figure 1.2. Processing elements communicate by means of shared memory. However, multiprocessor systems are typically implemented by utilizing an interconnection network as shown in Figure 1.3. The shared memory is divided into M memory modules. The N processing elements in the system can access these memory modules by using an interconnection network. Each processing element contains a processor and some local memory.

Since multiprocessor systems utilize fine grain parallelism (compared to multicomputer systems) the task interaction overhead should be kept to a minimum. This means that the network latency should be small (typically

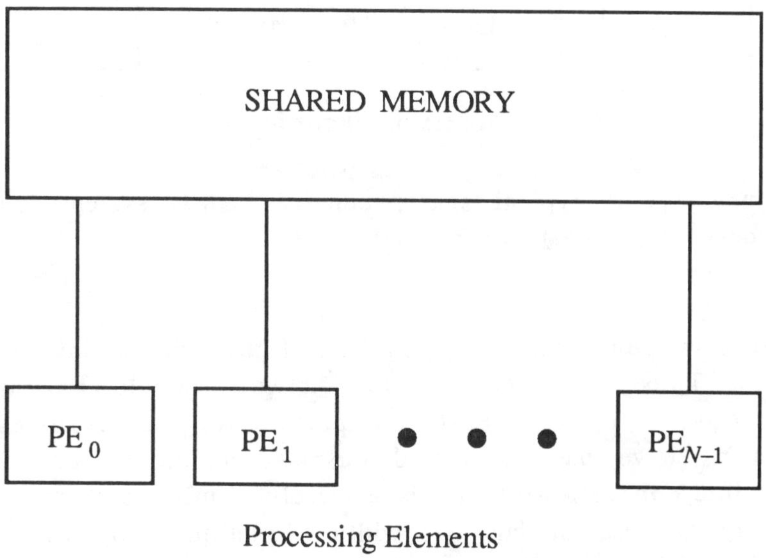

Figure 1.2 Shared-memory model

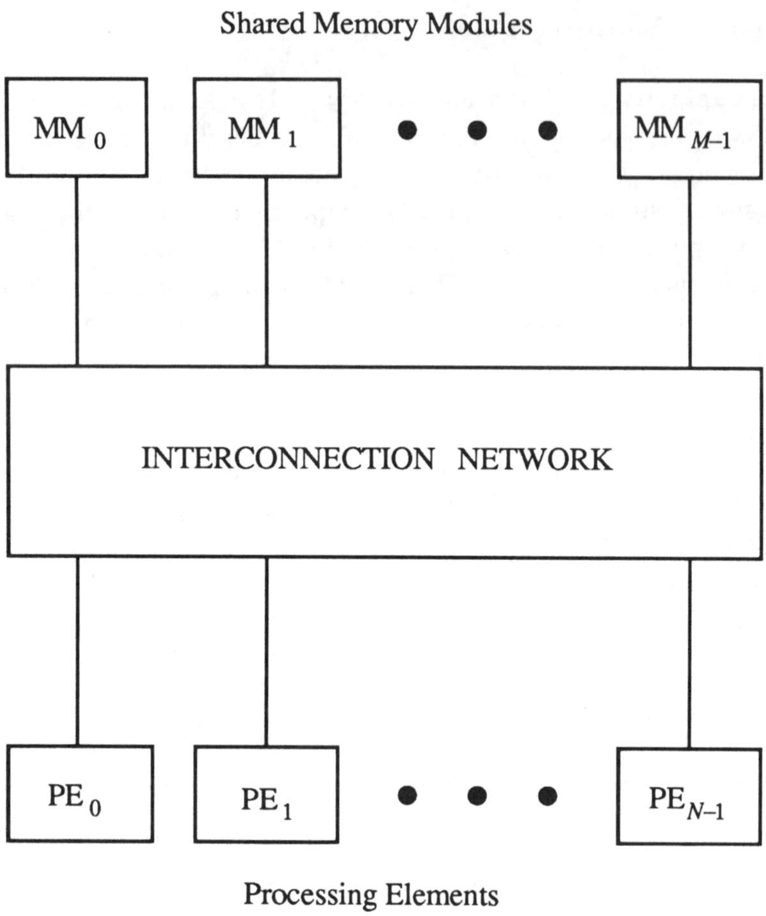

Figure 1.3 A typical shared-memory MIMD system (multiprocessor system)

within a few instruction cycles of the processing elements). Thus the interconnection network should be faster. Although several early experimental multiprocessor systems have used a shared bus as an interconnect, such an interconnection network severely limits system scalability because of bus bandwidth limitations. To avoid this problem, it is common to provide concurrent access to all M memory modules, provided there are enough processing elements requesting access to memory modules and no two processors wish to access the same memory module. For example, such concurrent access can be provided if we use the crossbar network as an interconnect. However, its cost is O(MN) making it too expensive for large multiprocessor systems. Current multiprocessor systems typically use a multistage interconnection network that belongs to the class of dynamic interconnection networks discussed in the next chapter (Section 2.2).

It should be noted that as the number of processors increases the interconnection network becomes the dominant component of the system, both in cost and performance. Therefore, it is important to design an interconnection network that is both efficient and cost-effective.

1.1.2.2. Multicomputer Systems

Multicomputer systems have no shared memory. These systems must communicate by means of explicit message passing. An interconnection network is utilized to facilitate this message passing function. Figure 1.4 depicts the structure of a multicomputer system. The processing elements, which are often referred to as nodes, typically consist of a microprocessor, local memory, and hardware support for message passing. For example, in the Intel iPSC system, each node contains 512K bytes of memory, an Intel 80286 microprocessor, an Intel 80287 floating-point coprocessor, and seven Ethernet transceiver chips to manage internode communication.

Since multicomputers are used with medium grain parallelism, the interconnection network does not have to be as fast as that for the multiprocessor systems. Typically, these systems use interconnection networks with point-to-point connections between nodes. Ideally, it is desirable to connect every node to every other node in the system so that messages can reach their destination in just one hop. However, such complete connection (the dual of the crossbar network discussed in Section 2.2.1) is not feasible for large systems because of its prohibitive cost.

As with the multiprocessor systems, the interconnection network plays a crucial role in determining the system scalability and performance. Again, designing an efficient and cost-effective interconnection network is very important.

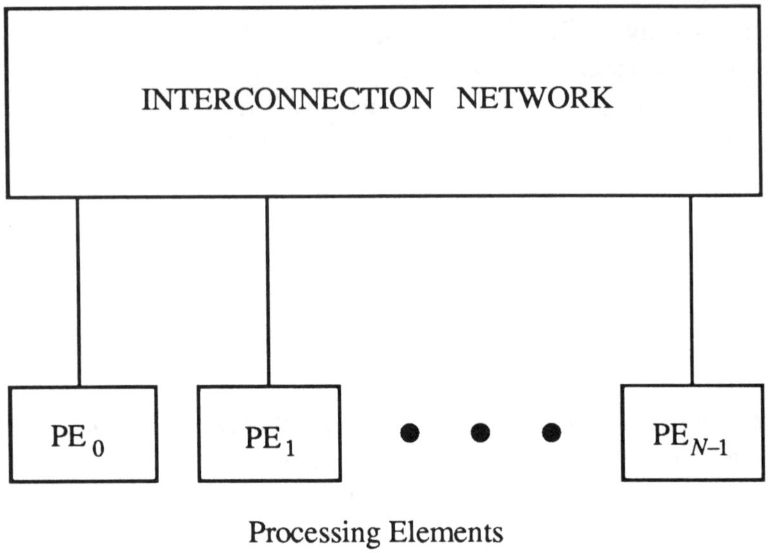

Figure 1.4 A typical distributed-memory MIMD system (multicomputer system)

1.2. General Purpose vs. Special Purpose Systems

There is a trade-off between system efficiency/complexity and the size of the application domain. Special purpose systems are very efficient and relatively simple in solving the problems for which they are designed (i.e., have a narrow domain of applications). On the other hand, general purpose systems encompass a wide range of applications but suffer from decreased speed, decreased hardware utilization, and increased software requirements. It is not yet clear whether the future parallel systems will be special purpose systems or general purpose systems or both. (In fact, there are, as yet, no widely accepted criteria to categorize parallel systems as special purpose or general purpose systems [SNYD 85].)

Harold Stone [STON 85] argues in favour of special purpose systems. He claims that the major advantage of general purpose systems is that they are economical because of their wide area of applicability. But, he argues, the economics of computer systems are changing rapidly because of VLSI and, that this change makes the special purpose systems economically viable.

Gajski [GAJS 85a], on the other hand, feels that there is room for both types of systems. His rationale is that the problem space is constantly expanding and the special purpose systems can only be designed to solve "mature" problems. Since the problem space is expanding, there are always new applications for which no "standard" solution techniques exists. Artificial intelligence may be an example of such an application area. For these applications, general purpose systems are a viable solution.

We believe that there is room for both types of systems. The present research effort to build general purpose multiprocessor and multicomputer systems, both in universities and in research labs, supports this position. Only multicomputer systems that belong to the general purpose category are considered in this monograph.

1.3. Outline of Text

The importance of developing efficient and cost-effective static interconnection networks for multicomputer systems has been established. Efficiency is often measured by the network latency. Ideally, we can minimize latency for a particular application if we know the exact communication requirements of the application program that is generating the message exchanges. Then we can minimize communication delay by providing a direct communication connection between the communicating nodes on which the tasks reside. That is, what is required is a match between the structure of the problem and the communication structure of the system (i.e., network topology). Such a close match can only be achieved for special purpose systems which have a narrow application domain. As an example, in image processing, it is known that it is possible to perform two-dimensional filtering efficiently using a two-dimensionally connected grid of processing elements (by assigning one processor per pixel) [HILL 85]. Here the mismatch between the problem structure and that of the architecture is minimal: the application is two-dimensional and the supporting architecture is two-dimensional.

With general purpose systems, achieving such a match is difficult, if not impossible. So in order to design an efficient and cost-effective interconnection network for general purpose systems, we have to exploit some fundamental phenomena underlying most (at least, a wide class of) applications. The chief characteristic that we exploit to derive an interconnection network is the locality in communication. Locality in memory referencing behaviour has been very successfully utilized in memory management schemes. We show that communication locality can also be effectively utilized in interconnection network design. For the rest of the monograph we concentrate on interconnection networks for general purpose multicomputer systems.

Chapter 2 presents necessary background material on interconnection networks. We discuss two classes of interconnection networks: dynamic interconnection networks and static interconnection networks. Since multicomputer systems typically use static interconnection networks, the emphasis here is on this type of network.

Hierarchical interconnection networks (HINs), which use a cluster-based organization, are introduced in Chapter 3. This chapter also presents performance analysis of a class of HINs. Both static analysis (where queueing delays are neglected) and queueing analysis are presented. In both cases, the HINs are shown to have a better cost-benefit ratio than the structures discussed in Chapter 2. This chapter concludes with a discussion of two performance enhancement schemes for HINs.

Chapter 4 studies the issue of how big "clusters" in HINs should be to achieve optimal performance. Clearly, the resolution of this issue depends on the characteristics of the workload that the HIN is going to support. This chapter considers five types of workload and, for each type of workload, gives optimum cluster sizes. The issue of the number of "levels" that a HIN should have is also considered.

In large parallel processing systems there is a possibility of many processors requesting access to the same data structure, or "service" by the same processor, at the same time. Such hot-spot contention creates congestion in the system, and this congestion becomes more serious as the number of processors involved increases. Chapter 5 discusses the impact of hot-spot contention in hypercube-based static interconnection networks. In order to reduce the adverse effect of hot-spot contention on system performance, two techniques have been proposed for multiprocessor systems: hardware combining [PFIS 85b] and software combining [YEW 87]. The effectiveness of the two corresponding schemes in reducing performance degradation due to hot-spot contention in multicomputer systems is presented. Both infinite and finite buffer cases are considered.

Fault-tolerance and reliability issues of binary hypercube-based HINs are considered in Chapter 6. It is shown by means of simulation that the reliabilities of binary hypercube-based HINs are intermediate between the two extremes provided by bidirectional ring and complete connection. Further, we consider two schemes to improve reliabilities of HINs. Both these schemes use hardware redundancy. We show that both these schemes provide substantial improvement in HIN reliabilities. This chapter also discusses the performance of the two schemes to improve fault-tolerance of binary hypercube-based HINs.

Routing algorithms for binary hypercube-based HINs are considered in Chapter 7. Four routing algorithms are considered: fixed, random, shortest queue, and retrograde routing. We derive bounds on message delay and saturation message generation rate and compare the performance of these routing algorithms in achieving these bounds. It is shown by means of analytical and simulation models that retrograde routing is not useful for asynchronous hypercube networks and the fixed routing results in unacceptable performance in most cases. The random routing provides substantially better performance than the fixed routing while the shortest queue routing provides performance close to the maximum attainable.

Finally, Chapter 8 concludes the monograph with some general observations on the efficacy of HINs.

Further Reading

Flynn's taxonomy looks at computer systems at a very high level. This simple classification has been enlarged in several different directions by including more details of system behaviour. For more details on this topic, the reader is referred to the following references: [ALMA 89], [DUNC 90], [ENSL 77], [GAJS 85b], [HAND 77], [HAYN 82], and [HWAN 84].

References

[AHUJ 83] S. Ahuja, "S/Net: A High-Speed Interconnect for Multiple Computers," *IEEE Selected Areas in Communications*, Vol. SAC-1, No. 5, November 1983, pp. 751-756.

[ALMA 89] G. S. Almasi and A. Gottlieb, *Highly Parallel Computing*, Benjamin/Cummings, Redwood City, California, 1989.

[BADR 86] H. G. Badr, D. Gelernter, and S. Podar, "An Adaptive Communications Protocol for Network Computers," *Performance Evaluation*, Vol. 6, March 1986, pp. 35-51.

[BATC 80] K. E. Batcher, "Design of a Massively Parallel Processor," *IEEE Trans. Computers*, Vol. C-29, No. 9, September 1980, pp. 836-840.

[BOUK 72] W. J. Bouknight, S. A. Danenberg, D. E. McIntyre, J. M. Randall, A. H. Sameh, and D. L. Slotnick, "The Illiac IV System," *Proc. IEEE*, Vol. 60, April 1972, pp. 369-379.

[BRAN 85] W. C. Brantley, K. P. McAuliffe, and J. Weiss, "RP3 Processor-Memory Element," *Proc. 1985 Int. Conf. Parallel Processing*, 1985, pp. 782-789.

[CROW 85] W. Crowther et al., "Performance Measurements on a 128-node Butterfly Parallel Processor," *Proc. 1985 Int. Conf. Parallel Processing*, 1985, pp. 531-540.

[DUNC 90] R. Duncan, "A Survey of Parallel Computer Architecture," *Computer*, Vol. 23, No. 2, February 1990, pp. 5-16.

[ENSL 77] P. H. Enslow, "Multiprocessor Organization," *ACM Computing Surveys*, Vol. 9, March 1977, pp. 103-129.

[FLYN 72] M. J. Flynn, "Some Computer Organizations and Their Effectiveness," *IEEE Trans. Computers*, Vol. C-21, No. 9, September 1972, pp. 948-960.

[FRAN 85] A. J. Frank, L. D. Wittie, and A. J. Bernstein, "Multicast Communication on Network Computers," *IEEE Software*, Vol. 2, No. 3, May 1985, pp. 49-61.

[GAJS 83] D. Gajski, D. Kuck, D. Lawrie, and A. Sameh, "CEDAR," Department of Computer Science, University of Illinois, Urbana, 1983. (Reprinted in *Tutorial on Supercomputers: Design and Applications*, (ed.) K. Hwang, IEEE Computer Society Press, 1983, pp. 251-275.)

[GAJS 85a] D. D. Gajski, "Does general Purpose Mean Good for Nothing?," in *Algorithmically Specialized Parallel Computers*, (eds.) L. Snyder, L. H. Jamieson, D. B. Gannon, and H. J. Siegel, Academic Press, 1985, pp. 249-250.

[GAJS 85b] D. D. Gajski and J. K. Peir, "Comparison of Five Multiprocessor Systems," *Parallel Computing*, Vol. 2, November 1985, pp. 265-282.

[GOTT 83] A. Gottlieb et al., "The NYU Ultracomputer – Designing a MIMD, Shared Memory Parallel Machine," *IEEE Trans. Computers*, Vol. C-32, No. 2, February 1983, pp. 175-189.

[HAND 77] W. Handler, "The Impact of Classification Schemes on Computer Architecture," *Proc. 1977 Int. Conf. Parallel Processing*, 1977, pp. 7-15.

[HAYE 86] J. P. Hayes, T. N. Mudge, Q. F. Stout, S. Colley, and J. Palmer, "Architecture of a Hypercube Supercomputer,"

Proc. 1986 Int. Conf. Parallel Processing, 1986, pp. 653-660.

[HAYN 82] L. S. Haynes, R. L. Lau, D. P. Siewiorek, and D. W. Mizell, "A Survey of Highly Parallel Computing," *Computer*, Vol. 15, No. 1, January 1982, pp. 9-24.

[HILL 85] W. D. Hillis, *The Connection Machine*, MIT Press, Cambridge, MA., 1985.

[HOCK 81] R. W. Hockney and C. R. Jesshope, *Parallel Computers*, Adam Hilger Ltd., Bristol, U.K., 1981.

[HWAN 84] K. Hwang and F. A. Briggs, *Computer Architecture and Parallel Processing*, McGraw-Hill, New York, 1984.

[LOVE 88] T. Lovett and S. Thakkar, "The Symmetry Multiprocessor System," *Proc. 1988 Int. Conf. Parallel Processing*, 1988, Vol. I, pp. 303-310.

[PFIS 85a] G. F. Pfister, W. C. Brantley, D. A. George, S. L. Harvey, K. P. Kleinfelder, E. A. Melton, V. A. Norton, and J. Wiess, "The IBM Research Parallel Processor Prototype (RP3): Introduction and Architecture," *Proc. 1985 Int. Conf. Parallel Processing*, 1985, pp. 764-771.

[PFIS 85b] G. F. Pfister and V. A. Norton, " 'Hot Spot' Contention and Combining in Multistage Interconnection Networks," *IEEE Trans. Computers*, Vol. C-34, No. 10, October 1985, pp. 943-948.

[RATT 85] J. Rattner, "Concurrent Processing: A New Approach in Scientific Computing," *Proc. AFIPS Conf.*, Vol. 54, 1985 NCC, pp. 157-166.

[REED 83] D. A. Reed and H. D. Schwetman, "Cost-Performance Bounds for Multimicrocomputer Networks," *IEEE Trans. Computers*, Vol. C-32, No. 1, January 1983, pp. 83-95.

[SEIT 85] C. L. Seitz, "The Cosmic Cube," *Comm. ACM*, Vol. 28, No. 1, January 1985, pp. 22-33.

[SNYD 85] L. Snyder, L. H. Jamieson, D. B. Gannon, and H. J. Siegel (eds.), *Algorithmically Specialized Parallel Computers*, Academic Press, 1985, pp. 243-246.

[STON 85] H. S. Stone, "Special-Purpose vs. General-Purpose Systems: A Position Paper," in *Algorithmically Specialized Parallel Computers*, (eds.) L. Snyder, L. H. Jamieson, D. B. Gannon, and H. J. Siegel, Academic Press, 1985, pp. 251-252.

[YEW 87] P. -C. Yew, N. -F. Tzeng, and D. H. Lawrie, "Distributing Hot-Spot Addressing in Large-Scale Multiprocessors," *IEEE Trans. Computers*, Vol. C-36, No. 4, April 1987, pp. 388-395.

2

Interconnection Networks

The interconnection network is an important component of a parallel processing system because, as discussed in Chapter 1, it must support communication between a large number of communicating entities (processing elements, memory modules, nodes). The architecture of a suitable interconnection network depends on various factors, including the amount and degree of communication. These factors are directly influenced by the application and the computational model used. For example, an interconnection network suitable for an SIMD machine may not be suitable for an MIMD machine. Section 2.1 discusses the main design issues involved in selecting an architecture of an interconnection network. Section 2.2 briefly presents details on dynamic interconnection networks, which are typically used in SIMD and shared-memory MIMD systems. Static interconnection networks, which are typically used in distributed-memory MIMD systems, are discussed in Section 2.3. Note that we are mainly concerned in this monograph with static interconnection networks. Section 2.4 gives a summary of the chapter.

2.1. Introduction

When a collection of processors are executing a parallel solution to a problem, there is often a need for the processors to exchange the results of their computations. Much of the power of the overall system may be wasted if the processors spend a considerable amount of time in communication. Thus there is need for the processors to communicate efficiently. The interconnection network is the means by which the various entities – processors, memory modules, etc. – communicate. In a uniprocessor environment, a single interconnection network like the time-shared bus may be sufficient. For multiple processor systems, as the number of processors increases, the interconnection network becomes the dominant component, in terms of both cost and performance of the system.

The interconnection network, therefore, is an important component of a parallel system. The suitability of an interconnection network for a target system depends on the kind of applications that the system is going to support. In selecting the architecture of an interconnection network, there are four design issues that should be considered [FENG 81]. These are mode of operation, control strategy, switching method, and network topology. These issues are discussed briefly (see [FENG 81] for a more detailed discussion).

- *Mode of Operation:* This refers to the type of communication used: *asynchronous* or *synchronous*. Synchronous mode of operation is characterized by a system-wide clock signal that is used by all devices in the system to operate in a lock-step fashion. Since the clock signal dictates the activities of the entire system, clock distribution is very crucial. Clock skew poses major problems in synchronizing large systems because each device in the system may not receive the clock signal at the same time [KUNG 88]. This may seriously affect system expandability. Further, this global synchronization causes problems of peak power[1] and fault-tolerance. In an asynchronous mode of operation, the clocking problem can be alleviated because no global clock is required.

Typically, SIMD machines use synchronous communication while the MIMD machines use asynchronous communication. For example, the Connection Machine, which is an SIMD machine, uses synchronous communication [HILL 85]. The NCUBE/ten [HAYE 86] and the Intel iPSC [RATT 85] systems, which are MIMD systems, operate in asynchronous mode.

- *Control Strategy:* This refers to how the routing is achieved. The two major types of control strategies are *centralized* control and *distributed* control. In a centralized control strategy, all routing information comes from the central controller. For large systems, this central controller may become a bottleneck that directly affects the overall system performance. Further, as with the global clock generator in synchronous systems, the existence of a single controller leads to fault-tolerance and system expandability problems.

  The distributed control strategy avoids these problems by allowing each device to do routing locally. The distributed control strategy results in a uniform device structure (i.e., all devices have the same structure) and improves system reliability substantially. For these reasons, distributed control is often preferred over centralized control.

- *Switching Method:* The two major switching methods are *circuit switching* and *packet switching*. In circuit switching, a circuit (i.e., a physical path) between pairs

---

[1] In large systems, synchronous transfer of data between large number of devices (i.e., data transfer occurring simultaneously between devices such as buffers) can lead to power supply induced noise problems due to large current surges as the components simultaneously change state.

of nodes is established and released asynchronously. In packet switching, packets of fixed size move through the stages of the network without actually establishing a complete path. In general, circuit switching is preferred for large data messages and packet switching is more efficient for short data messages. When the load is light (and when the amount of data to be transmitted is large enough to make circuit switching worthwhile), circuit switching is faster than packet switching because transmission occurs in parallel on each link of the path between the source and destination nodes. The performance of circuit switching, however, degrades rapidly as load increases [BADR 86]. A third method, called *staged circuit switching* (or similar "wormhole" routing [DALL 87, DALL 90]), combines aspects of circuit switching and packet switching [ARAN 85]. When the load is light, staged circuit switching behaves like circuit switching and at heavy loads it behaves like packet switching.

- *Network Topology:* Network topologies can be classified into two groups: *static* and *dynamic*. In a static topology, links are passive, and cannot be reconfigured to provide direct connections between different pairs of nodes. In a dynamic topology, links can be reconfigured dynamically. The dynamic networks are also called reconfigurable switching networks. Dynamic topologies have most often been used in SIMD and multiprocessor systems and the static topologies in multicomputer systems, although some could be used with the other type of architecture. Dynamic interconnection networks are discussed in the next section and static interconnection networks are discussed in Section 2.3.

Interconnection networks can be classified by one of these design issues. The most commonly used classifications are based on the last two design issues. A combination of these design issues is also used to classify interconnection networks [BHUY 89]. Several surveys have summarized work on this topic [e.g., BROO 83, FENG 81, SIEG 79, MASS 79, ANDE 75].

2.2. Dynamic Interconnection Networks

Dynamic interconnection networks typically involve a switching element of some sort to allow for dynamic reconfiguration of the network. There have been a variety of networks proposed in the literature. These networks represent a trade-off between cost and performance. In this section, we briefly discuss the following dynamic interconnection networks (presented in order of increasing cost and performance).

- Bus networks
- Single-stage shuffle-exchange networks
- Multistage shuffle-exchange networks
- Crossbar networks

2.2.1. Bus and Crossbar Networks

These two networks represent two extremes on the cost-performance spectrum. The crossbar network of size $N \times N$, shown in Figure 2.1, requires as many as N^2 switching elements, but the associated delay is independent of the size of the network. This network has the additional advantage of being a *non-blocking* network because it can achieve any permutation (i.e., any input-output connection pattern). However, since its cost increases in direct proportion to the square of the number communicating elements, this network is not practical for large parallel systems.

The bus structure, on the other hand, is the least expensive of the four networks considered here. In this sense, this network represents the other extreme on the cost-performance spectrum. There are several disadvantages associated with this structure. Since several processors share the common bus, the bandwidth available to each processor is inversely proportional to the number of processors. Thus the associated delay increases in direct proportion to the number of processors. In addition, bus loading factors may limit the number of processors to a modest number. Furthermore, a single shared bus causes problems of diminished fault-tolerance. To alleviate these problems, multiple bus structures have been proposed. However, link and switch costs increase as $O(MN)$ if there are M busses for connecting N nodes. Nevertheless, multiple bus structures are the subject of considerable research activity [LANG 82, DAS 85, TOWS 86, MUDG 87].

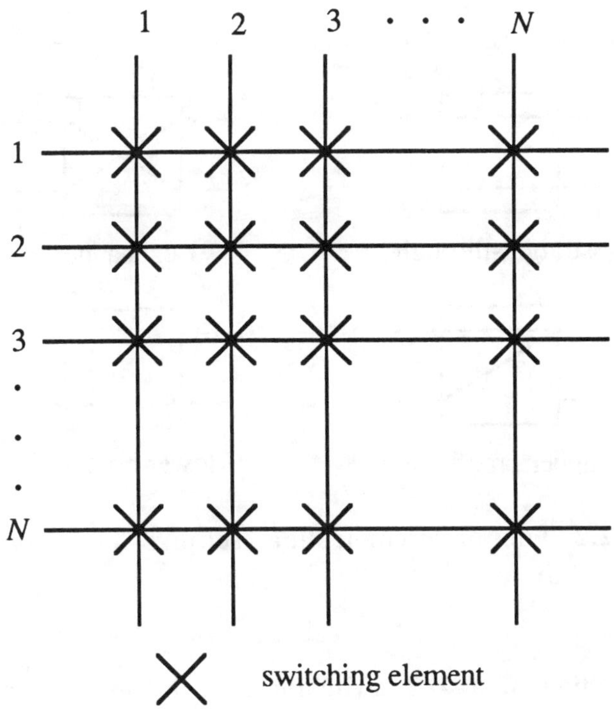

Figure 2.1 Crossbar interconnection network

2.2.2. Shuffle-Exchange Networks

These networks organize a set of switching boxes into stages. Depending on the number of stages used to construct a network, they can be classified as single-stage or multistage networks. Each box is essentially an exchange device that permits dynamic reconfiguration of the network. Here we consider only 2×2 switching boxes. In such a box, there are two inputs and two outputs. Four possible switch settings are shown in Figure 2.2: *straight-through*, *exchange*, *upper broadcast*, and *lower broadcast*. A two-function switching box is capable of achieving either the straight-through or exchange settings. A four-function box can perform any of the four settings. Network performance varies depending on the type of switching box used. In the remainder of this section, we assume a two-function switching box.

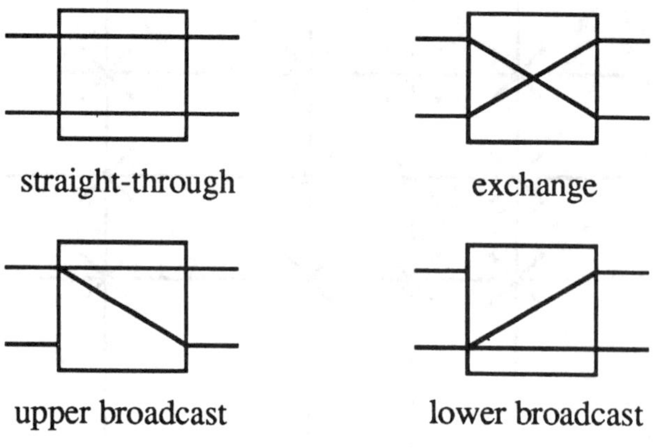

Figure 2.2 Four interconnection settings of a two-by-two switching box

The setting of a 2×2 switching box is determined by two control bits. If the control bit is '1' the input is connected to the lower output port; if the control bit is '0' the input is connected to the upper output port. Thus, of the four possible control bit combinations of a 2×2 switch, two combinations – 01 and 10 – result in straight-through and exchange settings. The remaining two combinations – 00 and 11 – result in conflict and one input must be blocked.

Figure 2.3 shows a single-stage shuffle-exchange network with $N = 8$ inputs/outputs. Note that the corresponding input and output lines are connected together (not shown in the figure). For example, the output line 000 is connected to the input line 000. Since the network uses 2×2 switching boxes, we need $N/2$ boxes to construct the network. This column of boxes is connected to inputs in perfect shuffle wiring pattern. The perfect shuffle is analogous to the process of perfectly interleaving the top half of a deck of cards with the bottom half as shown in Figure 2.4.

We will now briefly describe the routing in a single-stage shuffle-exchange network. In this network we have to use packet switching. There are buffers at the outputs of the switching boxes. The messages may have to recirculate through the single stage several times before reaching their final destinations. For this reason, these networks are also called *recirculating* networks.

We will describe a simple distributed routing scheme. This scheme is *distributed* because switch setting decisions are made locally at each switch (as opposed to being made by a centralized controller). The destination address of the message itself serves as control information that is used to set switch settings. Assume that each message maintains a recirculation count information *RCNT* with it. Every time a message arrives at a switching box, the bit in the destination address that is *RCNT* positions from the most significant bit (i.e., leftmost bit) will be used as the control bit. Suppose node 000 sends a message to node 111. The control bit information (shown underlined) used in routing this message to the destination node is given below.

$\underline{1}11$ during first round
$1\underline{1}1$ during second round
$11\underline{1}$ during third round

Thus, during the first round, the message is at the upper input port of the top switch. Since the control bit is '1', this is routed to the lower output port of that switch. Disregarding the buffers, the message reaches node 001 (i.e., at the upper input port of the second switch from top). Again, since the control bit for the second round is

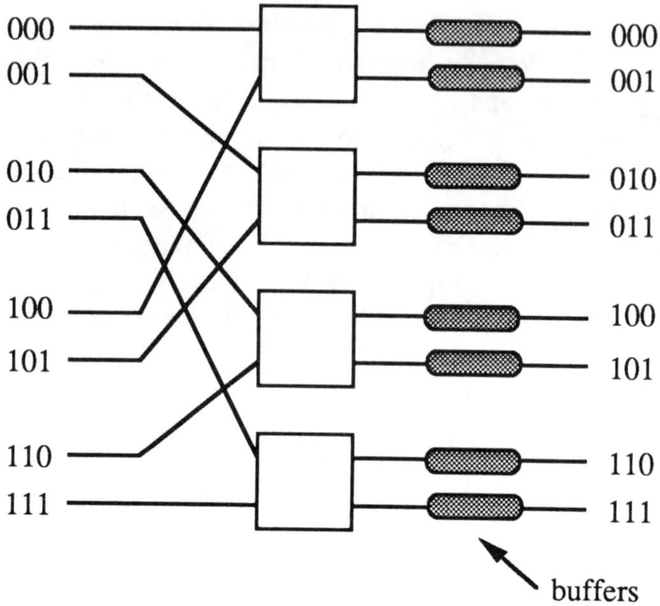

Figure 2.3 A single-stage shuffle-exchange network.

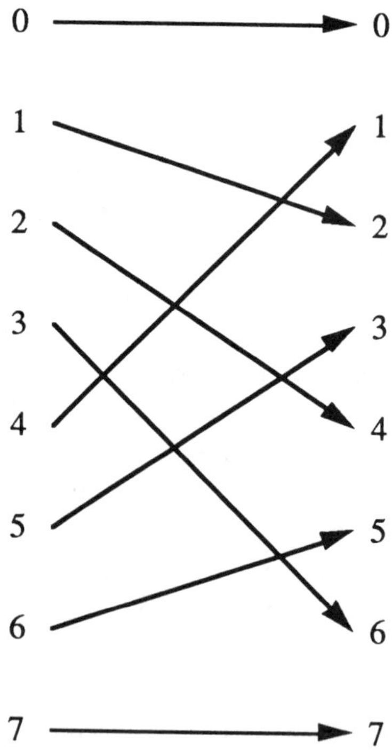

Figure 2.4 The perfect shuffle for $N = 8$.

also '1', the message is routed to the lower output port arriving at node 011 (i.e., at the upper input port of the bottom switch). Since the control bit for the third round is '1', the message finally reaches its destination.

It can be seen from the above description that a message reaches its final destination in *at most* $\log_2 N$ passes. For example, when $N = 8$, a message requires a maximum of 3 passes through the single stage.

In a multistage network, we use $\log_2 N$ stages (each stage is similar to the single-stage network discussed above) as shown in Figure 2.5. This increases hardware cost by a factor of $\log_2 N$ compared to the single-stage network. The messages still experience delay proportional to $\log_2 N$. However, unlike in the single-stage network, *all* messages require a constant $\log_2 N$ steps. However, the bandwidth is $\log_2 N$ times larger for the multistage network because messages can be pipelined in this network. In contrast, in a single-stage network, all $\log_2 N$ passes must be completed before the next batch of messages can be accepted. An additional advantage is that both packet switching and circuit switching can be used in multistage networks.

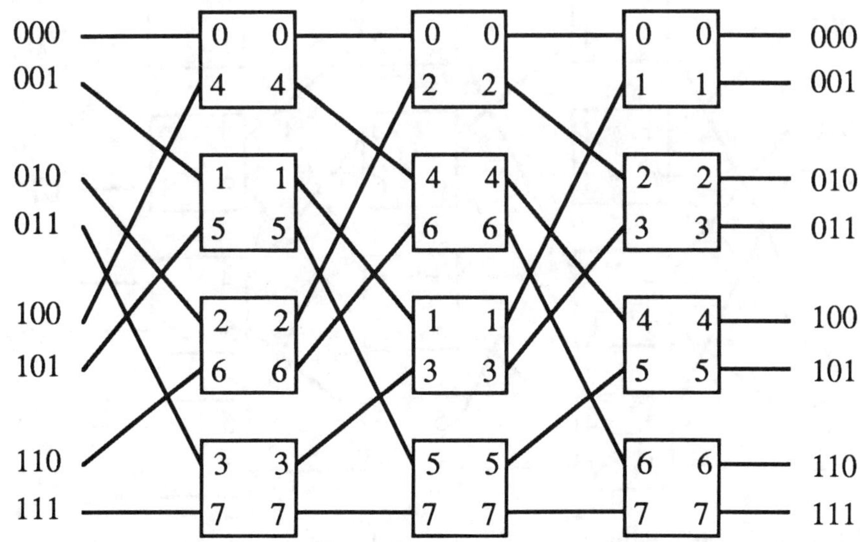

Figure 2.5 A multistage shuffle-exchange network

Message routing in this network is similar to that in the single-stage network. The destination address can be used to set switch settings to route the message to the final destination. Figure 2.6 shows routing of a message from node 101 to node 000 (shown by dotted line). Since all bits in the destination address are 0's, at every switching box, the message is routed to the upper output port. This network, in contrast to the crossbar network, is a *blocking* network. For example, in Figure 2.6, the message path blocks another message path from node 001 to 011.

Several networks have been proposed based on shuffle and exchange routing functions. These include the banyan [GOKE 73], *n*-cube [PEAS 77], Omega [LAWR 75], Benes [BENE 65], and delta networks [PATE 81]. Many of these networks have been shown to be topologically equivalent [WU 80]. These networks differ in the type of switching box used (for example, the Omega network uses a four-function switching box) and the type of control strategy used (i.e., *individual stage control* or *individual box control* or *partial stage control* etc.). More details on these networks can be found elsewhere in the literature [HWAN 84, ALMA 89].

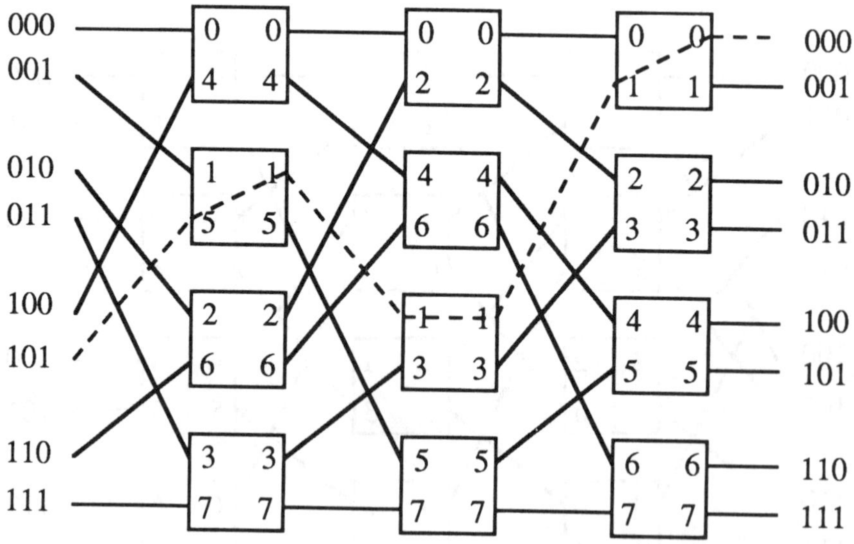

Figure 2.6 Routing in a multistage shuffle-exchange network

2.3. Static Interconnection Networks

Several static interconnection networks are presented in this section. To restrict the scope of our discussion, we focus our attention on link-based structures. For each structure, two measures that are useful for comparison purposes are included. One is the number of links used by the structure. This indicates network cost. The other measure, which indicates network performance, is the average internode distance. The following discussion assumes that messages are uniformly distributed across all the nodes (i.e., no locality in communication is assumed).

2.3.1. Ring Networks

A ring network, shown in Figure 2.7, can be one of two types: *bidirectional* or *unidirectional*. A unidirectional ring relays messages from node to node one way around the loop. In a bidirectional ring, messages can be relayed in both directions. In a unidirectional ring, messages traverse an average internode distance of approximately $N/2$ links where N is the number of nodes in the ring network. The corresponding value for the bidirectional ring network is $N/4$.

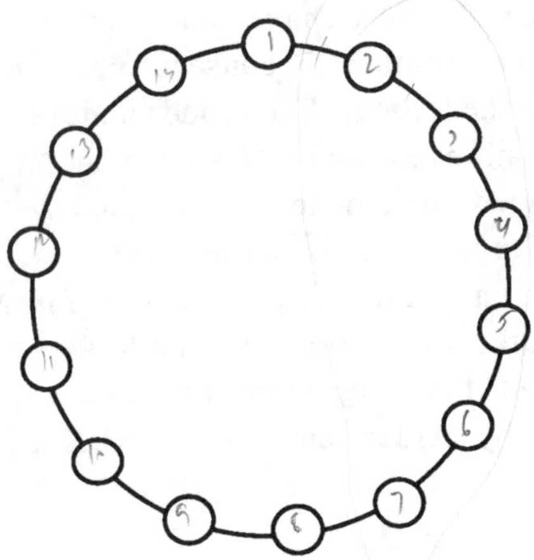

Figure 2.7 Ring network

Each node in this network has a degree[2] of 2. However, since the average internode distance increases linearly with N, the ring is limited to small numbers of nodes. Further, unless redundant paths are added, rings are unreliable. In a unidirectional ring, a single link or node failure leaves the system non-functional. In a bidirectional ring, failure of two nodes or links induces a partition of the network.

The ring network requires the minimum number of links, except for the binary tree, but the average internode distance increases in direct proportion to the number of nodes in the network. This network represents one extreme among the spectrum of networks considered here. The complete connection network, described in Section 2.3.2, represents the other extreme. Ring networks have been used in Local Area Networks. This topology has also been in a dataflow system [GURD 85] and in a multicomputer system [KUSH 82].

The chordal ring [ARDE 81], shown in Figure 2.8, improves the fault-tolerance of the ring network by adding redundant paths in the structure. This is accomplished by introducing *chordal links* between nodes of the simple ring, which also reduce the maximum number of links that must be traversed to reach a destination node.

In a chordal ring network, every node has one of these chordal links, so each node has a degree of 3. A chordal ring with degree 3 must have an even number of nodes. Let the nodes be numbered consecutively 0, 1, 2,..., $N-1$ clockwise round the clock. Each odd node i is connected by chordal link to an even node $(i+w) \bmod N$, and each even node j is connected to a node $(j-w) \bmod N$. The value w is called *chord length* and is assumed to be an odd integer. Figure 2.8 shows a chordal ring network for $N = 14$ and $w = 5$. In this network, the chord of length w is repeated every two nodes around the ring (said to have a *period* of 2). It has been shown by Arden and Lee [ARDE 81] that the opti-

---

[2]Informally, *degree* refers to the number of link connections of a node.

mal chord length for a given diameter[3] k, where k is odd and greater than or equal to 7, is given by $w_{opt}(k) = k + 4$ and the number of nodes in the network is given k^2+3k-6. For a 64-node network (i.e., $k = 7$), $w_{opt} = 11$. A generalized chordal ring can also be obtained by increasing the degree of each node and using varying chord lengths [DOTY 84].

In the chordal ring network, there is more than one shortest path between most pairs of nodes in the network. Routing in this topology is more involved than in a simple ring network. We omit the details here and refer the reader to [ARDE 81] for a discussion of routing in chordal ring networks.

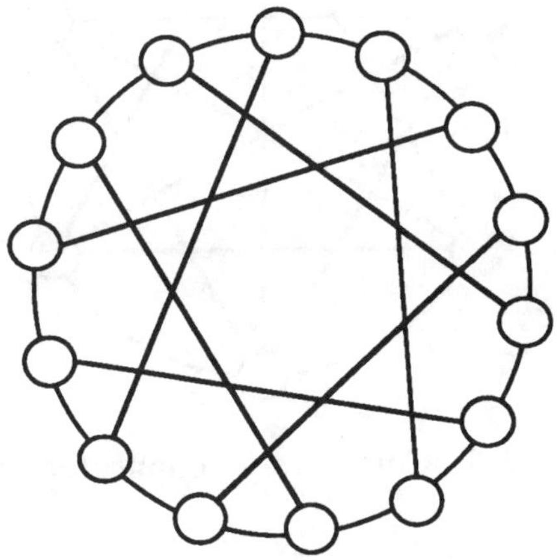

Figure 2.8 Chordal ring network

2.3.2. Completely Connected Networks

In this topology, shown in Figure 2.9, there is a dedicated link between each pair of nodes. Thus, in a N-node network, each node has a degree of $(N-1)$. The number of links in such a network is $N(N-1)/2$. Such networks are

---

[3]*Diameter* of a network is defined as the maximum distance between a pair of nodes in the network, where distance is the shortest path length between the nodes.

rarely used for large N because link cost grows as N^2. The use of optical technology may allow for greater values of N [SAWC 87]. Furthermore, the degree of each node is not fixed as in the ring networks. This causes problems with system expansion. As with the ring networks, this network is included for comparison purposes only. It requires the maximum number of links but provides minimum average internode distance among the networks considered. Routing in a completely connected network is trivial.

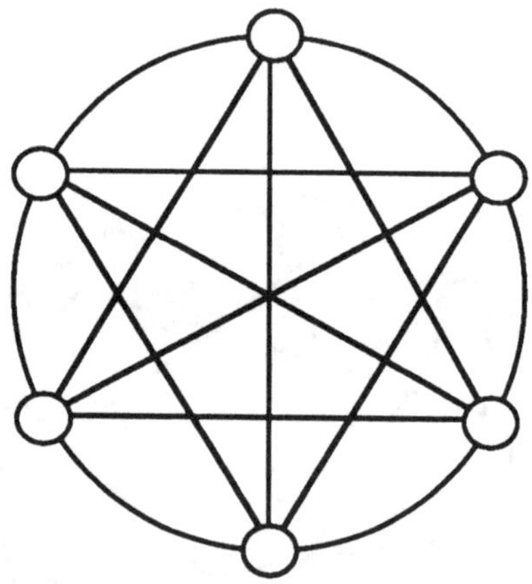

Figure 2.9 Completely connected network

2.3.3. Tree Networks

This interconnection structure [HORO 81, HARR 77], shown in Figure 2.10, is most suitable for tree-structured computations (multi-input, single-output) such as finding the maximum of a set of elements. The link costs grow only linearly with N. The average internode distance in a tree network increases slowly as the logarithm of network size N. As with ring networks, tree-based networks use fixed degree nodes. For the binary tree network, the degree is less than or equal to 3. The leaf nodes have a degree of 1, the root node has a degree of 2, and the internal nodes have a degree of 3.

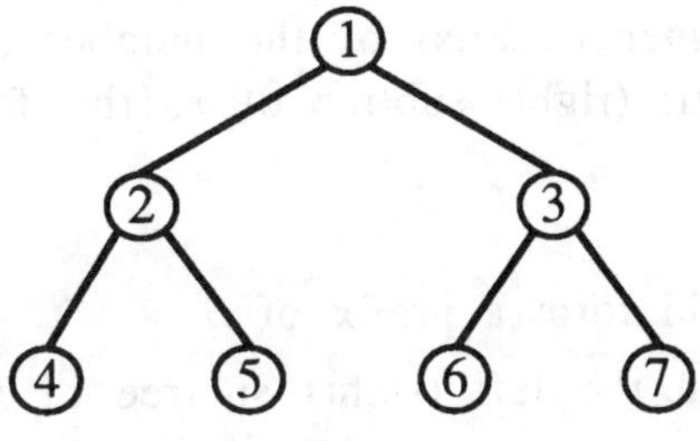

Figure 2.10 Binary tree network

There are several problems with the tree structure. First, message traffic density through single nodes, at or near the root, becomes very high assuming uniform communication among the nodes in the network. This would result in considerable queueing delay at these nodes. Wittie [WITT 81] shows that for binary trees, the message traffic density is the highest in the second level of nodes. For all other trees, with branching factor greater than two, traffic density is the highest at the root. Second, a tree structure is not reliable because it is minimally connected. For example, a single link or node failure can partition the network into two disjoint subnetworks.

Routing

Suppose that node x has a message destined for node B ($\neq x$). Note that the message might have been generated by node x itself or node x might have received it on its way to the destination node. In either case, the message is forwarded down the tree if the destination node is in the left (right) subtree of node x; otherwise, the message is passed up the tree to the parent node of node x.

To determine if node B is in the left (right) subtree of node x, assume that the nodes in the tree are numbered conventionally (i.e., number the root node 1 and number the left and right children of node y as $2y$ and $2y+1$, respectively – see Figure 2.10). It is then straightforward to see that nodes at level i (assume that the root node is at level 1) have numbers, expressed in binary form, that are i bits long. The left and right children of a node have a '0' or '1' appended to their parent's number. Let $|x|$ represent the length (i.e., number of bits) of the number of node x. Then, if B is in the left (right) subtree of x, the following must be true:

- $|x| < |B|$
- x should form a prefix of B
- B is in the left (right) subtree of x if $(|x|+1)$th bit from left in B is '0' ('1')

As an example, consider routing a message from node 3 (11) to node 4 (100). Since 11 is not a prefix of 100, the message is forwarded to the parent node (node 1). Since node 1 forms a prefix of 100 and the second bit from left is '0', the message is passed to node 2 (10). At node 2, the message is again forwarded to the left child because 10 is a prefix of 100 and the third bit from left is '0'. At the final destination node the message is consumed.

Variations

One way to lessen the congestion near the root and to reduce the consequences of a failure of a node or link is to provide extra links. Usually, these additional links are used to connect nodes at the same level in the tree (i.e., all additional links are "horizontal" links). We discuss two variations of the binary tree network.

The X-tree network [DESP 78] is a simple binary tree with all nodes at each level connected by a ring (Figure 2.11). The X-tree network requires a maximum degree of 5. Of course, the root and leaf nodes have a degree less than this.

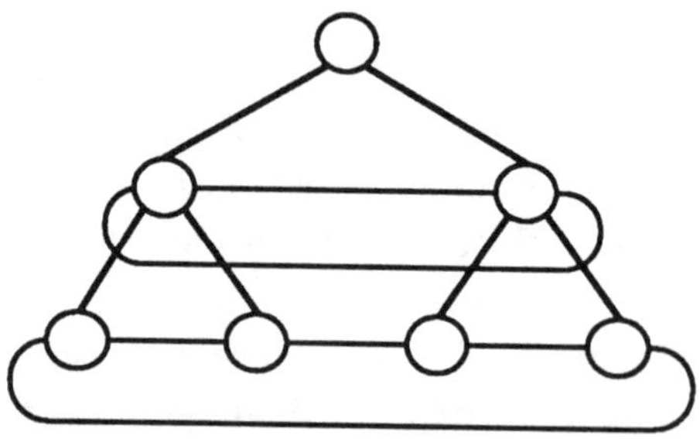

Figure 2.11 The X-tree network

Hypertrees [GOOD 81] provide an alternative way of adding these "horizontal" links to the binary tree structure (Figure 2.12). The hypertree combines the best features of the binary tree and the hypercube (discussed in Section 2.3.5). These links are chosen to be the hypercube connections and they always link nodes that have their binary addresses differing in only one address bit. While each node could be connected to more than one node depending on the level (for example, node 4 at level 2 could be connected to nodes 5 and 6), each node is restricted to having only one additional link connection so that the degree of each node remains fixed. This additional link is selected such that it minimizes the internode distance between the two nodes. For more details on the hypertree construction and routing, see [GOOD 81]. Note that the hypertree networks need a maximum degree of 4.

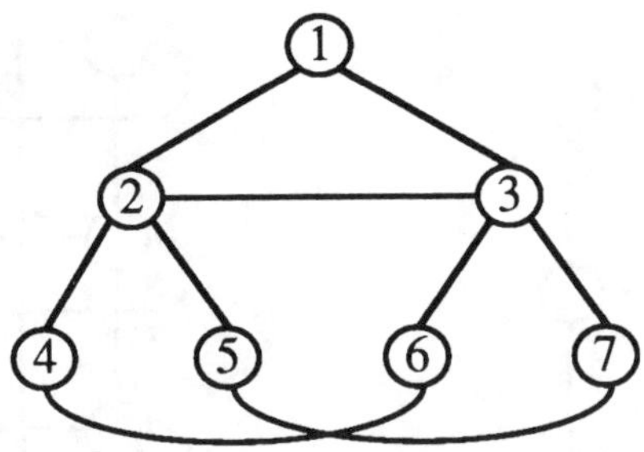

Figure 2.12 Hypertree network

2.3.4. Mesh and Torus

The mesh-connected parallel computer is an important parallel processing organization that has been used for the design of a number of supercomputing systems, such as the Illiac IV[4] [BARN 68, BOUK 72] and the MPP [BATC 80]. Several algorithms have been designed specifically for

[4] Strictly speaking, the Illiac mesh network is the chordal ring network discussed in Section 2.3.1.

mesh-connected computers [e.g., THOM 77, NASS 79, NASS 80, STOU 83, BOXE 89]. A two-dimensional, 3-wide mesh is shown in Figure 2.13a. In general, a mesh can be a W-wide, D-dimensional structure. Most algorithms use two-dimensional meshes, with W varying as needed to ensure the desired number of nodes N $(=W^2)$. A modified version of the mesh, with end-around connections as shown in Figure 2.13b, is called a torus. An advantage of the torus is that this network is symmetric (i.e., all nodes are identical in structure). The number of links in a (W, D) torus is given by DW^D. Note that the mesh is asymmetric because the nodes along the border are different from the rest. This symmetric property of the torus greatly simplifies its analysis. Wittie [WITT 81] presents an analysis of the torus and shows that the average message path length in a (W, D) torus is $(DW/4)$.

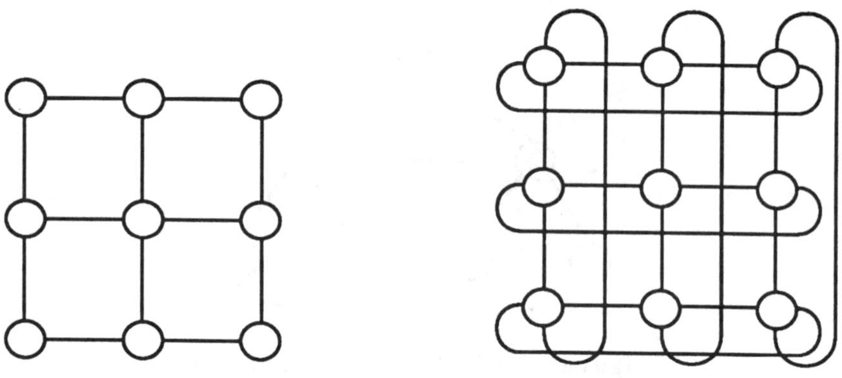

(a) (b)

Figure 2.13 Mesh and torus networks

Routing in these networks is done simply one dimension at a time. For example, assume that we are sending a message in a two-dimensional network from node (a, b) to node (c, d). The message is first forwarded to node (c, b) along one dimension (note that routing within a dimension is similar to routing in a simple ring network) and then it is moved along the other dimension from node (c, b) to node (c, d). Note that this simple routing algorithm uses a shortest path between the source and destination nodes to transmit messages.

There are two ways in which network size $N = W^D$ can be increased.

(1) Dimension D may be fixed and width W may grow as $N^{1/D}$, or
(2) Width W may be fixed and D may increase as log N.

Each method has advantages and disadvantages. If W grows as $N^{1/D}$, the number of connections per node is constant. The same module can be used regardless of network size. However, message delay increases relatively rapidly, as the Dth root of N. If W is fixed as N increases, the average message delay increases only slowly as D increases with log N, but connection costs grow as N log N, and, in particular, the number of connections per node grows as log N. Slow growth in message delay is very desirable. Allowing increases in the number of connections per node, however, would mean a standard node would have to include as many local ports as were required for the largest possible dimension. After D had reached this level, N could be increased only by changing W, causing a corresponding increase in message delays.

2.3.5. Binary Hypercube Networks

The binary hypercube is a special case of mesh network in which each dimension contains only two nodes (i.e., it is (2, D) mesh network). A D-dimensional hypercube contains 2^D nodes. Let the nodes be numbered from 0 to 2^D-1. There is a link between two nodes if their binary numbers (i.e., addresses) differ in only one bit (see Figure 2.14). Thus, expressing the numbers in binary form, each bit represents a dimension. In the three-dimensional case, we have nodes from 000 (0) through 111 (7), connected as shown in Figure 2.14c. The number of links in a D-dimensional network is $D2^{D-1}$. The average internode distance is $D2^{D-1}/2^D-1$. For large N this is approximately equal to $D/2$ where $D = \log_2 N$.

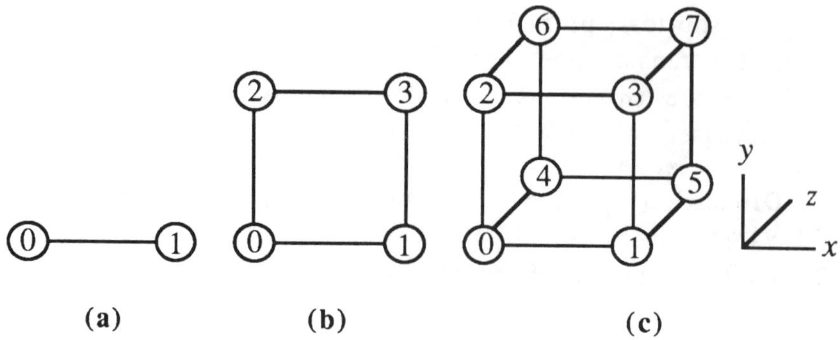

Figure 2.14 Binary hypercube networks (*a*) one-dimensional network; (*b*) two-dimensional network; (*c*) three-dimensional network

Routing in a binary hypercube network is similar to that in a mesh/torus network. However, since each dimension is limited to two nodes, the routing function can be simplified. Note that moving a message along a dimension eliminates the difference in the corresponding address bit. Thus, if a message is to be routed from node A to node B, then the exclusive-or (**xor**) of the source and destination addresses contains 1's only in those dimensions in which the message must traverse in order to reach the destination node. For example, if $A = 101$ and $B = 011$, then A **xor** $B = 110$. Thus the message must traverse once in the y-direction and once in the z-direction. There can be several variations depending on how we choose the order of dimensions to be traversed. Chapter 7 discusses various routing algorithms and their impact on performance.

A disadvantage with the binary hypercube is that it is harder (than with meshes) to expand the system size. A mesh can be increased in size by keeping D fixed and by increasing W. In the binary hypercube, W is fixed. Nevertheless, the binary hypercube is used, for example, in the Connection Machine [HILL 85] and the Cosmic Cube [SEIT 85]. Several commercial systems such as the Intel iPSC [RATT 85] and the NCUBE/ten [HAYE 86] are also based on the binary hypercube.

2.3.6. Cube-Connected Cycle

The cube-connected cycle (CCC) [PREP 81] avoids the problems of system expansion associated with the binary hypercube structure. In the CCC network, each node connects to three links independent of the system size. The CCC can be derived from the binary hypercube by replacing each node by a D-node cycle. A three-dimensional CCC is shown in Figure 2.15. A CCC of dimension D contains $D2^D$ nodes and requires $3D2^{D-1}$ links. Each node is connected to exactly three others by dedicated links: two links (called cycle-links) to neighbours on the same cycle and one link (called a cross-link) crossing the hypercube in one of the D dimensions to the corresponding node in another cycle.

Analysis of this structure [WITT 81] shows that the average internode distance is approximately $(7D/4)-3$ links. The corresponding value for the binary hypercube is approximately $D/2$. Note, however, that the CCC of dimension D has D times more nodes than does the binary hypercube.

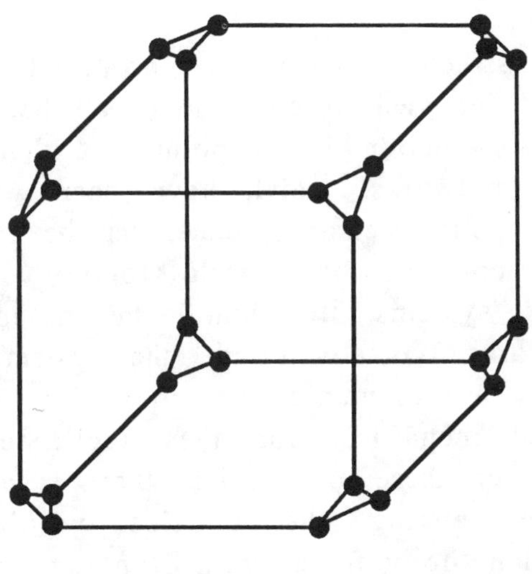

Figure 2.15 Three-dimensional cube-connected-cycles network

The routing algorithm for the CCC network is similar to that for the hypercube network [WITT 81]. To facilitate routing, the node with a cross-link in the ith dimension should be considered as being in the ith position in each cycle. The routing algorithm to send a message from node A to node B in the CCC of dimension D is as follows. The addresses of nodes A and B can be expressed as a cycle position P followed by a coordinate in a D-dimensional binary hypercube: $PC_0C_1 \ldots C_{D-1}$, where $0 \leq P \leq (D-1)$. A check is made as to whether the addresses of nodes A and B differ in coordinate C_P, where P is the cycle position of node A. If the coordinates differ, the message can be routed along the Pth dimension cross-link to a new node with the same index as node A except in the C_P coordinate. If the Pth coordinates are equal, but the message has not yet reached the cycle of the final destination (B) (i.e., not all the binary coordinates match), a cycle-link is used to move to the node in the next position within the same cycle. This new node may then apply this algorithm to send the message on its next hop (if needed).

2.3.7. Other Structures

Several other structures have been proposed in the literature. It is not intended to cover them all here. Rather, the purpose of this section is to point out that dynamic or reconfigurable networks, which have been widely applied to SIMD and multiprocessor systems, can be easily modified to derive a corresponding static topology suitable for multicomputer systems. It should be noted that these dynamic networks typically divide the system entities that are involved in communication into two groups, e.g., processors and memories, and they facilitate communication only between these groups, i.e., there is no support for communication among the entities within a group. Therefore, when deriving a static topology in which all entities belong to only one group, it is necessary to combine in some form the two groups of entities in the original scheme and obtain a closed or circular network.

As an example of this strategy, two sample networks are described here.

The R-ary N-cube [DALL 90, REED 87a, REED 87b] is derived from Pease's [PEAS 77] indirect binary N-cube. In this network, N is the number of levels and RN is the number of nodes at each level. The network contains RN^2 nodes, each connected to $2R$ other nodes. As discussed in the last paragraph, the cube is closed, i.e., the top and bottom rows shown in Figure 2.16 are the same.

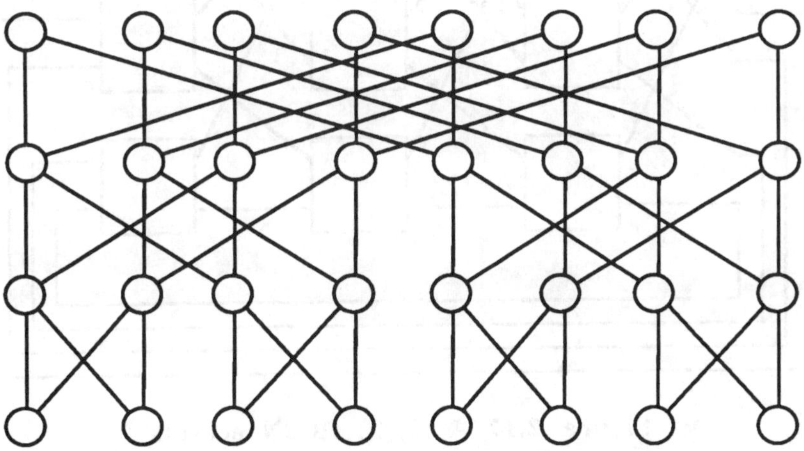

Figure 2.16 R-ary N-cube network

The second example is the homogeneous circular shuffle network (HCSN) [TRIP 86]. This is a circular form of the multistage shuffle-exchange network (see Figure 2.5), with switching nodes considered as processors. HCSN can be specified by two parameters: r and b. An HCSN of (r, b) has r columns with b^{r-1} processors in each column, and thus rb^{r-1} processors in the entire system. Processors in HCSN are homogeneous with b input ports and b output ports. Figure 2.17 is an example of an HCSN. More details on this network can be found in [TRIP 86].

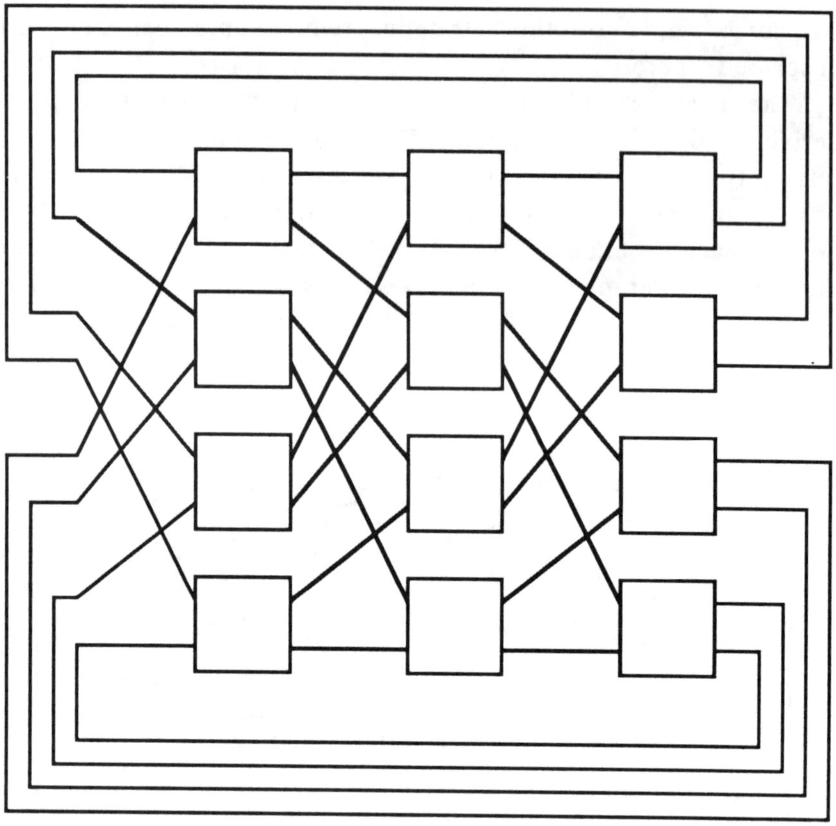

Figure 2.17 A (3, 2) HCSN network

2.4. Summary

This chapter has presented an introduction to interconnection networks. We have discussed both dynamic and static interconnection networks. Since distributed-memory multicomputer systems typically use static interconnection networks, the emphasis of our discussion has been on static interconnection networks.

We have presented several static interconnection networks. These provide a range of choices on the cost-performance spectrum. For reasons discussed in the next chapter, these networks may not be suitable for building large-scale multicomputer systems. The next chapter presents hierarchical interconnection networks as a cost-effective means of interconnecting large numbers of processors in multicomputer systems.

Further Reading

Our discussion of dynamic interconnection networks has been rather brief. We have included several references to survey articles on this other related topics. The following references provide additional information: [SIEG 90], [KOTH 87]. Performance of interconnection networks have been discussed in [REED 87a], [REED 87b], and [BHUY 89]. A detailed comparison of various link-oriented static interconnection networks, discussed in this chapter, is given in [DAND 90]. Performance comparison of multicomputer networks is also given in [AGRA 86], [REED 87a], and [WITT 81].

References

[AGRA 86] D. P. Agrawal, V. K. Janakiram, and G. C. Pathak, "Evaluating the Performance of Multicomputer Configurations," *Computer*, Vol. 19, 1986, pp. 23-37.

[ALMA 89] G. S. Almasi and A. Gottlieb, *Highly Parallel Computing*, Benjamin/Cummings, Redwood City, California, 1989.

[ANDE 75] G. A. Anderson and E. D. Jensen, "Computer Interconnection Structures: Taxonomy, Characteristics, and Examples," *ACM Comput. Surveys*, Vol. 7, No. 4, December 1975, pp. 197-213.

[ARAN 85] M. Arango, H. G. Badr, and D. Gelernter, "Staged Circuit Switching," *IEEE Trans. Computers*, Vol. C-34, No. 2, February 1985, pp. 174-180.

[ARDE 81] B. W. Arden and H. Lee, "Analysis of Chordal Ring Network," *IEEE Trans. Computers*, Vol. C-30, No. 4, April 1981, pp. 291-295.

[BADR 86] H. G. Badr, D. Gelernter, and S. Podar, "An Adaptive Communications Protocol for Network Computers," *Performance Evaluation*, Vol. 6, March 1986, pp. 35-51.

[BARN 68] G. H. Barnes, R. Brown, M. Kato, D. Kuck, D. Slotnick, and R. Stokes, "The Illiac IV Computer," *IEEE Trans. Computers*, Vol. C-17, No. 8, August 1968, pp. 746-757.

[BATC 80] K. E. Batcher, "Design of a Massively Parallel Processor," *IEEE Trans. Computers*, Vol. C-29, No. 9, September 1980, pp. 836-840.

[BENE 65] V. E. Benes, *Mathematical Theory of Communication Networks and Telephone Traffic*, Academic Press, New York, 1965.

[BHUY 89] L. N. Bhuyan, Q. Yang and D. P. Agrawal, "Performance of Multiprocessor Interconnection Networks," *Computer*, Vol. 21, No. 2, February 1989, pp. 25-37.

[BOUK 72] W. J. Bouknight, S. A. Danenberg, D. E. McIntyre, J. M. Randall, A. H. Sameh, and D. L. Slotnick, "The Illiac IV System," *Proc. IEEE*, Vol. 60, April 1972, pp. 369-379.

[BOXE 89] L. Boxer and R. Miller, "Dynamic Computational Geometry on Meshes and Hypercubes," *J. Supercomputing*, Vol. 3, 1989, pp. 161-191.

[BROO 83] G. Broomell and J. R. Heath, "Classification Categories and Historical Development of Circuit Switching Topologies," *ACM Comput. Surveys*, Vol. 15, No. 2, June 1983, pp. 95-133.

[DALL 87] W. J. Dally and C. L. Seitz, "Deadlock-free Message Routing in Multiprocessor Interconnection Network," *IEEE Trans. Computers*, Vol. C-36, No. 5, May 1987, pp. 547-553.

[DALL 90] W. J. Dally, "Performance Analysis of k-ary n-cube Interconnection Networks," *IEEE Trans. Computers*, Vol. C-39, No. 6, June 1990, pp. 775-785.

[DAND 90] S. P. Dandamudi, "A Comparison of Link-Oriented Multicomputer Networks" Research Note, School of Computer Science, Carleton University, Ottawa, Ontario K1S 5B6, Canada, 1990.

[DAS 85] C. Das and L. N. Bhuyan, "Bandwidth Availability of Multiple Bus Multiprocessors," *IEEE Trans. Computers*, Vol. C-34, No. 10, October 1985, pp. 918-926.

[DESP 78] A. M. Despain and D. A. Patterson, "X-Tree: A Tree Structured Multiprocessor Computer Architecture," *Proc. 5th Symp. on Comp. Arch.*, 1978, pp. 144-151.

[DOTY 84] K. W. Doty, "New Designs for Dense Processor Interconnection Networks," *IEEE Trans. Computers*, Vol. C-33, No. 5, May 1984, pp. 447-450.

[FENG 81] T-Y. Feng, "A Survey of Interconnection Networks," *Computer*, Vol. 14, No. 12, December 1981, pp. 12-27.

[GOKE 73] L. R. Goke and G. J. Lipovski, "Banyan Networks for Partitioning Multiprocessor Systems," *Proc. 1st Ann. Symp. on Comput. Arch.*, December 1973, pp. 21-28.

[GOOD 81] J. R. Goodman and C. H. Sequin, "Hypertree: A Multiprocessor Interconnection Topology," *IEEE Trans. Computers*, Vol. C-30, No. 12, December 1981, pp. 923-933.

[GURD 85] J. R. Gurd, C. C. Kirkham, and I. Watson, "The Manchester Prototype Dataflow Computer," *Comm. ACM*, Vol. 28, No. 1, January 1985, pp. 34-52.

[HARR 77] J. A. Harris and D. R. Smith, "Hierarchical Multiprocessor Organizations," *Proc. 4th Symp. on Comput. Arch.*, March 1977, pp. 41-48.

[HAYE 86] J. P. Hayes, T. N. Mudge, Q. F. Stout, S. Colley, and J. Palmer, "Architecture of a Hypercube Supercomputer," *Proc. 1986 Int. Conf. Parallel Processing*, 1986, pp. 653-660.

[HILL 85] W. D. Hillis, *The Connection Machine*, MIT Press, Cambridge, MA.,1985.

[HORO 81] E. Horowitz and A. Zorat, "The Binary Tree as an Interconnection Network: Applications to Multiprocessor Systems and VLSI," *IEEE Trans. Computers*, Vol. C-30, No. 4, April 1981, pp. 247-253.

[HWAN 84] K. Hwang and F. A. Briggs, *Computer Architecture and Parallel Processing*, McGraw-Hill, New York, 1984.

[KOTH 87] S. C. Kothari, "Multistage Interconnection Networks for Multiprocessor Systems," in *Advances in Computers*, Vol. 26, Academic Press, 1987, pp. 155-199.

[KUNG 88] S. Y. Kung, *VLSI Array Processors*, Prentice-Hall, Englewood Cliffs, NJ, 1988.

[KUSH 82] T. Kushner, A. Y. Wu, and A. Rosenfeld, "Image Processing on ZMOB," *IEEE Trans. Computers*, Vol. C-31, No. 10, October 1982, pp. 943-951.

[LANG 82] T. Lang, M. Valero, and I. Alegre, "Bandwidth of Crossbar and Multiple Bus Connections for

Microprocessors," *IEEE Trans. Computers*, Vol. C-31, No. 12, December 1982, pp. 1227-1233.

[LAWR 75] D. Lawrie, "Access and Alignment of Data in an Array Processor," *IEEE Trans. Computers*, Vol. C-24, No. 12, December 1975, pp. 1145-1155.

[MASS 79] G. M. Masson, G. C. Gingher, and S. Nakamura, "A Sampler of Circuit Switching Networks," *Computer*, Vol. 12, No. 6, June 1979, pp. 32-48.

[MUDG 87] T. N. Mudge, J. P. Hays, and D. C. Winsor, "Multiple Bus Architectures," *Computer*, Vol. 20, No. 6, June 1987, pp. 42-48.

[NASS 79] D. Nassimi and S. Sahni, "Bitonic Sort on a Mesh-Connected Parallel Computer," *IEEE Trans. Computers*, Vol. C-28, No. 1, January 1979, pp. 2-7.

[NASS 80] D. Nassimi and S. Sahni, "Finding Connected Components and Connected Ones on a Mesh-Connected Parallel Computer," *SIAM J. Computing*, Vol. 9, No. 4, November 1980, pp. 744-757.

[PATE 81] J. A. Patel, "Performance of Processor-Memory Interconnections for Multiprocessors," *IEEE Trans. Computers*, Vol. C-30, 1981, pp. 771-780.

[PEAS 77] M. C. Pease, "The Indirect Binary n-Cube Microprocessor Array," *IEEE Trans. Computers*, Vol. C-26, No. 5, May 1977, pp. 458-473.

[PREP 81] F. P. Preparata and J. Vuillemin, "The Cube-Connected-Cycles: A Versatile Network for Parallel Computation," *Comm. ACM*, Vol. 24, No. 5, May 1981, pp. 300-309.

[RATT 85] J. Rattner, "Concurrent Processing: A New Approach in Scientific Computing," *Proc. AFIPS Conf.*, Vol. 54, 1985 NCC, pp. 157-166.

[REED 87a] D. A. Reed and D. C. Grunwald, "The Performance of Multicomputer Interconnection Networks," *Computer*, Vol. 20, No. 6, June 1987, pp. 63-73.

[REED 87b] D. A. Reed and R. M. Fujimoto, *Multicomputer Networks: Message-Based Parallel Processing*, MIT Press, Cambridge, MA.,1987.

[SAWC 87] A. A. Sawchuk, B. K. Jenkins, C. S. Raghavendra, and A. Varma, "Optical Crossbar Networks," *Computer*, Vol. 20, No. 6, June 1987, pp. 50-60.

[SEIT 85] C. L. Seitz, "The Cosmic Cube," *Comm. ACM*, Vol. 28, No. 1, January 1985, pp. 22-33.

[SIEG 79] H. J. Siegel, "Interconnection Networks for SIMD Machines," *Computer*, Vol. 12, No. 6, June 1979, pp. 57-66.

[SIEG 90] H. J. Siegel, *Interconnection Networks for Large-Scale Parallel Processing*, McGraw-Hill, New York, 1990.

[STOU 83] Q. F. Stout, "Mesh-Connected Computers with Broadcasting," *IEEE Trans. Computers*, Vol. C-32, No. 9, September 1983, pp. 826-830.

[THOM 77] C. D. Thompson and H. T. Kung, "Sorting on a Mesh-Connected Parallel Computer," *Comm. ACM*, Vol. 20, No. 4, April 1977, pp. 263-271.

[TOWS 86] D. Towsley, "Approximate Models of Multiple Bus Microprocessor Systems," *IEEE Trans. Computers*, Vol. C-35, No. 3, March 1986, pp. 220-227.

[TRIP 86] S. K. Tripathi and S. -T. Huang, "Distributed Resource Scheduling for a Large Scale Network of Processors: HCSN," *Proc. 6th Int. Conf. Distributed Computing Systems*, IEEE Computer Society Press, 1986, pp. 321-327.

[WITT 81] L. D. Wittie, "Communication Structures for Large Networks of Microcomputers," *IEEE Trans. Computers*, Vol. C-30, No. 4, April 1981, pp. 264-273.

[WU 80] C. -L. Wu and T. -Y. Feng, "On a Class of Multistage Interconnection Networks," *IEEE Trans. Computers*, Vol. C-29, No. 8, August 1980, pp. 694-702.

3

Hierarchical Interconnection Networks

This chapter presents the proposed hierarchical interconnection networks. Hierarchical interconnection networks (HINs) are intuitively appealing when a large number of processors are to be connected for the reasons described in Section 3.1. Several hierarchical interconnection networks have been proposed in the literature. Most of these are two-level hierarchical networks. Section 3.2 presents details on some of these networks. Section 3.3 presents the structure of the HINs considered in this monograph. The advantages and disadvantages associated with these HINs are discussed in Section 3.4. A performance analysis of a class of HINs is presented in Section 3.5. This analysis includes both static analysis (i.e., queueing delays are neglected) and queueing analysis. In both cases, the hierarchical networks are shown to have better cost-benefit ratios than the corresponding non-hierarchical networks discussed in Chapter 2. The impact of two performance enhancement schemes – replication of links and improved routing algorithms – on hierarchical interconnection network performance is presented in Section 3.6. Finally, Section 3.7 gives a summary of the performance of HINs.

3.1. Motivation for Hierarchical Interconnection Networks

There are many possible static interconnection networks for multicomputer systems. Some examples, discussed in Chapter 2, are the linear array, bidirectional ring (BR), star, complete connection (CC), dual-bus hypercube [WITT 81], binary hypercube (BH), tree [HARR 77, DESP 78, HORO 81, GOOD 81], and the cube-connected-cycle (CCC) [PREP 81]. These provide a range of choices on the cost/performance spectrum. Table 3.1 summarizes some major points on the spectrum. At one extreme are completely connected networks that provide direct communication between any pair of nodes at the cost of using a number of links that grows with the square of the number of nodes. At the other extreme are ring-like networks which require a number of links that is proportional to the number of nodes, but in which the average internode distance increases in direct proportion to the number of nodes. Bus structures exhibit performance similar to that of the ring networks.

A significant intermediate point on the cost-performance spectrum is represented by hypercube networks. Hypercube networks allow the average distance between any pair of nodes to be O(log N) through a structure in which each node is directly attached to O(log N) other nodes.

There are two main motivations for HINs:

(*i*) to reduce link cost, and

(*ii*) to provide a framework for integrating several network topologies.

Table 3.1 Trade-offs involved in static interconnection networks

Type of network	Number of links	Average inter-node distance
Complete connection	$O(N^2)$	O(1)
Hypercube	O(N log N)	O(log N)
Ring	O(N)	O(N)

First, for very large systems, the number of links needed with a conventional network such as the hypercube may become prohibitively large. This, among other things, imposes a limit on system expansion. Therefore, future systems may be designed to minimize the number of links because most of the system space may be filled with wires [HILL 85].

As an example, consider the NCUBE/ten system [HAYE 86], which organizes 1024 nodes as a binary hypercube. Each node in this system has a total of 20 half-duplex link connections. Using custom-made VLSI chips, the designers could pack as many as 64 nodes on a single 16"×22" printed-circuit board (PCB). The total system consists of 16 such PCBs, and inter-PCB connections require as many as 512 wires from each PCB. (The NCUBE/ten actually uses 640 wires to allow connections to I/O devices.) We can readily identify from this description that an increasing number of links has two important implications for system design. First, as the system size increases, the number of wires required to establish link connections within a PCB (the on-PCB wires) increases. This increases demand for PCB area, which might result in a reduction in the number of nodes that could be placed on a PCB. Second, the number of wires needed to establish inter-PCB connections (the inter-PCB wires) also increases. While the space may not be as critical a problem with these connections, packaging constraints may impose a limit. For the NCUBE/ten system, Figure 3.1 shows the distribution of on-PCB wires to establish the necessary binary hypercube link connections and inter-PCB wires as a function of system size N. Both these types of links increase proportionally to log N and at the same rate. Therefore, minimizing both the types of wires is important for system expansion.

One way to achieve this reduction in the required number of links is to exploit the locality that exists in communication patterns. Hierarchical structures provide a natural way to exploit this communication locality. It is important to note that only locality as a general phenomenon present in many parallel computations is exploited; HINs are not tailored for specific forms of locality or particular

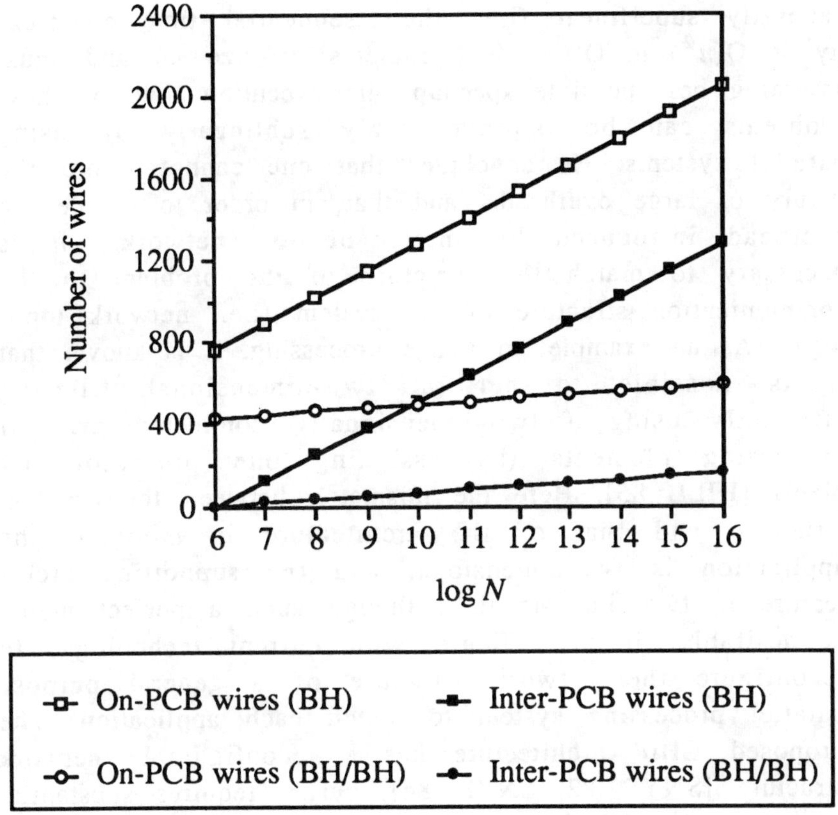

Figure 3.1 Distribution of on-PCB and inter-PCB wires in the BH and BH/BH networks (the PCB is assumed to have 64 nodes as in the NCUBE/ten system; the BH/BH network uses a cluster size of 8)

applications. An analogy can be made with cache or memory management; in these domains as well, a general property of computations (temporal and spatial localities in this case) is exploited without tailoring for specific forms of these phenomenon which might be found in particular applications.

Second, there are a number of compelling interconnection network topologies; each has advantages and disadvantages, and each is most appropriate for its own set of applications. Snyder [SNYD 86] argues that the problems that are of interest in the context of parallel systems are generally superlinear (i.e., their sequential time complexity is $O(n^2)$ to $O(n^4)$ for problems of size n) and thus, assuming best possible speedup, the execution time of these problems can be improved only sublinearly by using parallel systems. He concludes that one cannot afford the luxury of large overheads, and that, in order to reduce the overhead introduced by interconnection networks, it is necessary to match the structure of the problem to the communication structure of the system (i.e., network topology). As an example, in image processing, it is known that it is possible to perform two-dimensional filtering efficiently using a two-dimensionally connected grid of processing elements (by assigning one processor per pixel) [HILL 85]. Here the mismatch between the problem structure and that of the architecture is minimal: the application is two-dimensional and the supporting architecture is two-dimensional. Although such a perfect match is desirable, it is difficult, with current technology, to reconfigure the network structure of a general purpose parallel processing system to match each application. The proposed CHiP architecture has a reconfigurable network structure [SNYD 82, SNYD 84], but it requires substantial advances in VLSI and packaging technologies. HINs provide an alternative way in which several topologies can be integrated using current technology.

3.2. Review of Previous Work

Hierarchical structure has long been used to exploit locality in system behaviour. One successful example is the memory hierarchy used to exploit locality in the memory referencing behaviour of programs. As well, several systems/network structures have been proposed/built with hierarchical structure. In this section, we briefly review previous work in this area and in the next section we present the structure of the hierarchical networks considered here.

Several systems have been proposed with HINs. The Cm* is a two-level hierarchical multiprocessor system

[SWAN 77a, SWAN 77b]. The Cm* is made up of 50 processor memory pairs called compute modules or cm's. They are grouped to form clusters containing up to 14 cm's. Communication within a cluster is via a parallel bus controlled by an address mapping processor termed a *Kmap*. There are five clusters and these communicate via an inter-cluster bus. The Cm* is extensible, either by adding processors to each cluster (up to a maximum of 14) or by increasing the number of clusters.

The Cedar system [GAJS 83] uses a bus interconnection between the processors within a cluster and the cluster memory they share, and a multistage interconnection network between all processors and a global memory shared among all clusters. The global multistage network is based on an extension of the Omega network [LAWR 75] and is similar in concept to the Omega network designed for the Burroughs FMP machine [BARN 81]. Abraham and Davidson [ABRA 86] present an analysis of the Cedar system organization.

Cluster-based multiprocessor systems using a crossbar network are also proposed by Agrawal and Mahgoub [AGRA 85]. They note that the cluster-based scheme provides results closer to a fully connected crossbar-based scheme if the concept of favourite memory (i.e., a processor accesses a favourite memory with high probability) is assumed to be applicable; otherwise, there is substantial degradation in performance (i.e., when memory requests are equally distributed throughout the system). In general, they conclude, a cluster-based scheme offers great potential for future supercomputer systems.

Carlson [CARL 85] proposes a two-level mesh hierarchy scheme: the mesh with a global mesh structure. It is shown that this structure allows dramatic improvement in the efficiency of executing computations organized as a binary tree and for linear recurrences, while for other computations, such as sorting, it offers no improvement.

A cluster structure using shared buses as the basic interconnection media has been proposed by Wu and Liu [WU 81]. Multiple levels of clustering may be present in their organization. Shared buses are used to interconnect the units within a cluster. Structural complexity analysis is given under the assumption of uniform message routing. However, they take message locality into consideration for topological optimization case studies. The locality is modelled by a single parameter LC (similar to the parameter α discussed in Section 3.5.1).

Hwang and Ghose [HWAN 87] have proposed cluster-based hierarchical networks, called *Hypernets*, that can use various building blocks such as the hypercubes, trees, and buses. Another cluster-based hierarchical organization has been proposed by Ghose and Desai [GHOS 89, GHOS 90] that is a two-level hierarchical network based on a hypercube network – the hierarchic cubic network (HCN). A brief comparison of these networks is given later in this chapter.

Hierarchical networks have also been proposed for large store-and-forward packet-switched computer networks [KLEI 77, KAMO 79].

3.3. The Structure of HINs

The hierarchical structure proposed in [DAND 90] is a cluster-based organization. Intuitively, the cluster organization can be viewed as follows: several nodes are grouped into a level 1 cluster; several level 1 clusters are grouped into a level 2 cluster etc. Interconnection networks used at different levels may have different topologies; further, the networks used at the same level may also be different from cluster to cluster. Figure 3.2 shows a two-level heterogeneous HIN: four different network topologies - the binary hypercube, the bidirectional ring, the torus, and the X-tree - are used to interconnect the four level 1 clusters. The level 2 network, which in this example is a complete connection network, links the interface nodes (shown shaded) of the four level 1 clusters.

In the rest of the monograph, for reasons of analytical tractability, we focus our attention to a restricted class of HINs called homogeneous HINs. The structure of the HINs

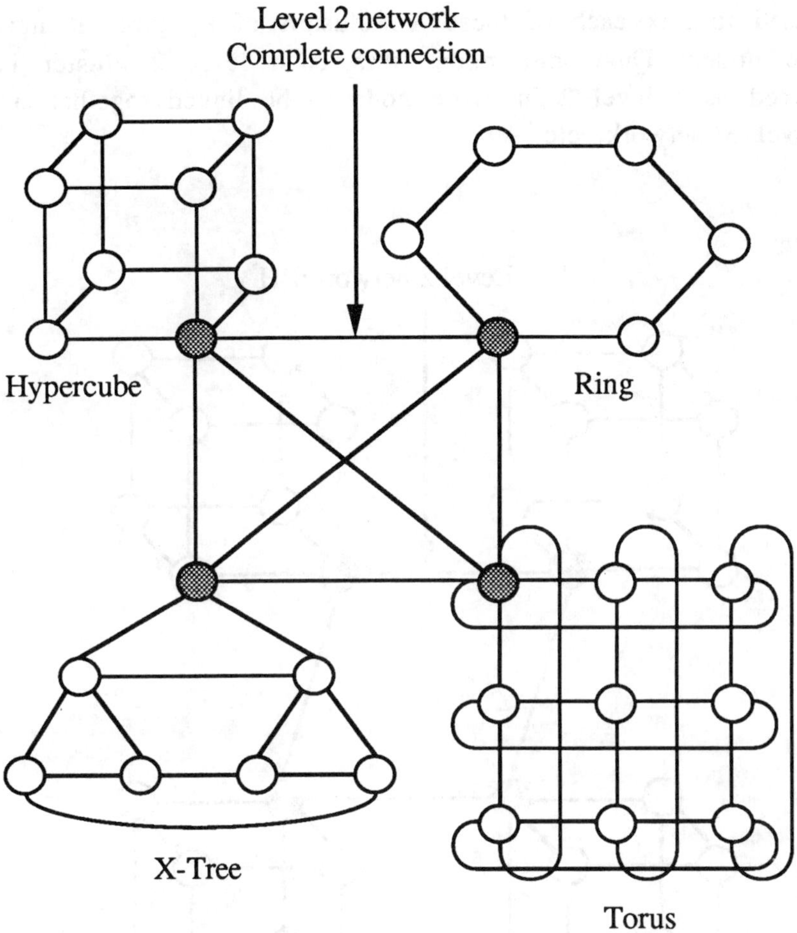

Figure 3.2 An example heterogeneous hierarchical interconnection network

considered here can be described informally as follows. Let N denote the total number of nodes in the network. These N nodes are divided into K_1 clusters of $n_1 = N/K_1$ nodes each. Each cluster of n_1 nodes is linked together by a level 1 interconnection network. Then one node from each cluster is selected to act as an interface node and these K_1 interface nodes are again divided into K_2 clusters of $n_2 = K_1/K_2$ nodes each. A level 2 interconnection network is used to link each of these K_2 clusters of n_2 level 1 interface nodes. Then, one node from each level 2 cluster is selected as a level 2 interface node to be linked together by a level 3 network, etc.

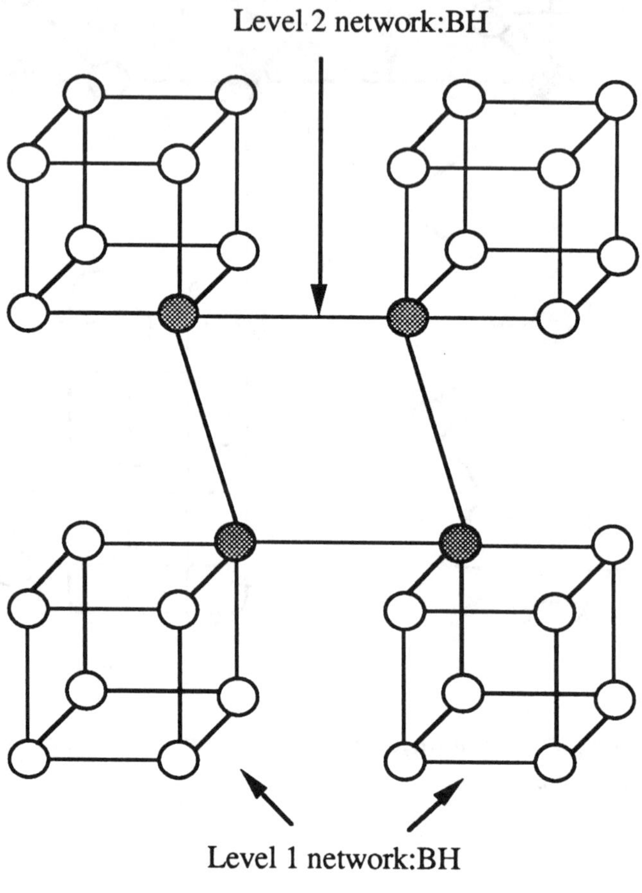

Figure 3.3 A BH/BH hierarchical interconnection network with a cluster size of 8 nodes

In the analysis presented in Section 3.5, all HINs are restricted to two levels. The analysis presented in Chapter 4 indicates that two levels is a pragmatic choice for the number of levels in a HIN design. It is further assumed that the same interconnection network is used in all clusters at level 1 and that all clusters are of the same size. Figure 3.3 shows an example homogeneous HIN with two levels, each level using a binary hypercube (BH) network. The notation "level 1 network/level 2 network" is used to identify a homogeneous HIN. For example, BH/BH identifies the HIN shown in Figure 3.3.

3.4. Advantages and Disadvantages of HINs

To fix our attention on the pros and cons of HINs, we concentrate on binary hypercube-based HINs (see Figure 3.3) in this section. An advantage of HINs is that they tend to reduce the number of on-PCB and inter-PCB wires substantially. This aspect of HINs is important in implementing large parallel systems. For example, consider the NCUBE/ten system discussed in Section 3.1. The use of the BH/BH HIN with a cluster size of 8 would greatly reduce the number of wires needed for inter-PCB connection (from 512 wires to 64 wires). Further, the number of on-PCB wires is also reduced from 1280 wires to 496 wires. Figure 3.1 shows the on-PCB and inter-PCB wire distribution for the BH/BH network that uses a cluster size of 8. (It will be shown later that this is the optimum cluster size for large systems under a cost-benefit model.) The use of the BH/BH network reduces the need for both types of wires substantially. This reduction in the number of link connections, as stated in Section 3.1, has two implications on system design. First, it reduces the demand for both chip area and PCB area. Thus, more nodes can be packed in a given PCB area. Second, since inter-PCB connection is greatly simplified, it is now feasible to increase the system size N substantially. This second factor is important in implementing large parallel systems.

Another advantage of HINs is that they reduce the degree (i.e., the number of links connected to a node) of the majority of nodes. For the binary hypercube-based HINs, the degree of the remaining nodes is the same as that of the corresponding non-hierarchical network. For example, consider a binary hypercube network with $N = 2^D$ nodes. The degree of each node in this network is D (assuming full-duplex links). In contrast, in a two-level BH/BH HIN with a cluster size of $n = 2^d$, only 2^{D-d} nodes will have a degree of D (the interface nodes), and the remaining nodes will have only a degree of d. If $N = 1024$ (i.e., $D = 10$) and $n = 8$ (i.e., $d = 3$), then the BH/BH HIN will have 896 nodes with degree 3 and 128 nodes with degree 10. This is in contrast to a degree of 10 for all 1024 nodes in the BH network.

Major disadvantages of HINs include the potentially high traffic rates on inter-cluster (i.e., level 2 network) links, and thus the potential degradation in performance, and the potential for diminished fault-tolerance[1] due to the special role played by interface nodes. However, the performance enhancements suggested in Section 3.6 appear to economically alleviate the problem of congestion on inter-cluster links. It is also shown in Chapter 6 that standard fault-tolerance techniques can be economically applied to the interface nodes to improve the reliability of the BH/BH HIN to close to that of the BH network (which, incidentally, provides reliabilities much like that of a complete connection [BHUY 86]).

3.4.1. Comparison with Other Networks

There are other methods to reduce the link cost and the degree of connection. Here we briefly compare the BH/BH HIN to the following three networks: the cube-connected-cycles (CCC) network [PREP 81], Hypernet [HWAN 87], and the HCN [GHOS 89, GHOS 90].

Figure 3.4a shows the link cost associated with the BH, BH/BH, CCC, 2-level Hypernet, and the HCN networks. For comparison purposes, the link costs of the bidirectional ring (BR) and the complete connection (CC) networks are

---

[1] Note that fault-tolerance is not as serious a problem with other hierarchical structures such as the Hypernet and the HCN.

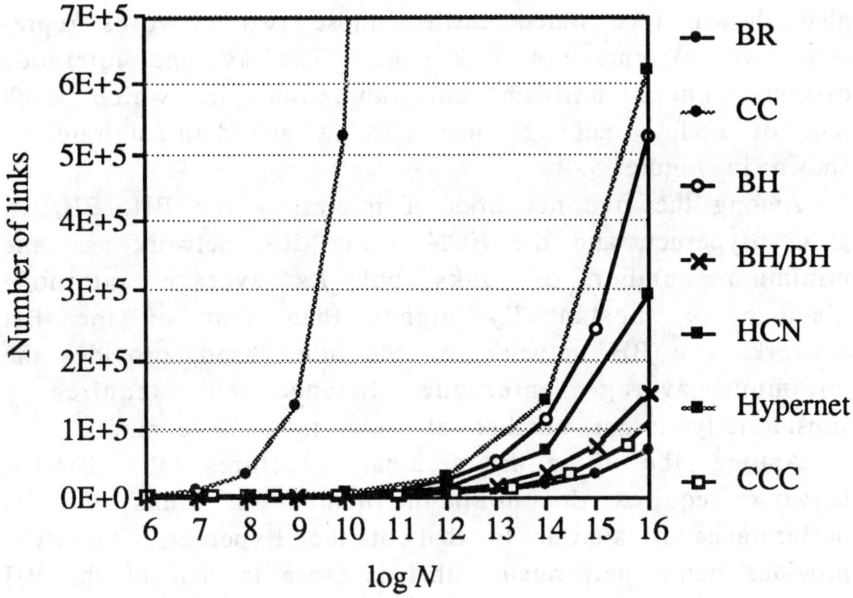

(a)

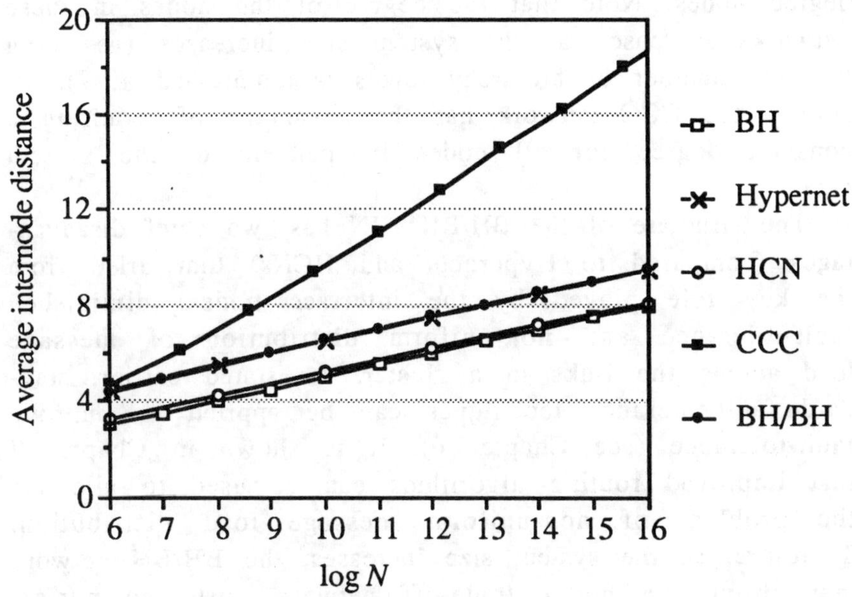

(b)

Figure 3.4 Link costs and the average internode distances of various interconnection networks

also shown. (As stated earlier, these two networks represent two extremes in link cost.) The average internode distance under uniform communication, in which each pair of nodes exchange messages at an identical rate, is shown in Figure 3.4b.

Among the five networks of interest – the BH, BH/BH, CCC, Hypernet, and the HCN – the CCC network uses the minimum number of links but its average internode distance is substantially higher than that of the BH network. The BH network, on the other hand, provides the minimum average internode distance but requires a substantially larger number of links to achieve this.

Among the three hierarchical structures, the BH/BH network requires the minimum number of links and its performance is similar to that of the Hypernet. The HCN provides better performance that is close to that of the BH network, but this network requires substantially more links to achieve this improvement. However, both the Hypernet and the HCN organizations utilize uniform degree nodes. Note that the degree of the nodes in these networks increases as the system size increases (assuming that the number of hierarchy levels is maintained at 2). Of course, the CCC network has the advantage of requiring a constant degree for all nodes independent of the system size.

The structure of the BH/BH HIN has two chief disadvantages (compared to Hypernets and HCNs) that arise from the key role played by the interface nodes: diminished fault-tolerance and non-uniform distribution of message load among the links in a cluster. As stated earlier, standard fault-tolerance techniques can be applied to improve fault-tolerance (see Chapter 6). It is shown in Chapter 7 that improved routing algorithms can be used to alleviate the problem of non-uniform message load distribution. Therefore, as the system size increases, the BH/BH network may provide a better trade-off between cost and performance. However, it should be noted that this type of structure may not be suitable for all applications.

3.5. Analysis of Hierarchical Interconnection Networks

This section analyses several example HINs, and, through this analysis, shows the advantages of HINs in comparison to non-hierarchical structures. In the analysis, the performance of a HIN is compared with that of a non-hierarchical (reference) network; here, a BH network is used. The HINs considered are BH/BH, BH/CCC, BH/BR, and BH/CC. It is obvious that the last two networks are not useful for large numbers of clusters, but they are included for comparison purposes only. The BH/BR uses the minimum number of links among the four hierarchical networks and the BH/CC provides the minimum average internode distance.

Section 3.5.1 presents a performance analysis of HINs assuming that there is no contention (i.e., no queueing). Analysis with contention is presented in Section 3.5.2. This section also presents the results of the simulation experiments that validate the queueing analysis.

3.5.1. Analysis with No Contention

Let N denote the total number of nodes in the network, n denote the number of nodes in a cluster, and K denote the number of clusters (i.e., K nodes participate in the level 2 network), where $N = Kn$. It is assumed here, for convenience of analysis, that N is evenly divisible by K. It is also assumed that a node can send messages to itself. Such an assumption is not strictly necessary; however, without this assumption, the resulting mathematical equations become more unwieldy without adding any additional insight into performance.

Let α be the probability of both source and destination nodes of a message being in the same cluster. Therefore, $(1-\alpha)$ represents the probability of inter-cluster communication. The larger the value of α (for a fixed cluster size), the stronger the locality in communication. Locality in communication has been characterized similarly by other researchers [WU 81]. It is further assumed that:

- Intra-cluster communication is uniformly random (i.e., a source node sends an intra-cluster message to each node within its cluster with equal probability).

- Inter-cluster communication is uniformly random (i.e., a source node sends an inter-cluster message to each other cluster with equal probability, and to each node within the destination cluster with equal probability).

It is difficult to predict what *specific* values of α one should expect in practice, but it is clear that a large number of parallel applications are in fact characterized by a communication structure that results in significant locality. The results of the following sections suggest that HINs yield superior performance to non-hierarchical networks over a wide range of α values, and thus should be generally useful.

3.5.1.1. Criteria for comparison of performance

Several performance measures have been proposed to evaluate communication structures for parallel systems [LEVI 85]. The following performance measures are used here to evaluate various interconnection networks. Similar measures have been used by other researchers [BHUY 83, AGRA 86, MCCR 86, KUHL 86, REED 87].

(1) *Link cost*: One goal is to minimize the link cost L as it limits the economical size of the network. The number of links is used to represent the link cost. Since bus-based structures are not treated here, the number of link connections need not be considered.

(2) *Average internode distance*: Another goal is to minimize the average internode distance P as it largely determines message transmission time and, hence, the effective computing rate. The number of links in the message transmission path is used as a measure of the internode distance.

(3) *LP product*: In general, trying to minimize one of the above two measures (say P) results in an increase in the other (in this case L). Therefore, a useful measure is $L \times P$, which should be minimized. The *LP* product really gives a cost-benefit ratio, with L representing the cost of the network and $1/P$ representing the benefit. Thus, benefit per unit cost can be maximized by minimizing the *LP* product. Similar performance measures are also used by other researchers [BHUY 83, MCCR 86].

(4) *LP ratio*: It is useful to compare the performance of an HIN to that of the reference network. The subscript 'H' is used to represent the performance measures of an HIN (e.g., L_H, P_H) and 'R' is used for the reference network (e.g., L_R, P_R). Then,

$$LP \text{ ratio} = \frac{L_H \times P_H}{L_R \times P_R} \tag{3.1}$$

Smaller *LP* ratios are preferred. A value of 1 for the *LP* ratio indicates that the HIN has the same *LP* product as the reference network. An *LP* ratio < 1 is desired as it indicates an improvement in performance (at least, with respect to the *LP* measure) associated with the HIN.

3.5.1.2. Analysis of the BH network

Consider a binary hypercube (BH) with $N = 2^D$ nodes, where D is the dimensionality of the hypercube. Since each node connects to D nodes in D dimensions, there are $D\,2^D$ link connections. Since each link provides two link connections, there are half as many links in the network. Thus

$$L_{BH} = D\,2^{D-1} \tag{3.2}$$

The average internode distance P_{BH} is now derived under the assumption of locality in communication.

Let $n = 2^d$. Then the address of a node, which is D bits long, can be divided into two groups. The d least significant bits identify a node within a cluster of nodes whose $(D-d)$ most significant bits are the same; these $(D-d)$ bits serve to identify the cluster. Then,

$$P_{BH} = \alpha P'_{BH} + (1-\alpha) P''_{BH} \tag{3.3}$$

where

P'_{BH} = average distance between two nodes within a cluster, and

P''_{BH} = average distance between two nodes that are in two different clusters.

The average internode distance within a cluster (recalling that we allow message source and destination to be the same node) is given by:

$$P'_{BH} = \frac{\sum_{i=0}^{d} \binom{d}{i} i}{2^d} = \frac{d}{2} \tag{3.4}$$

To compute P''_{BH}, choose an arbitrary source node. Recall that the D address bits are divided into two groups. In computing P''_{BH}, it should be noted that in the most significant $(D-d)$ bits the source and destination node addresses should not be the same (the lower d bits may be the same). Let *NumNodes* (i, j) be the number of destination nodes at a distance $i + j$ from the source node, where the distance i $(i > 0)$ is contributed by the most significant $(D-d)$ bits and the distance j $(j \geq 0)$ is contributed by the least significant d bits. Since

$$NumNodes\ (i, j) = \binom{D-d}{i}\binom{d}{j}$$

and the number of destination nodes (in a different cluster) reachable from the source is $2^D - 2^d$, the average distance travelled by an inter-cluster message is given by

$$P''_{BH} = \frac{\sum_{i=1}^{D-d}\sum_{j=0}^{d}\left\{\binom{D-d}{i}\binom{d}{j}(i+j)\right\}}{2^D - 2^d}$$

$$= \frac{\sum_{j=0}^{d}\binom{d}{j}\left[\sum_{i=1}^{D-d}\binom{D-d}{i}i\right] + \sum_{i=1}^{D-d}\binom{D-d}{i}\left[\sum_{j=0}^{d}\binom{d}{j}j\right]}{2^D - 2^d}$$

This expression can be simplified by using the following two facts about binomial coefficients:

$$\sum_{i=0}^{N}\binom{N}{i} = 2^N$$

and

$$\sum_{i=0}^{N} i\binom{N}{i} = N\ 2^{N-1}$$

Then,

$$P''_{BH} = \frac{2^d\left[(D-d)2^{(D-d-1)}\right] + \left[2^{D-d} - 1\right]\left[d\ 2^{d-1}\right]}{2^D - 2^d}$$

$$= \frac{D\ 2^{D-1} - d\ 2^{d-1}}{2^D - 2^d} \tag{3.5}$$

Eqs. (3.3), (3.4), and (3.5) then give

$$P_{BH} = \alpha\left[\frac{d}{2}\right] + (1-\alpha)\left[\frac{D2^{D-1} - d\,2^{d-1}}{2^{D} - 2^{d}}\right] \tag{3.6}$$

It should be noted that $D = \log N$ and $d = \log n = \log (N/K)$.

3.5.1.3. Analysis of the BH/BH hierarchical network

This network uses the BH network at both levels. From each cluster, one node participates in the level 2 BH. This node serves as the interface node between the two levels. The number of links in this structure is

$$L_{BH/BH} = K\left[d\,2^{d-1}\right] + (D-d)\,2^{(D-d-1)} \tag{3.7}$$

Since $K = 2^{D-d}$,

$$L_{BH/BH} = d\;2^{D-1} + (D-d)\,2^{D-d-1}$$

The average internode distance of an HIN is given by

$$P_{H} = \alpha(P_{level1}) + (1-\alpha)[2P_{level1} + P_{level2}] \tag{3.8}$$

where

P_{level1} = average internode distance of the network at level 1 (this distance is computed by assuming that a node can send messages to itself); and

P_{level2} = average internode distance of the network at level 2 (this distance is computed by assuming that a node cannot send messages to itself).

For the HIN under consideration,

$$P_{level1} = \frac{d}{2}.$$

$P_{level 2}$ can be computed from Eq. (3.4), yielding

$$P_{level 2} = \frac{\sum_{i=1}^{D-d} \binom{D-d}{i} i}{2^{D-d} - 1} = \frac{(D-d)\, 2^{D-d-1}}{2^{D-d} - 1} \tag{3.9}$$

Therefore, using Eq. (3.8)

$$P_{BH/BH} = \alpha \left[\frac{d}{2}\right] + (1-\alpha)\left[2\frac{d}{2} + \frac{(D-d)\, 2^{D-d-1}}{2^{D-d} - 1}\right]$$

$$= \alpha \left[\frac{d}{2}\right] + (1-\alpha)\left[\frac{(D+d)\, 2^{D-1} - d\, 2^{d}}{2^{D} - 2^{d}}\right]$$

3.5.1.4. Analysis of the BH/BR hierarchical network

This network uses a bidirectional ring as the level 2 network. The number of links in this HIN is

$$L_{BH/BR} = K \left[d\, 2^{d-1}\right] + K$$

where K is the number of clusters in the network. Eq. (3.8) is used to compute the average internode distance. Since the level 1 network is a BH,

$$P_{level 1} = \frac{d}{2}.$$

$P_{level 2}$ is given by

$$P_{level 2} = \begin{cases} \dfrac{K+1}{4} & \text{if } K \text{ is odd} \\[2ex] \dfrac{K^2}{4(K-1)} & \text{if } K \text{ is even} \end{cases}$$

Thus, the average internode distance is

$$P_{BH/BR} = \begin{cases} \alpha\left[\dfrac{d}{2}\right] + (1-\alpha)\left[d + \dfrac{K+1}{4}\right] & \text{for } K \text{ odd} \\ \\ \alpha\left[\dfrac{d}{2}\right] + (1-\alpha)\left[d + \dfrac{K^2}{4(K-1)}\right] & \text{for } K \text{ even} \end{cases}$$

3.5.1.5. Analysis of the BH/CC hierarchical network

For this network it is easy to derive the following:

$$L_{BH/CC} = K\left[d\,2^{d-1}\right] + \frac{K(K-1)}{2}$$

and,

$$P_{BH/CC} = \alpha\left[\frac{d}{2}\right] + (1-\alpha)(d+1)$$

It is clear from the last equation that the average internode distance is dependent only on the size of the cluster and not on the number of clusters.

3.5.1.6. Analysis of the BH/CCC hierarchical network

Let D_c be the dimensionality of the (level 2) CCC network. Then, the number of nodes in the level 2 network (equal to the number of clusters K in the HIN) is $D_c\,2^{D_c}$ and the number of links is $3D_c\,2^{D_c-1}$. The total number of nodes N is $D_c\,2^{D_c+d}$, and the number of links is

$$L_{BH/CCC} = K\left(d\,2^{d-1}\right) + 3D_c\,2^{D_c-1}$$

The average internode distance, without self-routing, in the CCC of dimensionality D_c is given by [WITT 81]

$$P_{level\,2} = \frac{7}{4}D_c - 3 + \frac{D_c+1}{2^{D_c-1}}$$

Then

$$P_{BH/CCC} = \alpha\left[\frac{d}{2}\right] + (1-\alpha)\left[d + \frac{7}{4}D_c - 3 + \frac{D_c + 1}{2^{D_c - 1}}\right]$$

3.5.1.7. Discussion of results

The average internode distance P and the LP ratio are shown in Figures 3.5-3.7 for some example hierarchical networks. All these networks have a cluster size $n = 16$. Figures 3.5 and 3.6 give P and LP ratio values for $N = 128$ and 1024, respectively. The value of α is varied from 0 to 1. For a system with 1024 nodes and for the configurations considered, the BH/BH network provides the best cost-performance ratio (i.e., the lowest LP ratio) for a wide range of α values. As α approaches 1, however, both the BH/BR and BH/CCC hierarchical networks provide a better LP ratio because these networks allocate fewer links to the rarely used (in this case) level 2 network. Note that even for $\alpha = 0$ (reflecting a context of strong "anti-locality"), the BH/BH network has an LP ratio of less than one. It should be noted, however, that as α approaches 0, the required message processing capacities of level 2 links increase, as will be shown in Section 3.5.2.4.

Figure 3.7 gives P and LP ratio values as functions of the total number of nodes in the network N for $\alpha = 0.8$. Again, n is fixed at 16 and the number of clusters K is increased to increase N. The graph of Figure 3.7a indicates that the average internode distance of the BH/BH hierarchical network is only about 10% higher than that of the BH reference network. The BH/BH hierarchical network, however, uses far fewer links than does the BH reference network, as shown in Figure 3.8. This reduction in the number of links used is directly proportional to N. This factor is important when designing large systems.

From the sample results presented here and from other results with varying parameter values, it appears that both BH/BH and BH/CCC hierarchical networks provide substantial improvements in cost-performance ratios (as measured

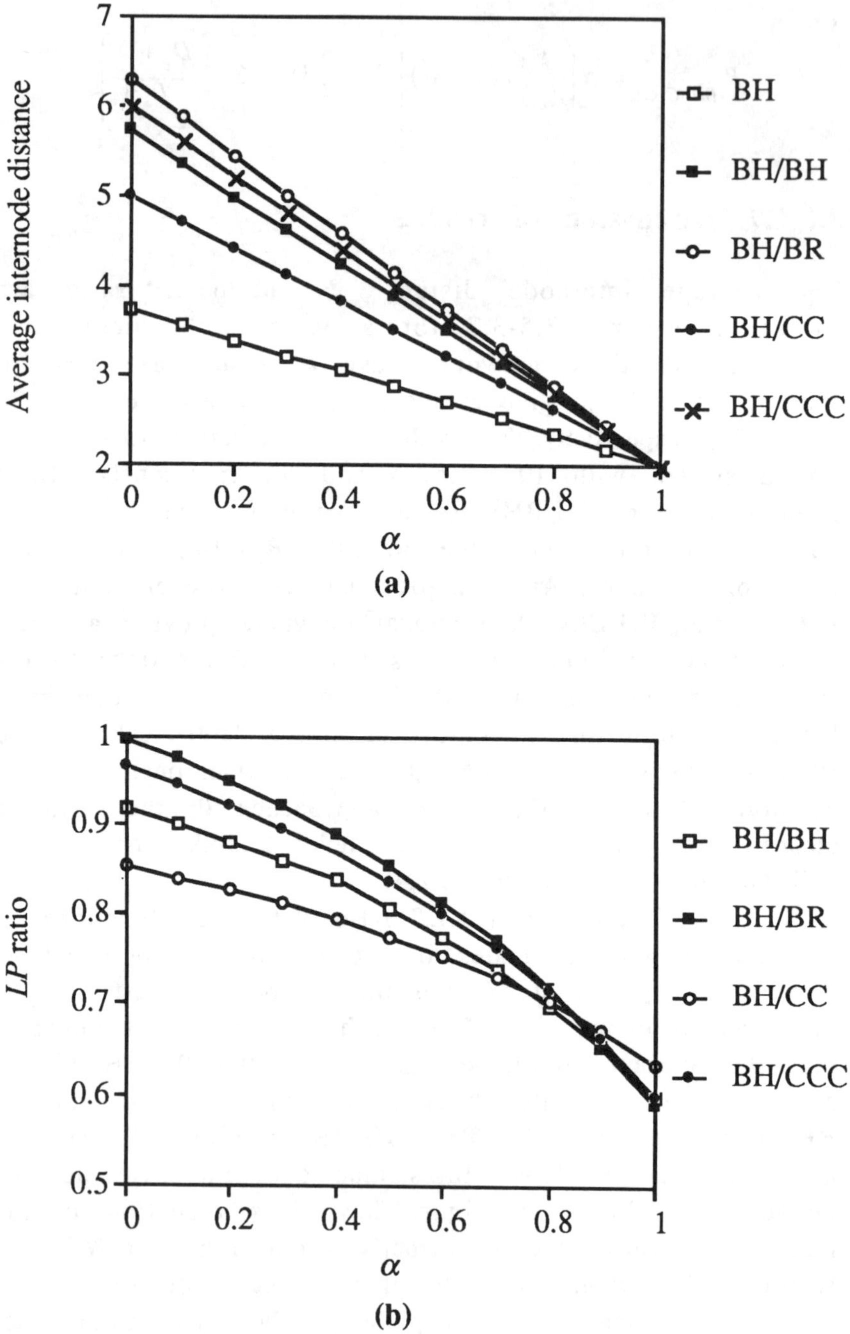

Figure 3.5 Average internode distance and the *LP* ratio of hierarchical networks (N = 128 and K = 8)

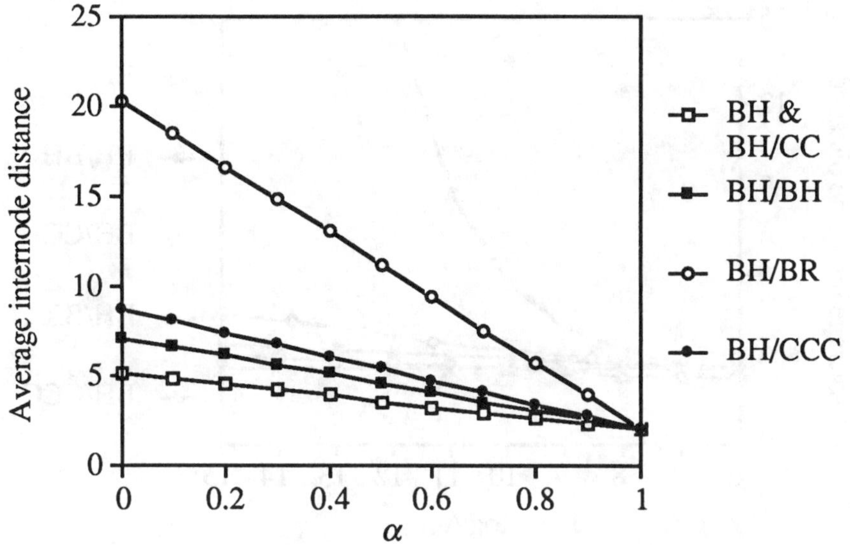

(a)

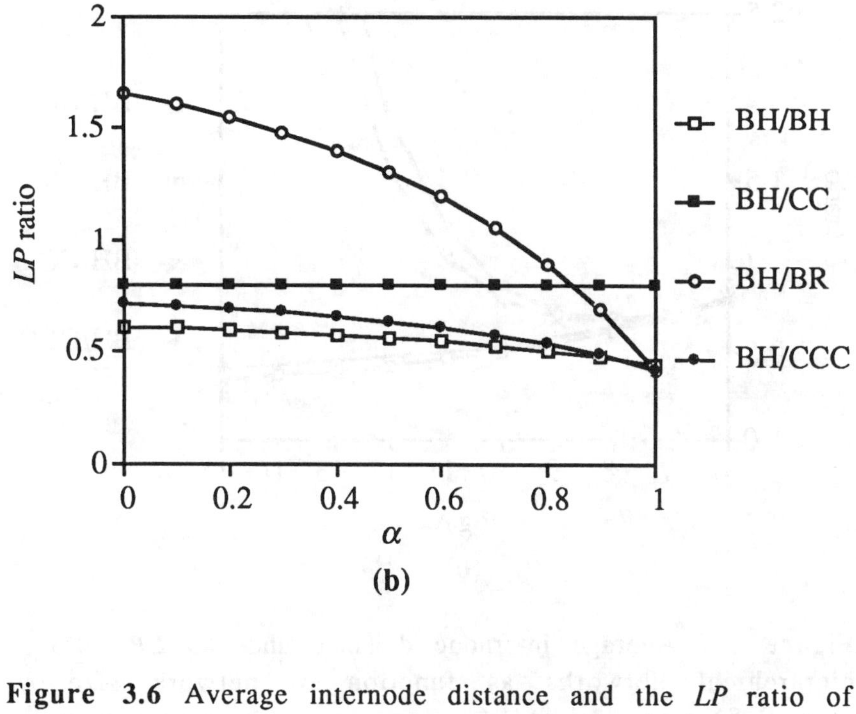

(b)

Figure 3.6 Average internode distance and the *LP* ratio of hierarchical networks (N = 1024 and K = 64)

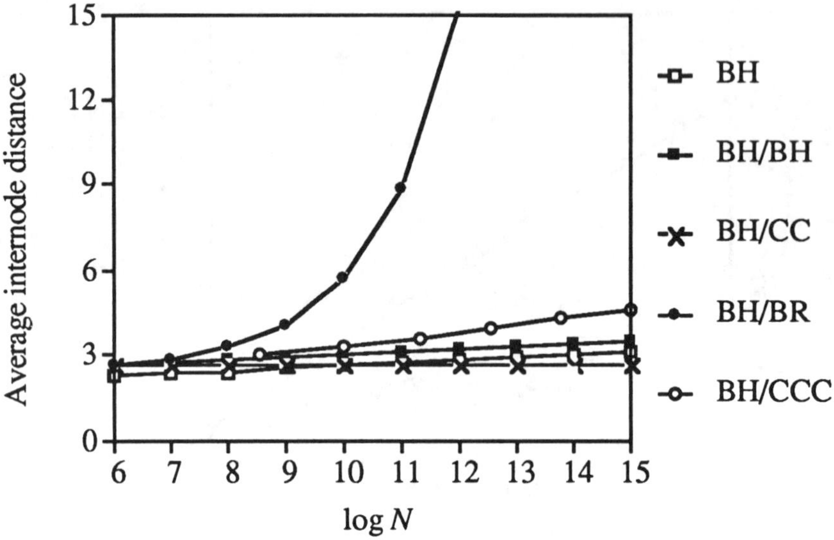

(a)

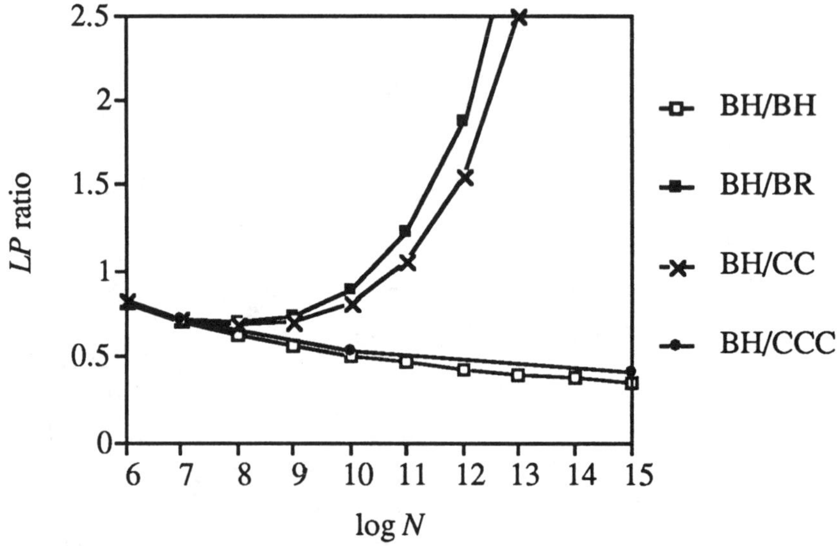

(b)

Figure 3.7 Average internode distance and the LP ratio of hierarchical networks as function of network size N ($\alpha = 0.8$)

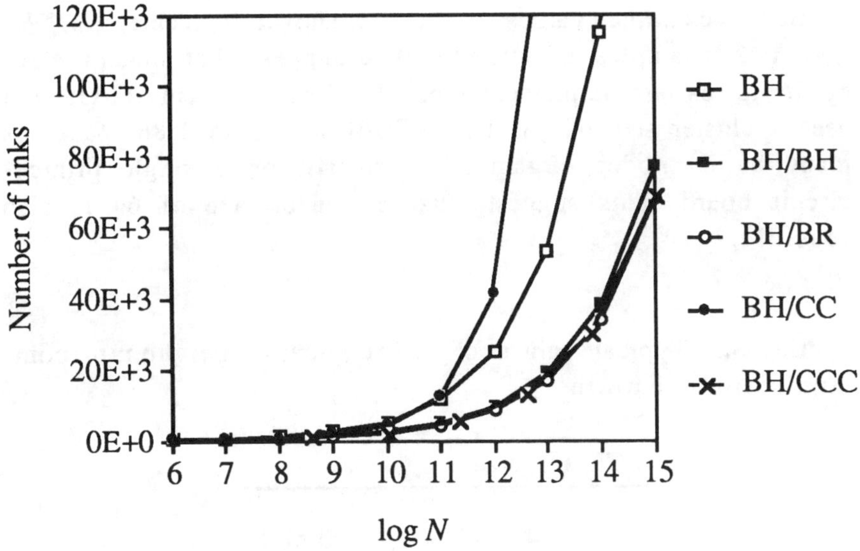

Figure 3.8 Link cost of various hierarchical networks

by the *LP* ratio) and that these improvements increase as the system size increases. The extent of these improvements depends significantly on the degree of locality in communication, as measured by α, but even for very small α some improvement is obtained.

Different applications may have greatly differing α values. It is useful to consider here, however, an example that illustrates for at least a class of applications what range of values would be likely. Consider applications that are naturally structured as two-dimensional meshes. Mesh-connected systems and correspondingly structured algorithms have been extensively studied in the literature [THOM 77, NASS 79, NASS 80, STOU 83, LEON 85, CARL 85, BOXE 89]. Such systems efficiently support nearest-neighbour communication in which each node communicates with four of its neighbouring nodes. Now, suppose that a cluster consists of a square sub-mesh of n nodes (i.e., a $\sqrt{n} \times \sqrt{n}$ mesh). It is straightforward to show that, for a mesh-structured computation on such a system,

$$\alpha = 1 - \frac{1}{\sqrt{n}}.$$

Some example values of α are shown in Table 3.2. We give two examples of systems that suggest that cluster sizes of 16 to 64 are implementable. The Cedar system [GAJS 83] uses a cluster size of 16. The NCUBE/ten [HAYE 86] packs as many as 64 nodes, organized as a BH, on a single printed-circuit board. This suggests that a cluster size of 64 is also feasible.

Table 3.2 Typical values of α for nearest-neighbour communication pattern

Cluster size n	α
4	0.500
9	0.670
16	0.750
25	0.800
36	0.830
49	0.860
64	0.875

3.5.2. Analysis with Contention

A very simple model is used for the queueing analysis. The "Markovian" and other similar assumptions that we use in this analysis are not at all "realistic", in that they do not reflect the behaviour of some given, particular application. Note, however, that it is not the goal here to accurately predict the performance of a particular system with some particular workload; rather, all that is desired is an "order of magnitude" evaluation of the relative performance of different types of systems. A large body of literature and experience with models of this type supports their usefulness [LAZO 84].

Each network link is assumed to be full-duplex. In our analysis, we conceptually replace each full-duplex link by two simplex links, each of which is modelled as a queueing centre [KLEI 75]. Expressions are derived for the average message delay on each link. The following assumptions are made about the network and its workload:

(i) Each node generates messages at rate λ and the times between message generations are exponentially distributed.

(ii) The node message generation processes are independent of each other.

(iii) Message service times are exponentially distributed; each link processes these messages at rate μ.

(iv) Each node has unbounded buffering capacity.

(v) Packet-switching is used for message transmission. (Packet-switching is used in several multicomputer systems such as the Cosmic Cube [SEIT 85] and the NCUBE/ten [HAYE 86].)

(vi) All messages are routed over the shortest path between the source and destination nodes. If more than one shortest path exists between a pair of nodes, it is assumed that random routing is used (i.e., each shortest path is selected with equal probability). Thus the routing scheme uses no information regarding the current state of the network. (The impact on performance of improved routing algorithms is briefly discussed in Section 3.6.2. More detailed study of routing algorithms is given in Chapter 7.)

To facilitate the queueing analysis, Kleinrock's independence assumption [KLEI 76] is used. This assumption states that each time a message arrives at a link, a new service time is generated for this message from the exponential service time distribution (i.e., there is no "memory" of message lengths from hop to hop). This assumption is often used in the delay analysis of communication networks [GOPA 81]. The results of the simulation experiments presented in Section 3.5.2.5 indicate that this assumption is reasonable in this context. This allows each simplex link to be modelled as an M/M/1 queueing centre [KLEI 75]. Our link model is shown in Figure 3.9.

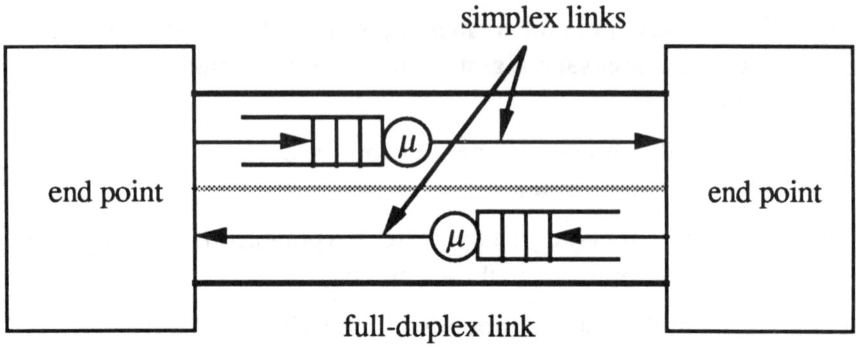

Figure 3.9 Queueing model for links

3.5.2.1. Analysis of the BH network

This section considers the BH network with N nodes. Initially, expressions are derived for the average number of messages Q in each (link) queue, the utilization ρ of each link and the average message delay R under the assumption of uniformly random communication, so as to illustrate the analysis technique. This technique is then applied to derive expressions for Q, ρ, and R under the assumption of locality in communication.

As stated, each simplex link is modelled as an M/M/1 queue. Let λ_{link} be the effective arrival rate of messages seen by a link. By the symmetry of the BH, λ_{link} is the same for all links.

Let $D = \log N$ denote the dimensionality of the BH. Then, each message travels $D/2$ links on average. Since messages are generated by each node at rate λ,

$$\text{Total rate at which messages visit links} = N\lambda\left[\frac{D}{2}\right]$$

Then, since there are $2D\ 2^{D-1}$ links (recall that each full-duplex link is counted twice here), and since $N = 2^D$, the effective message arrival rate seen by each link is

$$\lambda_{link} = \frac{2^D \lambda \left[\frac{D}{2}\right]}{2D\ 2^{D-1}} = \frac{\lambda}{2} \tag{3.10}$$

The utilization ρ of each link and the average message queue length Q at each link are given by

$$\rho = \frac{\lambda_{link}}{\mu} = \frac{\lambda}{2\mu} \tag{3.11}$$

and

$$Q = \frac{\rho}{1-\rho} \tag{3.12}$$

The delay encountered by messages at each link is given by

$$\frac{Q}{\lambda_{link}} = \frac{1}{\mu - \lambda_{link}} \tag{3.13}$$

Therefore, the average message delay under uniform communication is given by

$$R = \frac{D}{2(\mu - \lambda_{link})} = \frac{D}{2\mu - \lambda}$$

When locality in communication is considered, λ_{link} will be different. Again, assume that the cluster size $n = 2^d$, the number of clusters $K = 2^{D-d}$, and α is the probability of intra-cluster communication. In this case, the links can be divided into two groups: cluster (CL) links and non-cluster (NCL) links. Cluster links are those that connect only the nodes within a cluster (i.e., nodes whose upper $(D-d)$ bits are the same) and non-cluster links are those that connect two nodes that are in two different conceptual clusters (i.e., nodes whose lower d bits are the same). Let μ_{CL} and μ_{NCL} be the message processing rates of cluster and non-cluster links, respectively (as will be seen later, it is desirable to allow these links to be of differing data rates). Furthermore, let $\lambda_{link,CL}$ and $\lambda_{link,NCL}$ be the message arrival rates at cluster and non-cluster links, respectively. For cluster links, the effective arrival rate $\lambda_{link,CL}$ is given by Eq. (3.10). To compute $\lambda_{link,NCL}$ it should be noted that each inter-cluster message uses, on average, $(P''_{BH} - d/2)$ non-cluster links, where P''_{BH} is given by Eq. (3.5). Since inter-cluster messages are generated at rate $(1\text{-}\alpha)\lambda$ by each node and since there are $2[D\,2^{D-1} - 2^{D-d}\,d\,2^{d-1}] = 2\,(D-d)\,2^{D-1}$ non-cluster links, $\lambda_{link,NCL}$ is given by

$$\lambda_{link,NCL} = \frac{(1-\alpha)\,\lambda 2^{D}\left[P''_{BH} - \frac{d}{2}\right]}{2(D-d)2^{D-1}}$$

$$= (1-\alpha)\,\lambda\,\frac{2^{D-1}}{2^{D}-2^{d}}$$

The mean queue length, link utilization, and delay at each link are given by Eqs. (3.11), (3.12), and (3.13) by using appropriate λ_{link} and μ values. The average message delay is given by

$$R_{BH} = \alpha\left[\frac{d}{2}\right]\Delta_{CL} + (1-\alpha)\left[\frac{d}{2}\,\Delta_{CL} + \left(\frac{(D-d)\,2^{D-1}}{2^{D}-2^{d}}\right)\Delta_{NCL}\right]$$

$$= \left[\frac{d}{2}\right]\Delta_{CL} + (1-\alpha)\left(\frac{(D-d)\,2^{D-1}}{2^{D}-2^{d}}\right)\Delta_{NCL}$$

where $\Delta_{CL} = \dfrac{1}{\mu_{CL} - \lambda_{link,CL}}$, and $\Delta_{NCL} = \dfrac{1}{\mu_{NCL} - \lambda_{link,NCL}}$.

3.5.2.2. Analysis of the BH/BH hierarchical network

In this network, one node from each cluster acts as an interface node. As in the analysis of the BH network, the links are divided into cluster and non-cluster links, and the message arrival rate for each type of link is derived.

In deriving $\lambda_{link,NCL}$, it should be noted that each inter-cluster message uses $(D-d)\,2^{D-d-1}/(2^{D-d}-1)$ non-cluster links, on average, and each cluster generates these messages at rate $(1-\alpha)\,\lambda\,2^{d}$. Therefore,

$$\lambda_{link,NCL} = \frac{2^{D-d}\,2^{d}\,(1-\alpha)\left[\dfrac{(D-d)\,2^{D-d-1}}{2^{D-d}-1}\right]}{2(D-d)\,2^{D-d-1}}$$

$$= \frac{2^{D-1}\,(1-\alpha)\,\lambda}{2^{D-d}-1}$$

The message load of inter-cluster messages is, however, not distributed equally among the links in a cluster. The cluster links closer to the interface node receive more inter-cluster messages than those that are not. Thus, $\lambda_{link,CL}$ is dependent on how close a link is to the interface node.

Let $H(s,t)$ be the distance between nodes s and t (i.e., the number of bits in which the addresses of s and t differ when expressed in binary form). Then we define a j-level link as a cluster link that connects a node at distance j from an interface node to a node at distance j-1 from the interface node. Then, the arrival rate of messages at a j-level link is given by

$$\lambda_{link,CL,j} = \lambda'_j + \lambda''_j$$

where

λ'_j = arrival rate (at a j-level link) due to intra-cluster messages, and

λ''_j = arrival rate (at a j-level link) due to inter-cluster messages.

Since the intra-cluster message load is equally distributed over the links within a cluster, λ'_j is given by

$$\lambda'_j = \frac{\alpha\lambda}{2} \qquad \text{for all } j$$

λ''_j is not the same for all the links in a cluster. It is given by

$$\lambda''_j = n\,\lambda(1-\alpha)\,p(j)$$

where $p(j)$ is the probability that an inter-cluster message gets routed through a j-level link on its way out of (or into) the cluster.

We now derive an expression for $p(j)$. An assumption of the model is that the routing algorithm utilizes all the shortest paths with equal probability. A set of links J exists, all of whose element links are j-level links that act as intermediate links for all inter-cluster messages generated by any source node within the cluster that is at a distance of at least j from the interface node. Therefore, the number of source nodes for which an element of J acts as an intermediate link is $2^d - \sum_{k=0}^{j-1}\binom{d}{k}$. Since there are $(d-j+1)\binom{d}{j-1}$ such intermediate links (i.e., the number of elements in J),

$$p(j) = \frac{2^d - \sum_{k=0}^{j-1}\binom{d}{k}}{(d-j+1)\binom{d}{j-1}2^d}$$

$$= \frac{\sum_{k=j}^{d}\binom{d}{k}}{(d-j+1)\binom{d}{j-1}2^d}$$

The utilization, mean queue length and mean delay of a j-level link are respectively:

$$\rho_j = \frac{\lambda_{link,CL,j}}{\mu_{CL}}$$

$$Q_j = \frac{U_j}{1 - U_j}$$

and

$$\Delta_j = \frac{1}{\mu_{CL} - \lambda_{link,CL,j}}$$

Now, analogously to Eq. (3.8), average message delay can be computed using

$$R_H = \alpha(R_{level1}) + (1-\alpha)(2R_{level1} + R_{level2})$$

where

R_{level1} = average message delay in the level 1 network

and

R_{level2} = average message delay in the level 2 network

This yields

$$R_{BH/BH} = \alpha \left[\frac{d}{2}\right] \Delta_{Avg} + (1-\alpha) \times \left[2\,\Delta_{CL-Avg} + \left(\frac{(D-d)2^{D-d-1}}{2^{D-d} - 1}\right) \Delta_{NCL-Avg}\right]$$

where

Δ_{Avg} = average delay, at a link, of an intra-cluster message

$$= \frac{1}{d\, 2^{d-1}} \sum_{j=1}^{d} \left\{ (d - j + 1) \binom{d}{j-1} \Delta_j \right\}$$

Δ_{CL-Avg} = average delay of an inter-cluster message in a cluster (summed over all the links traversed within the cluster)

$$= \sum_{j=1}^{d} \left\{ \Delta_j (d - j + 1) \binom{d}{j-1} p(j) \right\}$$

and,

$\Delta_{NCL-Avg}$ = average delay, at a link, of an inter-cluster message in the level 2 network

$$= \frac{1}{\mu_{NCL} - \lambda_{link,NCL}}$$

3.5.2.3. Analysis of other hierarchical networks

This section presents the analysis of BH/BR, BH/CC, and BH/CCC hierarchical networks. The analysis is very similar to that presented in the previous section for the BH/BH network. Since only the level 2 network differs, it is obvious that $\lambda_{link,CL,j}$ and thus Δ_j, Δ_{Avg} and $\Delta_{CL\text{-}Avg}$ remain the same as that derived for the BH/BH network. The following expressions can be derived for $\lambda_{link,NCL}$.

For the BH/BR network:

$$\lambda_{link,NCL} = \begin{cases} 2^{d-1} \lambda (1 - \alpha) \left[\dfrac{K + 1}{4} \right] & \text{if } K \text{ is odd} \\ \\ 2^{d-1} \lambda (1 - \alpha) \left[\dfrac{K^2}{4(K - 1)} \right] & \text{if } K \text{ is even} \end{cases}$$

For the BH/CC network:

$$\lambda_{link,NCL} = \frac{2^d \lambda (1 - \alpha)}{K - 1}$$

For the BH/CCC network:

$$\lambda_{link,NCL} = \frac{2^d \lambda(1-\alpha)}{3}\left[\frac{7}{4}D_C - 3 + \frac{D_C + 1}{2^{D_C - 1}}\right]$$

Note that the number of clusters K is given by $D_C 2^{D_C}$. The average message delays are given below.

$$R_{BH/BR} = \begin{cases} \alpha\left[\frac{d}{2}\right]\Delta_{Avg} + (1-\alpha)\times \\ \quad \left[2\Delta_{CL-Avg} + \left(\frac{K+1}{4}\right)\Delta_{NCL-Avg}\right] & \text{if } K \text{ is odd} \\ \alpha\left[\frac{d}{2}\right]\Delta_{Avg} + (1-\alpha)\times \\ \quad \left[2\Delta_{CL-Avg} + \left(\frac{K^2}{4(K-1)}\right)\Delta_{NCL-Avg}\right] & \text{if } K \text{ is even} \end{cases}$$

$$R_{BH/CC} = \alpha\left[\frac{d}{2}\right]\Delta_{Avg} + (1-\alpha)\left[2\Delta_{CL-Avg} + \Delta_{NCL-Avg}\right]$$

$$R_{BH/CCC} = \alpha\left[\frac{d}{2}\right]\Delta_{Avg} + (1-\alpha)\times$$

$$\left[2\Delta_{CL-Avg} + \left(\frac{7}{4}D_c - 3 + \frac{D_c + 1}{2^{D_c - 1}}\right)\Delta_{NCL-Avg}\right]$$

where Δ_{Avg}, Δ_{CL-Avg}, and $\Delta_{NCL-Avg}$ are defined as before.

3.5.2.4. Discussion of results

A large number of experiments with varying input parameter values have been performed to assess the performance of the various network architectures under the above queueing analysis. Some sample results that were thought to be representative of those obtained are presented in this section.

Figure 3.10a depicts the delays involved in BH, BH/BH, BH/CCC, and BH/CC networks for the following system parameters: $\lambda = 1$, $\mu_{CL} = \mu_{NCL} = 3$, $d = 3$, $D = 9$, and $D_c = 4$ ($N = 512$). The results for the BH/BR hierarchical network are not included in this plot as the non-cluster links (i.e., the links in the level 2 network) saturate at this load.

Figure 3.10b depicts the *LR* ratio which is defined similar to the *LP* ratio except that the average message delay is used instead of the average internode distance. It should, however, be noted that the *LR* ratio is a function of network parameters such as λ, μ_{CL} and μ_{NCL}. The *LR* ratio improves as α increases. In the BH/CCC network, links in the level 2 network saturate for small values of α, and thus, *R* and *LR* ratio values for this network are shown for $\alpha \geq 0.8$ only.

In Figure 3.10, the value of α is restricted to $\alpha \geq 0.5$. For α values below this range, the non-cluster links of the hierarchical networks saturate with the stated parameter values. It is clear that HINs yield superior performance only if there is locality in communication. The value of α above which the HINs become cost effective depends on several factors such as λ, μ_{CL}, μ_{NCL}, and the system and cluster sizes.

Figure 3.11 gives *R* and *LR* ratio values as a function of the total number of nodes in the network *N*. The value of *N* is increased by keeping *n* fixed at 16 (i.e., $d = 4$) and by increasing the number of clusters. The parameters used are: $d = 4$, $\lambda = 1$, $\mu_{CL} = \mu_{NCL} = 3$, and $\alpha = 0.8$. For the BH/CCC network, μ_{NCL} is chosen as $\mu_{NCL} = i\,\mu_{CL}$, where *i* is an integer greater than 0 and may vary with *N*. The value of *i* selected is such that the resulting link utilization of the level 2 network links is less than 80%. This increase in μ_{NCL} is taken care of in the network cost by multiplying the number of level 2 links by *i*. Both BH/BH and BH/CCC networks offer substantial cost-performance ratio improvements for large systems. These conclusions are similar to those obtained with the static analysis (Section 3.5.1.7). However,

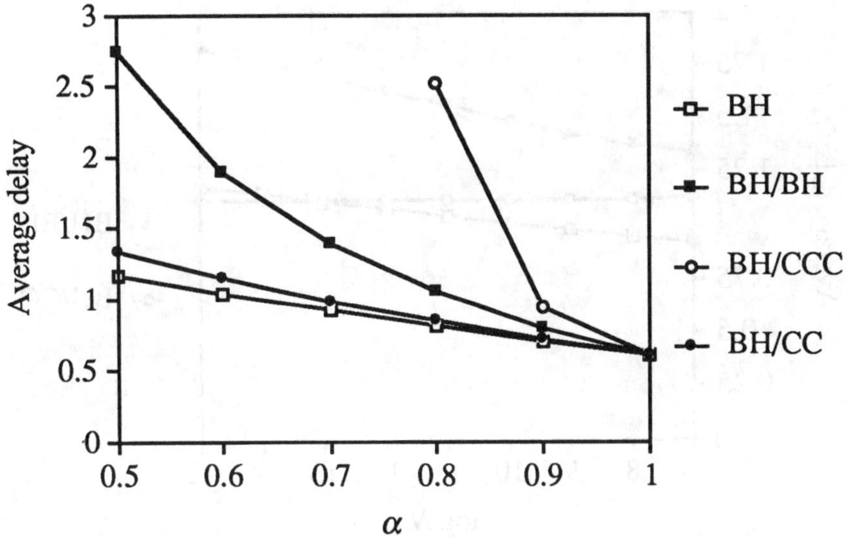

(a)

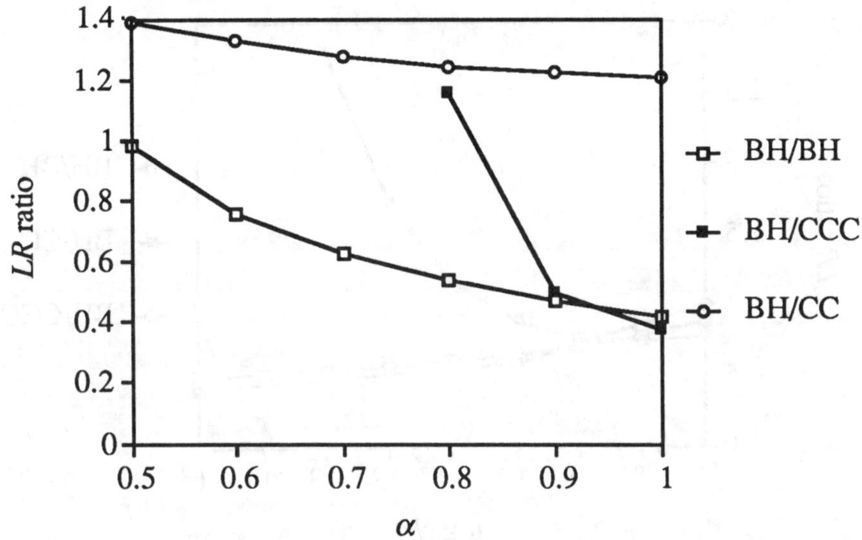

(b)

Figure 3.10 Average message delay and the *LR* ratio of hierarchical networks as a function of α

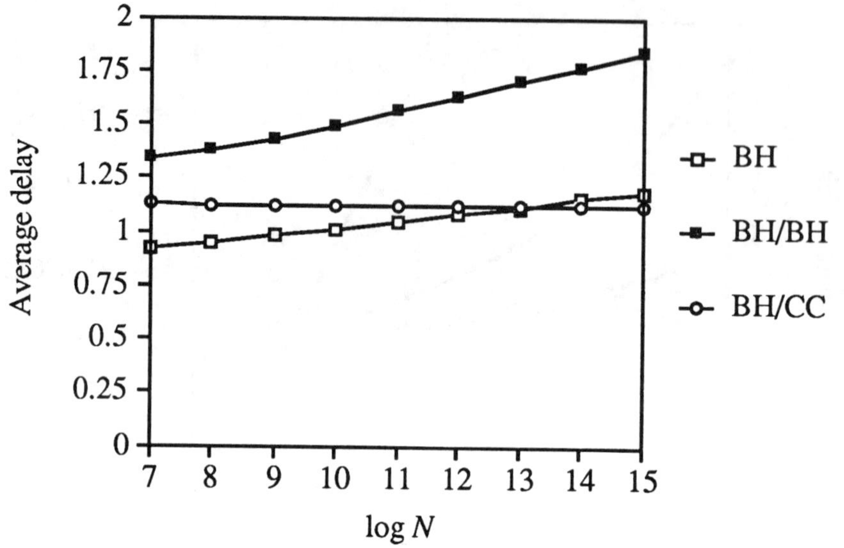

(a)

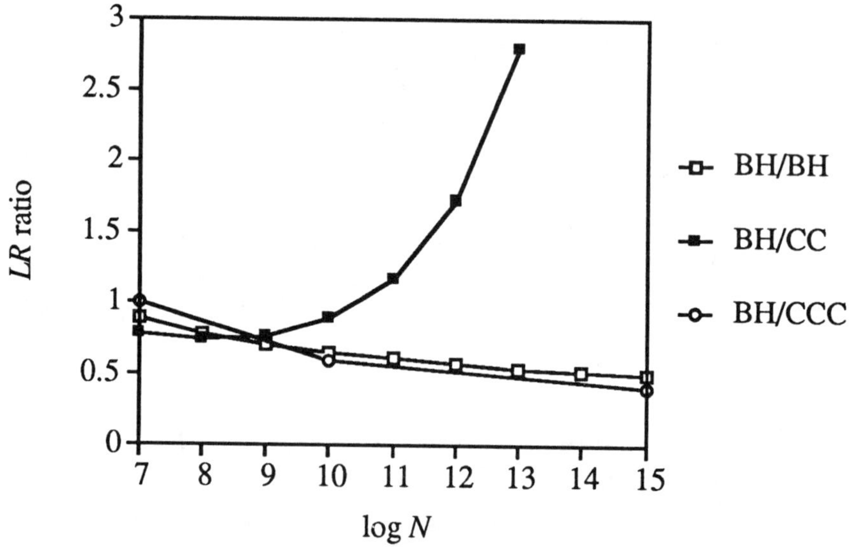

(b)

Figure 3.11 Average message delay and the *LR* ratio of hierarchical networks as a function of network size *N*

for large N, the BH/CCC network requires much higher message service rates for the non-cluster links than does the BH/BH network.

3.5.2.5. Validation of the queueing analysis

To facilitate the queueing analysis, it was assumed that whenever a message arrives at a link on its path to its destination, a new service time is generated from the exponential service time distribution. In a real system, of course, the messages would retain their service times, which reflect the lengths of the messages, from the times they are generated to the times they arrive at their destinations. A simulation model was constructed that reflected this reality, and, therefore, allowed validation of the independence assumption used in the analysis. In all other respects, the simulation model matched the analytic model.

Two networks - BH and BH/BH - were selected for simulation experiments. For each network, two plots are presented. One plot gives average delay as a function of α and the other plot gives average delay as a function of the network size N. The value of α is varied from 0.5 to 1.0 in steps of 0.1 and $\log_2 N$ is varied from 5 to 8. The results for the BH network are presented in Figure 3.12 and those for the BH/BH network are given in Figure 3.13. It can be seen from these plots that the results obtained from the analytical formulas match closely those obtained by simulation, thus justifying the use of Kleinrock's independence assumption in this context.

3.6. Performance Enhancements

The performance of HINs can be improved in several ways. This section briefly describes two of these. Section 3.6.1 discusses the improvement possible by replicating links in the level 2 network while the following section presents the impact of improved routing algorithms. A detailed discussion of routing algorithms is given in Chapter 7.

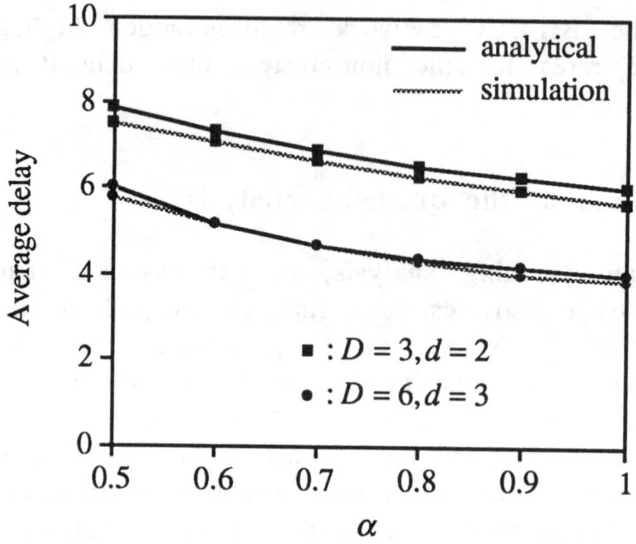

(a)

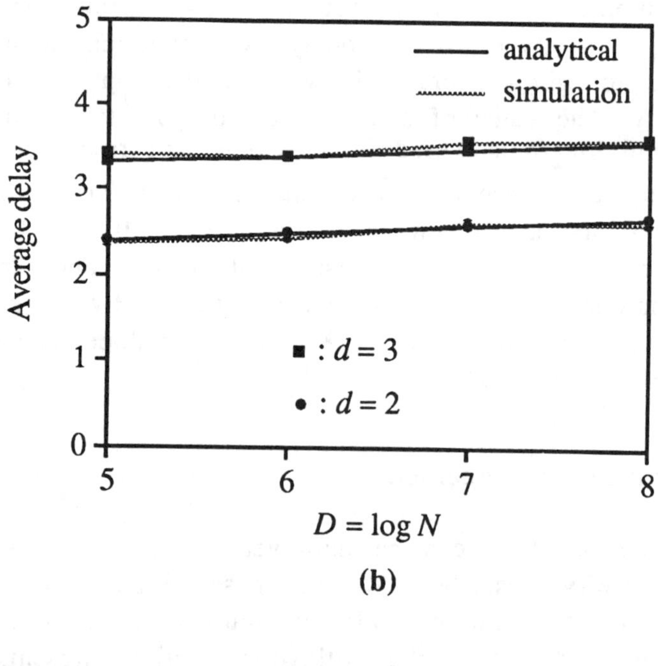

(b)

Figure 3.12 Comparison of analytical and simulation results for the BH network

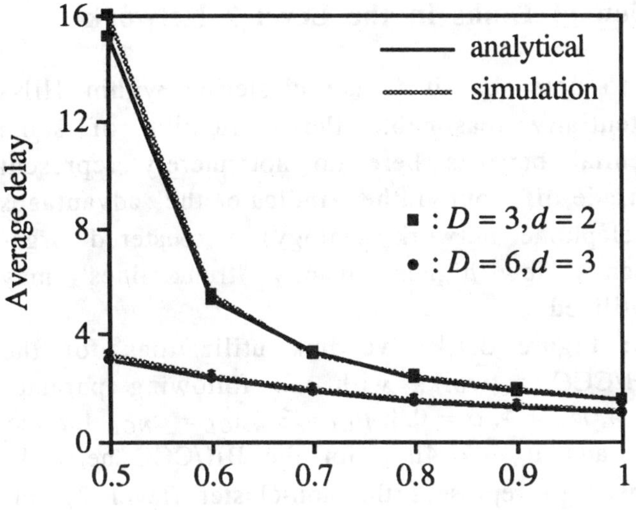

(a)

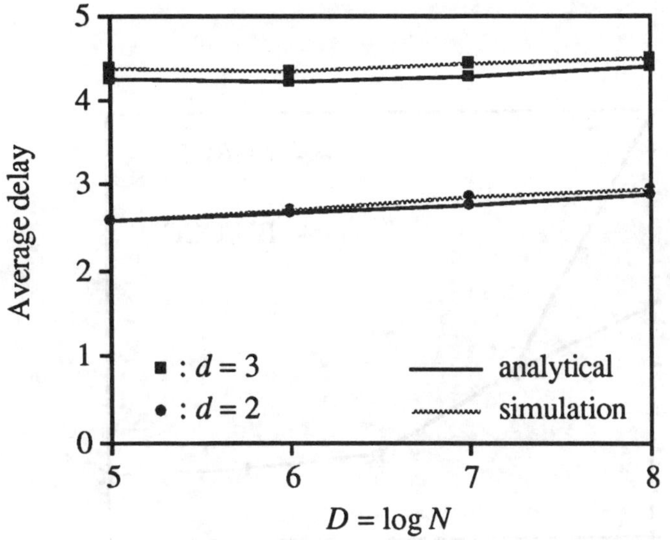

(b)

Figure 3.13 Comparison of analytical and simulation results for the BH/BH network

3.6.1. Replication of Links in the Level 2 Network

It is important to note that it is the clustering within HINs that makes potentially reasonable the replication of some links. The potential benefits here do not merely represent a cost-benefit trade-off, but rather indicate the advantages of (to use a telephone network analogy) a clustered organization in which a few higher capacity "trunk lines" may be profitably utilized.

The plots in Figure 3.14 give link utilizations for the BH/BH and BH/CCC networks with the following parameters: D = 15, d = 4, D_c = 4, α = 0.8, μ_{CL} = 3, $\mu_{CL} = \mu_{NCL}$ for the BH/BH network, and $\mu_{NCL} = 4\mu_{CL}$ for the BH/CCC network. Here j = 0 is used to represent the non-cluster (level 2) links. This plot suggests that by replicating the links in the level 2 network, effectively increasing μ_{NCL}, the average delay can be reduced. If the reduction in the average delay compensates for the increase in the number of links, the overall LR ratio improves (decreases). This section investi-

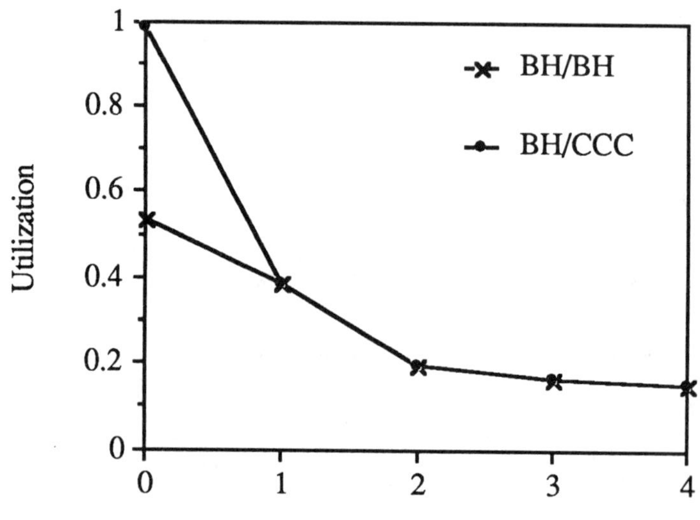

Figure 3.14 Link utilization of the BH/BH and BH/CCC networks (link level 0 represents the non-cluster links)

gates the effect of this replication on the performance of HINs.

Figure 3.15 shows the impact of replicating links in the level 2 network for the BH/BH and BH/CCC networks. The parameters used are: $d = 4$, D = 15, $\lambda = 1$, $\mu_{CL} = 3$, and $\alpha = 0.8$. The value of μ_{NCL} is varied to change the ratio μ_{NCL} / μ_{CL}. The μ_{NCL} / μ_{CL} ratio gives the number of parallel wires used to implement a logical link. These plots suggest that there is an optimum value ("knee") for μ_{NCL} at which the *LR* ratio is the smallest. Ideally, we would like to design the level 2 network such that the operating point is at or close to the knee. For the BH/BH network, the *LR* ratio is the smallest (allowing only integral μ_{NCL} / μ_{CL} ratios) when $\mu_{NCL} = 2\ \mu_{CL}$; for the BH/CCC network, it is the smallest when $\mu_{NCL} = 8\ \mu_{CL}$. It is important to note that the knee is quite broad indicating that there are several operating points that are nearly optimal. Thus, designing a network for near-optimum performance would apparently be straightforward.

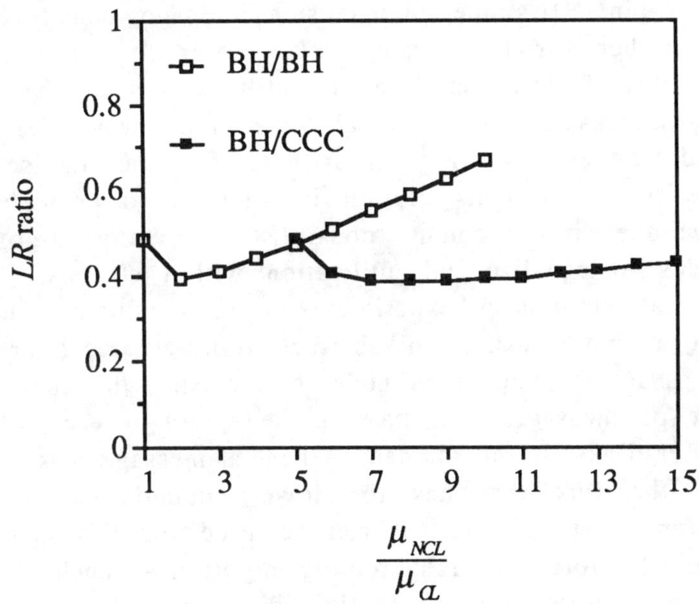

Figure 3.15 Impact of replicating links within the level 2 network

It appears from these data that the BH/CCC network can potentially achieve very similar *LR* ratios as for the BH/BH network, but that this requires a much greater replication of links in the level 2 network. In this example, the links in the level 2 network of the BH/CCC network require a replication factor that is four times that of the corresponding links in the BH/BH network.

3.6.2. Impact of Improved Routing Algorithms

The queueing analysis and the simulation experiments described in Section 3.5.2.5 used a routing algorithm that chooses randomly among shortest paths. In this routing algorithm, if a message at a node can be routed towards its destination on any of l links attached to the node, one of these l links is selected randomly. This works comparatively well with the BH network (under the assumed workload) because both intra- and inter-cluster messages are uniformly distributed over the links within a cluster. However, in HINs the inter-cluster message density tends to be higher for the cluster links closer to the interface node. Thus, if these links can be utilized less by the intra-cluster messages, the overall message delay can be reduced. Several routing algorithms can be devised to achieve this goal. This section is intended to estimate the performance improvement possible with any algorithm that tries to equalize link utilization within clusters.

Several simulation experiments were conducted on the BH/BH network using an abstract routing algorithm that works as follows. For each node in a cluster, the cumulative number of messages that have passed through each of the d cluster links is maintained. When a message has to be routed, the link that has the lowest cumulative message count (among the links that can be used for this message) is selected. Note that real routing algorithms (such as one based on "shortest-queue" routing discussed in Chapter 7) could be expected to perform somewhat better.

Many experiments were done with different parameters. Selected results are presented in Figure 3.16 that illustrate well the outputs of these experiments. The upper two curves are for D = 6, d = 3, λ = 1, μ_{CL} = 1.5, and μ_{NCL} = 3; the lower two curves are for D = 3, d = 2, λ = 1, μ_{CL} = 1.5, and μ_{NCL} = 3. In general, the improvement in performance increases with increasing utilizations of the most heavily utilized links (as may be caused by increasing the cluster size, decreasing α, and/or by increasing λ). For example, when α = 0.5, the average message delay for the larger network reduces from 15.2 to 6.3 since, in this case, the cluster links connected to the interface node have a utilization of

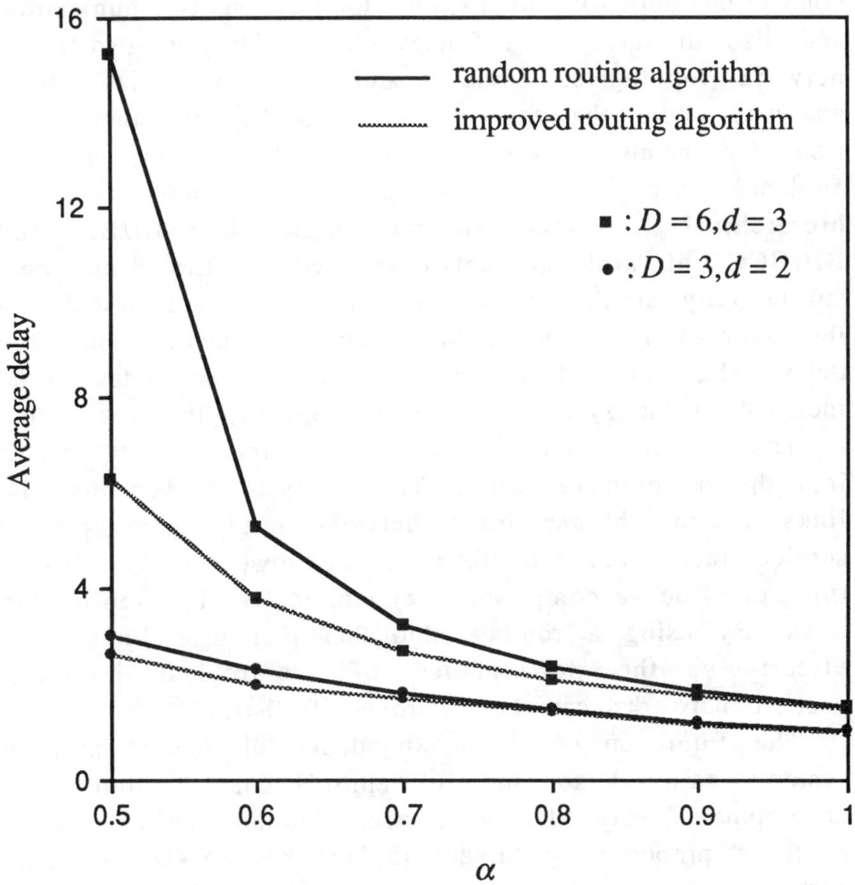

Figure 3.16 Effect of improved routing algorithm on the BH/BH network

94% when using the random routing algorithm. For the same network, when $\alpha = 0.6$, these links have a utilization of 82% and the average message delay reduces from 5.3 to 3.8. These results suggest that implementing improved routing algorithms would quite likely be worthwhile. A more detailed study of routing algorithms is given in Chapter 7.

3.7. Summary

This chapter has presented the use of hierarchical interconnection networks to exploit locality in communication, and also to serve as a framework for integrating different network topologies. Some example networks have been analysed under the assumption of locality in communication. By means of static analysis and queueing analysis, evidence was presented suggesting the suitability of the hierarchical networks. In particular, the BH/BH and BH/CCC hierarchical networks reduce the link cost substantially at the expense of only moderately increasing the average internode distance and the average message delay. Thus, hierarchical networks allow more nodes to be included in the system when constrained by the link cost.

The queueing analysis provided a much deeper insight into the performance issues. This analysis showed that the links in the higher level network might need greater service rates than the links in the lower level network; this can be accomplished economically by replicating links. By using a routing algorithm that uses links more effectively, the performance of hierarchical interconnection networks can be improved further.

The future may see an abundance of special purpose systems tailored to specific applications. Technological developments may also yield reconfigurable systems much as those proposed by Snyder [SNYD 82, SNYD 84], with performance superior to to those of the static hierarchical networks discussed here. Hierarchical networks, however, provide tailoring to a general phenomenon underlying many parallel computations ("locality") while remaining "general purpose", with current technology.

Further Reading

This chapter discussed performance of a cluster-based hierarchical interconnection networks. However, several other types of hierarchical networks have been proposed in the literature. The reader is referred to the following references for additional information: [HWAN 87], [LAKS 88], [GHOS 89], [GHOS 90], and [WU 81].

Acknowledgement

Material presented in this chapter is partly based on [DAND 90].

References

[ABRA 86] S. G. Abraham and E. S. Davidson, "A Communication Model for Optimizing Hierarchical Multiprocessor Systems," *Proc. 1986 Int. Conf. Parallel Processing*, 1986, pp. 467-474.

[AGRA 85] D. P. Agrawal and I. E. O. Mehgoub, "Performance Analysis of Cluster-Based Supersystems," *Proc. 1st Int. Conf. on Supercomputing Systems*, St. Petersburg, Florida, IEEE Computer Society Press, 1985, pp. 593-602.

[AGRA 86] D. P. Agrawal, V. K. Janakiram and G. C. Pathak, "Evaluating the Performance of Multicomputer Configurations," *Computer*, Vol. 19, No. 5, May 1986, pp. 23-37.

[BARN 81] G. H. Barnes and S. F. Lundstrom, "Design and Validation of a Connection Network for Many-Processor Multiprocessor Systems," *Computer*, Vol. 14, No. 12, December 1981, pp. 31-41.

[BHUY 83] L. N. Bhuyan and D. P. Agrawal, "Design and Performance of Generalized Interconnection Networks,"

IEEE Trans. Computers, Vol. C-32, No. 12, December 1983, pp. 1081-1090.

[BHUY 86] L. N. Bhuyan and C. R. Das, "Dependability Evaluation of Multicomputer Networks," *Proc. 1986 Int. Conf. Parallel Processing,* 1986, pp. 576-583.

[BOXE 89] L. Boxer and R. Miller, "Dynamic Computational Geometry on Meshes and Hypercubes," *J. Supercomputing,* Vol. 3, 1989, pp. 161-191.

[CARL 85] D. Carlson, "The Mesh With A Global Mesh: A Flexible, High-Speed Organization for Parallel Computation," *Proc. 1st Int. Conf. on Supercomputing Systems,* St. Petersburg, Florida, IEEE Computer Society Press, 1985, pp. 618-627.

[DAND 90] S. P. Dandamudi and D. L. Eager, "Hierarchical Interconnection Networks for Multicomputer Systems," *IEEE Trans. Computers,* Vol. C-39, No. 6, June 1990, pp. 786-797.

[DESP 78] A. M. Despain and D. A. Patterson, "X-Tree: A Tree Structured Multiprocessor Computer Architectures," *Proc. 5th Symp. on Comp. Arch.,* 1978, pp. 144-151.

[FULL 78] S. H. Fuller et al., "Multi-Microprocessors: An Overview and Working Example," *Proc. IEEE,* Vol. 66, 1978, pp. 216-228.

[GAJS 83] D. Gajski, D. Kuck, D. Lawrie, and A. Sameh, "CEDAR," Department of Computer Science, University of Illinois, Urbana, 1983. (Reprinted in *Tutorial on Supercomputers: Design and Applications,* (ed.) K. Hwang, IEEE Computer Society Press, 1983, pp. 251-275.)

[GHOS 89] K. Ghose and K. R. Desai, "The HCN: A Versatile Interconnection Network Based on Cubes," *Proc. Supercomputing Conf.,* 1989, pp. 426-435.

[GHOS 90] K. Ghose and K. R. Desai, "The Design and Evaluation of the Hierarchical Cubic Network," *Proc. 1990 Int. Conf. Parallel Processing,* 1990, Vol. 1, pp. 355-362.

[GOOD 81] J. R. Goodman and C. H. Sequin, "Hypertree: A Multiprocessor Interconnection Topology," *IEEE Trans. Computers,* Vol. C-30, No. 12, December 1981, pp. 923-933.

[GOPA 81] G. Gopal and J. W. Wong, "Delay Analysis of Broadcast Routing in Packet-Switching Networks," *IEEE Trans. Computers*, Vol. C-30, No. 12, December 1981, pp. 915-922.

[HARR 77] J. A. Harris and D. R. Smith, "Hierarchical Multiprocessor Organizations," *Proc. 4th Symp. on Comput. Arch.*, March 1977, pp. 41-48.

[HAYE 86] J. P. Hayes, T. N. Mudge, Q. F. Stout, S. Colley, and J. Palmer, "Architecture of a Hypercube Supercomputer," *Proc. 1986 Int. Conf. Parallel Processing*, 1986, pp. 653-660.

[HILL 85] W. D. Hillis, *The Connection Machine*, MIT Press, Cambridge, MA., 1985.

[HORO 81] E. Horowitz and A. Zorat, "The Binary Tree as an Interconnection Network: Applications to Multiprocessor Systems and VLSI," *IEEE Trans. Computers*, Vol. C-30, No. 4, April 1981, pp. 247-253.

[HWAN 87] K. Hwang and J. Ghose, "Hypernet: A Communication Efficient Architecture for Constructing Massively Parallel Computers," *IEEE Trans. Computers*, Vol. C-36, No. 12, December 1987, pp. 1450-1466.

[KAMO 79] F. Kamoun and L. Kleinrock, "Stochastic Performance Evaluation of Hierarchical Routing for Large Networks," *Computer Networks*, Vol. 3, 1979, pp. 337-353.

[KLEI 75] L. Kleinrock, *Queueing Systems: Volume 1*, Wiley, New York, 1975.

[KLEI 76] L. Kleinrock, *Queueing Systems: Volume 2*, Wiley, New York, 1976.

[KLEI 77] L. Kleinrock and F. Kamoun, "Hierarchical Routing for Large Networks," *Computer Networks*, Vol. 1, 1977, pp. 155-174.

[KUHL 86] J. G. Kuhl and S. M. Reddy, "Fault-Tolerance Considerations in Large, Multiple-Processor Systems," *Computer*, Vol. 19, No. 3, March 1986, pp. 56-67.

[LAKS 88] S. Lakshmivarahan and S. K. Dhall, "A New Hierarchy of Hypercube Interconnection Schemes for Parallel Computers," *J. of Supercomputing*, Vol. 2, 1988, pp. 81-108.

[LAWR 75] D. Lawrie, "Access and Alignment of Data in an Array Processor," *IEEE Trans. Computers*, Vol. C-24, No. 12, December 1975, pp. 1145-1155.

[LAZO 84] E. D. Lazowska, J. Zahorjan, G. S. Graham, and K. C. Sevcik, *Computer System Performance*, Prentice-Hall Inc., Englewood Cliffs, 1984.

[LEIS 85] C. E. Leiserson, "Fat-Trees: Universal Networks for Hardware Efficient Supercomputing," *IEEE Trans. Computers*, Vol. C-34, No. 10, October 1985, pp. 892-901.

[LEON 85] D. D. Leondorf, "Development and Use of an Asynchronous MIMD Computer for Finite Element Analysis," in *Algorithmically Specialized Parallel Computers*, (eds.) L. Snyder, L. H. Jamieson, D. B. Gannon, and H. J. Siegel, Academic Press, 1985, pp. 213-222.

[LEVI 85] S. P. Levitan, "Evaluation Criteria for Communication Structures in Parallel Architectures," *Proc. 1985 Int. Conf. Parallel Processing*, 1985, pp. 147-154.

[MCCR 86] C. D. McCrosky, "Message Passing in Synchronous Hypercubes," Tech. Rep. 86-4, Department of Computational Science, University of Saskatchewan, Saskatoon, 1986 (to appear in *Computer System Science and Engineering*).

[NASS 79] D. Nassimi and S. Sahni, "Bitonic Sort on a Mesh-Connected Parallel Computer," *IEEE Trans. Computers*, Vol. C-28, No. 1, January 1979, pp. 2-7.

[NASS 80] D. Nassimi and S. Sahni, "Finding Connected Components and Connected Ones on a Mesh-Connected Parallel Computer," *SIAM J. Computing*, Vol. 9, No. 4, November 1980, pp. 744-757.

[PREP 81] F. P. Preparata and J. Vuillemin, "The Cube-Connected-Cycles: A Versatile Network for Parallel Computation," *Comm. ACM*, Vol. 24, No. 5, May 1981, pp. 300-309.

[RATT 85] J. Rattner, "Concurrent Processing: A New Approach in Scientific Computing," *Proc. AFIPS Conf.*, Vol. 54, 1985 NCC, pp. 157-166.

[REED 83a] D. A. Reed, "Queueing Network Models of Multimicrocomputer Networks," *Proc. 1983 ACM SIGMETRICS Conf. on Measurement and Modeling of*

Computer Systems, Minneapolis, Minnesota, 1983, pp. 190-197.

[REED 83b] D. A. Reed and H. D. Schwetman, "Cost-Performance Bounds for Multimicrocomputer Networks," *IEEE Trans. Computers,* Vol. C-32, No. 1, January 1983, pp. 83-95.

[REED 87] D. A. Reed and D. C. Grunwald, "The Performance of Multicomputer Interconnection Networks," *Computer,* Vol. 20, No. 6, June 1987, pp. 63-73.

[SEIT 85] C. L. Seitz, "The Cosmic Cube," *Comm. ACM,* Vol. 28, No. 1, January 1985, pp. 22-33.

[SNYD 82] L. Snyder, "Introduction to the Configurable Highly Parallel Computer," *Computer,* Vol. 15, No.1, January 1982, pp. 47-56.

[SNYD 84] L. Snyder, "Supercomputers and VLSI: The Effect of Large-Scale Integration on Computer Architecture," *Advances in Computers,* Vol. 23, Academic Press, 1984, pp. 1-33

[SNYD 86] L. Snyder, "Type Architectures, Shared Memory, and The Corollary of Modest Potential," *Ann. Rev. Comput. Sci.,* Vol. 1, 1986, pp. 289-317.

[STOU 83] Q. F. Stout, "Mesh-Connected Computers with Broadcasting," *IEEE Trans. Computers,* Vol. C-32, No. 9, September 1983, pp. 826-830.

[SWAN 77a] R. J. Swan, S. H. Fuller, and D. Siewiorek, "Cm* – A Modular, Multi-Microprocessor," *Proc. of the National Computer Conference,* 1977, pp. 39-46. (Reprinted in *Tutorial on Parallel Processing,* (eds.) R. H. Kuhn and D. A. Padua, IEEE Computer Society Press, 1981, pp. 146-153.)

[SWAN 77b] R. J. Swan, A. Bechtolsheim, K. -W. Lai, and J. K. Ousterhout, "The Implementation of the Cm* Multi-Microprocessor," *Proc. of the National Computer Conference,* 1977, pp. 645-655. (Reprinted in *Tutorial on Parallel Processing,* (eds.) R. H. Kuhn and D. A. Padua, IEEE Computer Society Press, 1981, pp. 154-164.)

[THOM 77] C. D. Thompson and H. T. Kung, "Sorting on a Mesh-Connected Parallel Computer," *Comm. ACM,* Vol. 20, No. 4, April 1977, pp. 263-271.

[WITT 81] L. D. Wittie, "Communication Structures for Large Networks of Microcomputers," *IEEE Trans. Computers,* Vol. C-30, No. 4, April 1981, pp. 264-273.

[WU 81] S. W. Wu and M. T. Liu, "A Cluster Structure as an Interconnection Network for Large Multimicrocomputer Systems," *IEEE Trans. Computers,* Vol. C-30, No. 4, April 1981, pp. 254-264.

4

Two Design Issues

This chapter discusses two design issues concerning HINs – the cluster size and the number of levels in the hierarchy. Initially, as in Chapter 3, two-level HINs are considered. In a two-level HIN, determining the optimum cluster size is an important design issue. Since the BH network offers a reasonable compromise between the number of links and the average internode distance (see Section 3.1), the BH/BH network is considered when addressing this question. The optimum cluster size for the BH/BH network is discussed in Section 4.2. Section 4.3 considers the impact on performance of increasing the number of levels in the HIN. A summary is given in the last section.

4.1. Introduction

The previous chapter has shown that HINs are cost effective. HINs reduce the link cost substantially at the expense of moderately increasing the average internode distance and the average message delivery time. This advantage of HINs has been quantified by two performance measures; in the static analysis, the *LP* ratio was used and in the queueing analysis, the *LR* ratio was used. Although the *LR* ratio is perhaps a more important cost-benefit ratio, it required significant additional simplifying assumptions regarding the workload, and, in addition, required a more complex analysis. Therefore, the *LP* ratio is used here as the performance measure of interest. The design approach advocated here is to use a static analysis to make decisions on the basic design issues such as the cluster size and the number of levels. A queueing analysis may then be used to design the link architecture (addressing questions such as appropriate link data rates, whether to use bit-serial links or parallel links, if parallel links are to be used how many physical links should represent a logical link, etc.).

The *LP* ratio is dependent on the underlying degree of locality in communication. Locality can be characterized in several ways, in addition to the simple method used earlier in Chapter 3. Let $\phi(l)$ denote the probability that a message is destined for some specific node that is l links away from the source node, l_{max} denote the maximum internode distance in the network, and $NumNodes(l)$ denote the number of nodes exactly l links away from a source node. Then, the average internode distance, P, is given by

$$P = \sum_{l=1}^{l_{max}} l \; \phi(l) \, NumNodes(l)$$

Different choices for $\phi(l)$ reflect differing degrees and types of locality, and lead to different average internode distances and, in turn, to different values of the *LP* ratio. Five types of distribution for $\phi(l)$ are considered in this chapter. These are:

(*i*) Uniform (UNIF)
(*ii*) Decreasing probability (DPF)
(*iii*) Overlapping sphere of locality (O-SOL)
(*iv*) Sphere of locality (SOL)
(*v*) Generalized sphere of locality (G-SOL)

For each type of locality characterization, expressions can be derived for the average internode distance, in terms of the parameters of the characterization. These expressions are complex, however, and thus optimum network designs are found numerically in the following sections.

4.2. The Optimum Cluster Size for the BH/BH Network

Let P_y^x be the average internode distance in network Y with a locality characterization of type X. For example, $P^{UNIF}_{BH/BH}$ represents the average internode distance in a BH/BH network with uniform communication. L_{BH} and $L_{BH/BH}$, which are independent of the message routing pattern, are given by Eqs. (3.2) and (3.7), respectively.

The following five subsections derive the average internode distances for the BH and BH/BH networks with each of the five locality characterizations discussed above. Here, $\phi(l)$ is consistently interpreted in terms of the distances within the reference network BH. Further, it is assumed that nodes do not send messages to themselves. Finally, in Section 4.2.6 these results are used to derive optimum cluster sizes.

4.2.1. Uniform Communication

In uniform communication, each pair of nodes i and j exchange messages at an identical rate. The assumption of uniform communication is appealing because one would expect real computations to be characterized by more locality, implying that the assumption should result in an upper bound on message path lengths. For the BH network with $N = 2^D$ nodes and uniform communication, $\phi(l)$ is given by

$$\phi(l) = \frac{1}{2^D - 1}$$

Then,

$$P_{BH}^{UNIF} = \frac{1}{2^D - 1}\sum_{l=1}^{D}\binom{D}{l} l = \frac{D2^{D-1}}{2^D - 1}$$

The average internode distance of an HIN, with uniform communication, is given by Eq. (3.8) with $\alpha = \frac{2^d-1}{2^D-1}$. For the BH/BH network, with clusters of size 2^d and $N = 2^D$ nodes, $P_{level1} = \frac{d\,2^{d-1}}{2^d-1}$ and P_{level2} is given by Eq. (3.9). This yields

$$P_{BH/BH}^{UNIF} = \alpha\left[\frac{d\,2^{d-1}}{2^d - 1}\right] + (1-\alpha)\left[d + \frac{(D-d)2^{D-d-1}}{2^{D-d} - 1}\right]$$

4.2.2. Decreasing Probability Communication

In this characterization of locality, the probability that a given message is destined for a node l links away from the source decreases as a smooth function of l. A wide variety of potentially suitable distribution functions exhibiting such behaviour exist. One such function is given by [REED 83, REED 87],

$$\phi(l) = \frac{Decay(a, l_{\max})}{NumNodes(l)}a^l \qquad 0 < a < 1,\quad 1 \le l \le D$$

where $Decay(a, l_{\max})$ is a normalizing constant chosen to ensure that the $\phi(l)$ sum to one. As a approaches one, the ϕ approximates a linearly increasing function of the distance from the source node. Conversely, as a approaches zero, ϕ approximates a nearest neighbour communication pattern. Choices of a between these two extremes lead to varying degrees of communication locality.

For the BH network,

$$Decay(a, D) = \frac{1-a}{a(1-a^D)}$$

and

$$\phi(l) = \left[\frac{1-a}{a(1-a^D)}\right]\frac{a^l}{\binom{D}{l}} \tag{4.1}$$

Therefore,

$$P_{BH}^{DPF} = \left[\frac{1-a}{a(1-a^D)}\right]\sum_{l=1}^{D} l\, a^l$$
$$= \frac{Da^{D+1} - (D+1)\,a^D + 1}{(1-a)\left[1-a^D\right]}$$

The derivation of $P_{BH/BH}^{DPF}$ can be divided into two parts.

$$P_{BH/BH}^{DPF} = P'_{BH/BH} + P''_{BH/BH} \tag{4.2}$$

where

$P'_{BH/BH}$ = that portion of the average internode distance contributed by messages whose source and destination nodes are within a cluster, and

$P''_{BH/BH}$ = that portion of the average internode distance contributed by messages whose source and destination nodes are in two different clusters.

Considering first $P'_{BH/BH}$, it is easy to derive that

$$P'_{BH/BH} = \sum_{l=1}^{d}\binom{d}{l}\, l\, \phi(l) \tag{4.3}$$

In computing $P''_{BH/BH}$ it is necessary to consider all 2^d nodes in a cluster. The address of a node is divided into two parts, the most significant $(D-d)$ bits giving the cluster number, and the least significant d bits representing a node within a cluster. The distance between a source node and a destination node is divided into four components: $i+j+k+m$. The term i represents the distance from the source node to the source cluster interface node, and j represents the distance in the level 2 network. The least significant d bits of the destination node are further divided into two groups: one group consists of those bits of the destination node corresponding to the bits of the source node address that differ from those of the source node cluster interface node, and the rest of the least significant bits form the other group. Then, k can be considered as representing the distance contributed by the former group of address bits and m as representing the distance contributed by the later group. Recall that $\phi(l)$ is interpreted in terms of the distances within the reference network (BH). The sum $i+j+k+m$ gives the distance in the BH/BH network that corresponds to a distance of $j+k+m$ in the BH network. $P''_{BH/BH}$ can then be derived as

$$P''_{BH/BH} = \frac{1}{2^d} \sum_{i=0}^{d} \sum_{j=1}^{D-d} \sum_{k=0}^{i} \sum_{m=0}^{d-i} \left\{ (i+j+k+m) \binom{d}{i} \binom{D-d}{j} \binom{i}{k} \binom{d-i}{m} \phi(j+k+m) \right\} \tag{4.4}$$

4.2.3. Overlapping Sphere of Locality

Any reasonable mapping of a distributed computation onto a multicomputer system should place those tasks that exchange messages with high frequency physically close to one another. One abstraction of this idea places each node at the centre of a sphere of locality [REED 83]. A given message is destined for a node within the source node's sphere of locality with some high probability α, and to some node outside the sphere of locality with the low probability $(1-\alpha)$. A message is destined for each node within the same category (either within or exterior to the sphere of locality) with identical probability. Let L be the maximum number of links a message may cross and remain in the sphere of locality centred at its source (i.e., L is the radius of the sphere). The number of nodes contained in a sphere of locality for the BH network is $\sum_{l=1}^{L}\binom{D}{l}$.

Then,

$$\phi(l) = \begin{cases} \dfrac{\alpha}{\sum_{l=1}^{L}\binom{D}{l}} & 1 \le l \le L \\ \dfrac{1-\alpha}{2^{D} - \sum_{l=0}^{L}\binom{D}{l}} & L < l \le D \end{cases} \tag{4.5}$$

P_{BH}^{O-SOL} is given by

$$P_{BH}^{O-SOL} = \frac{\alpha\sum_{l=1}^{L}\binom{D}{l}l}{\sum_{l=1}^{L}\binom{D}{l}} + \frac{(1-\alpha)\sum_{l=L+1}^{D}\binom{D}{l}l}{\sum_{l=L+1}^{D}\binom{D}{l}}$$

$P_{BH/BH}^{O-SOL}$ is given by Eqs. (4.2), (4.3) and (4.4) by using Eq. (4.5) for $\phi(l)$.

4.2.4. Sphere of Locality

Another similar but distinct form of locality characterization, called sphere of locality (SOL), divides the total number of nodes N into K *disjoint* groups of n nodes each. All nodes within a group share the same sphere of locality that comprises the nodes within that group. In contrast, in O-SOL, each node has its own distinct sphere of locality. A message is destined for a node within the same sphere of locality as the source node with some high probability α, and to some node in a different sphere of locality with probability $(1-\alpha)$. A message is destined for each node within the same category (either within or exterior to the sphere of locality) with identical probability. Chapter 3 has used the same characterization of locality. Locality in communication has also been characterized similarly by other researchers [WU 81].

P_{BH}^{SOL} is given by (similar to Eq. (3.6)),

$$P_{BH}^{SOL} = \alpha\left[\frac{s2^{s-1}}{2^{s}-1}\right] + (1-\alpha)\left[\frac{D2^{D-1} - s2^{s-1}}{2^{D} - 2^{s}}\right]$$

For the BH/BH network, the average internode distance is given by

$$P_{BH/BH}^{SOL} = \alpha P_{iSOL} + (1-\alpha) P_{oSOL} \qquad (4.6)$$

where

P_{iSOL} = average distance between two nodes in the same sphere of locality, and

P_{oSOL} = average distance between two nodes in different spheres of locality.

Consider the following two cases: (*i*) $d \le s$, and (*ii*) $d \ge s$.

Case (i): $d \le s$

Since $d \le s$, the number of clusters within a sphere of locality is 2^{s-d}. In this case, P_{iSOL} can be derived as

$$P_{iSOL} = \beta P_{CL-avg} + (1-\beta)\left[2P'_{CL-avg} + P_{NCL-avg}\right]$$

where

β= fraction of messages between two nodes in the same sphere of locality that also lie within the same cluster;

P_{CL-avg} = average internode distance in a cluster;

P'_{CL-avg} = average number of links traversed in the source (or destination) cluster by messages whose source and destination nodes lie within the same sphere of locality, but in different clusters;

$P_{NCL-avg}$ = average number of links traversed in the level 2 network by messages whose source and destination nodes lie within the same sphere of locality, but in different clusters.

It is straightforward to derive that

$$\beta = \frac{2^d - 1}{2^s - 1},$$

$$P_{CL-avg} = \frac{d\,2^{d-1}}{2^d - 1},$$

$$P'_{CL-avg} = \frac{d}{2},$$

and

$$P_{NCL-avg} = \frac{(s-d)2^{s-d-1}}{2^{s-d} - 1}.$$

Therefore,

$$P_{iSOL} = \left[\frac{d2^{d-1}}{2^s - 1}\right] + \left[\frac{2^s - 2^d}{2^s - 1}\right]\left\{d + \frac{(s-d)2^{s-d-1}}{2^{s-d} - 1}\right\}$$

P_{oSOL} can be derived similarly and is given by

$$P_{oSOL} = d + \frac{(D-s)2^{D-s-1}}{2^{D-s}-1}$$

Case (ii): $d \geq s$

For this case,

$$P_{iSOL} = \frac{s2^{s-1}}{2^{s}-1}$$

and

$$P_{oSOL} = \left[\frac{2^{d}-2^{s}}{2^{D}-2^{s}}\right]\left\{\frac{d2^{d-1}-s2^{s-1}}{2^{d}-2^{s}}\right\} + \left[1-\frac{2^{d}-2^{s}}{2^{D}-2^{s}}\right]\left\{2\frac{d}{2}+\frac{(D-d)2^{D-d-1}}{2^{D-d}-1}\right\}$$

$$= \left[\frac{d2^{d-1}-s2^{s-1}}{2^{D}-2^{s}}\right] + \left[\frac{2^{D}-2^{d}}{2^{D}-2^{s}}\right]\left[d+\frac{(D-d)2^{D-d-1}}{2^{D-d}-1}\right]$$

4.2.5. Generalized Sphere of Locality

A disadvantage with SOL and O-SOL is that they assume uniformly random message routing within and without a sphere of locality. The generalized sphere of locality (G-SOL) model removes this assumption. In this model, instead of using just two levels of locality, a layered model is used. The total number of nodes is divided into disjoint spheres of locality, which are then each divided into subspheres of locality, and so on. Thus, the G-SOL locality model generalizes the SOL locality model. Each node is at the centre of a locality containing only itself, said to be a layer 0 locality. A message from this node is destined to a node within its containing layer i locality, but not within its containing layer $i-1$ locality, with probability α_i (and to each node within this layer with equal probability); locality implies that $\alpha_j \geq \alpha_k$ if $0 < j < k$. Since a node may not send messages to itself in this model, $\alpha_0 = 0$.

Since spheres of locality at varying layers may contain varying numbers of nodes, this locality model provides much flexibility. For the BH-based networks under consideration, it is convenient to assume that the number of nodes in a layer i locality is 2^i. This is done by grouping together nodes with related addresses. A set of nodes belong to a layer i locality if the most significant $(D-i)$ bits of their addresses are the same. Let $F(i)$ be the probability of a message from a node being destined for some node in its containing level i locality. From the definition of α_k,

$$F(i) = \sum_{k=0}^{i} \alpha_k .$$

As an example of how this characterization of communication locality could be applied, consider nearest-neighbour communication in which each node communicates with its four neighbouring nodes in a two-dimensional torus with $N = 2^D$ nodes. If D is even, then the torus is $2^{D/2} \times 2^{D/2}$; if D is odd, it is $2^{(D+1)/2} \times 2^{(D-1)/2}$. In such a structure, $F(i)$ can be computed as follows, assuming again that layer i localities are to contain 2^i nodes. If i is even, a layer i locality represents a square mesh of $2^{i/2} \times 2^{i/2}$; if i is odd, a layer i locality represents a mesh of $2^{(i+1)/2} \times 2^{(i-1)/2}$. Then, it is easy to derive $F(i)$, $0 < i < D$, as

$$F(i) = \begin{cases} 1 - \dfrac{1}{\sqrt{2^i}} & \text{if } i \text{ is even} \\[2ex] 1 - \dfrac{1.5}{\sqrt{2^{i+1}}} & \text{if } i \text{ is odd} \end{cases}$$

Some sample $F(i)$ values are shown in Table 4.1 for a 1024-node torus. It should be noted that this characterization of communication locality only approximately represents the true locality (nearest-neighbour communication) that is present.

Table 4.1 Example $F(i)$ values for a 1024-node torus

i	number of nodes in a layer i locality ($= 2^i$)	$F(i)$
1	2	0.25
2	4	0.50
3	8	0.625
4	16	0.75
5	32	0.8125
6	64	0.875
7	128	0.90625
8	256	0.9375
9	512	0.953125
10	1024	1

With the G-SOL type of distribution, $P_{BH}^{G\text{-}SOL}$ can be derived as

$$P_{BH}^{G-SOL} = \sum_{i=1}^{D}[F(i) - F(i-1)]P_{avg}(i)$$

where $P_{avg}(i)$ is the average internode distance between a source node and the nodes that are in the containing layer i locality but not in the containing layer $(i-1)$ locality. Note that such nodes must have addresses that differ in the $(i-1)$th least significant bit in comparison to the source node address, but whose $(D-i)$ most significant bits match those of the source node address. Since the number of potential destination nodes at a distance $(j+1)$ from the source node, where j ($j \geq 0$) is contributed by the least significant $(i-1)$ bits and the '1' is contributed by the $(i-1)$th least significant bit, is equal to $\binom{i-1}{j}$, $P_{avg}(i)$ is given by

$$P_{avg}(i) = \frac{\sum_{j=0}^{i-1} \left\{ \binom{i-1}{j} (j+1) \right\}}{2^{i} - 2^{i-1}} = \frac{i+1}{2}$$

For the BH/BH network, the average internode distance is given by

$$P^{G-SOL}_{BH/BH} = P'_{BH/BH} + P''_{BH/BH}$$

where

$P'_{BH/BH}$ = that portion of the average internode distance contributed by messages whose source and destination nodes are within the source cluster, and

$P''_{BH/BH}$ = that portion of the average internode distance contributed by messages whose source and destination nodes are in two different clusters.

$P'_{BH/BH}$ and $P''_{BH/BH}$ can be derived as

$$P'_{BH/BH} = \sum_{i=1}^{d} [F(i) - F(i-1)] P_{avg}(i)$$

and,

$$P''_{BH/BH} = \sum_{i=d+1}^{D} [F(i) - F(i-1)] P''_{avg}(i)$$

where $P''_{avg}(i)$ is defined in a similar manner as $P_{avg}(i)$, but is conditioned on source and destination nodes being in distinct clusters. Since all destination nodes have to be nodes that are in the layer i locality containing the source node, but not in the layer $i-1$ locality, the ith address bit of all these destination nodes should differ from the corresponding bit in the address of the message source node. The number of clusters composed of such nodes is 2^{i-d-1}. Thus, $P''_{avg}(i)$ is given by

$$P''_{avg}(i) = \frac{\sum_{j=0}^{d} \sum_{k=0}^{i-d-1} \sum_{m=0}^{d} \left[\binom{d}{j} \binom{i-d-1}{k} \binom{d}{m} (j+k+m+1) \right]}{2^d 2^{i-d-1} 2^d}$$

where j represents the number of links travelled by a message to reach the interface node in the source cluster, k represents the number of links travelled in the level 2 network and m represents the number of links travelled from the interface node in the destination cluster to the destination node. The '1' represents the distance contributed by the ith address bit. This expression can be simplified to yield

$$P''_{avg}(i) = \frac{d+i+1}{2}$$

This yields

$$P^{G-SOL}_{BH/BH} = \sum_{i=1}^{d} [F(i) - F(i-1)](i+1)/2 + \sum_{i=d+1}^{D} [F(i) - F(i-1)](d+i+1)/2$$

4.2.6. Discussion of Results

Some sample results of the analysis done so far are presented in Figures 4.1-4.5 for the five types of locality characterization. For each characterization, the system size is varied from 2^7 to 2^{16}. Each figure consists of two plots; one plot gives the optimum cluster size as a function of the network size, and the other gives the *LP* ratios when that optimum cluster size is utilized.

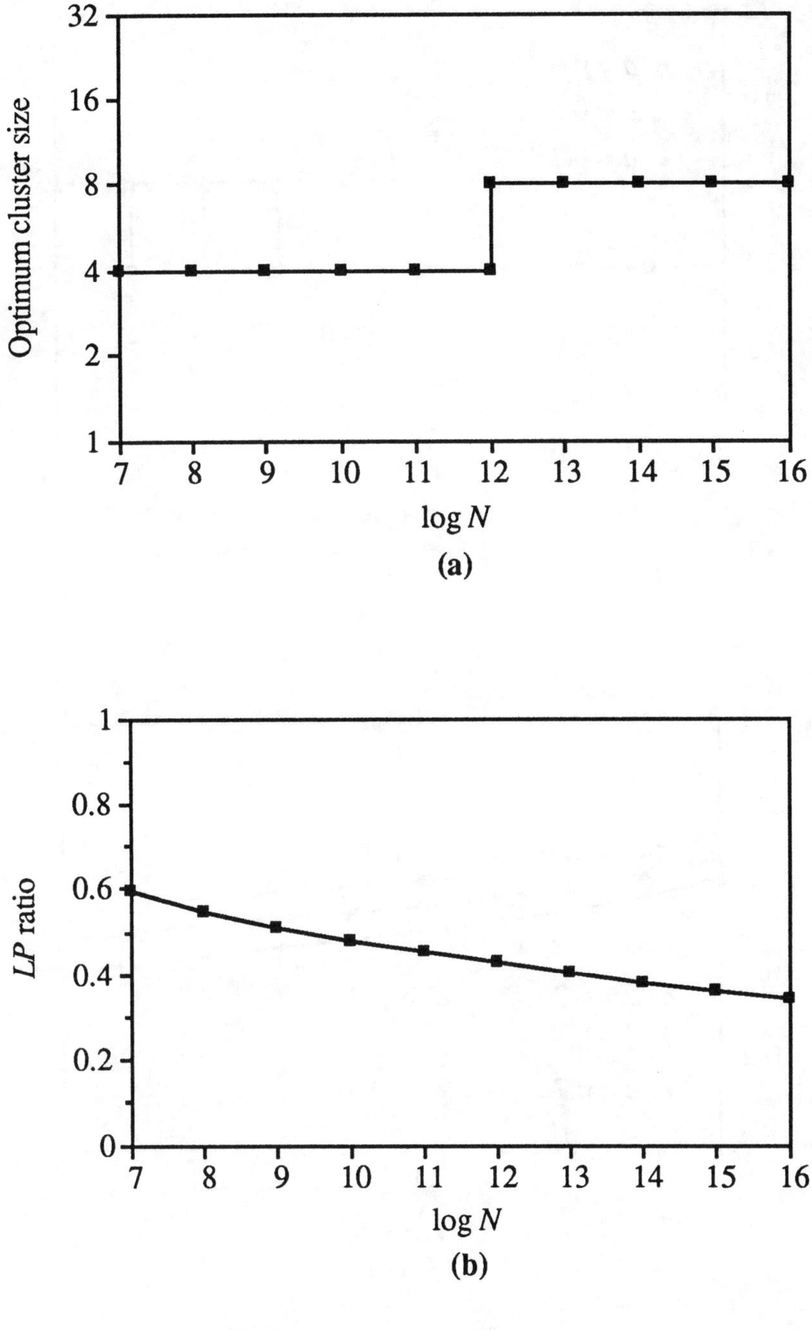

Figure 4.1 Optimum cluster size and the corresponding *LP* ratio for the BH/BH network (UNIF)

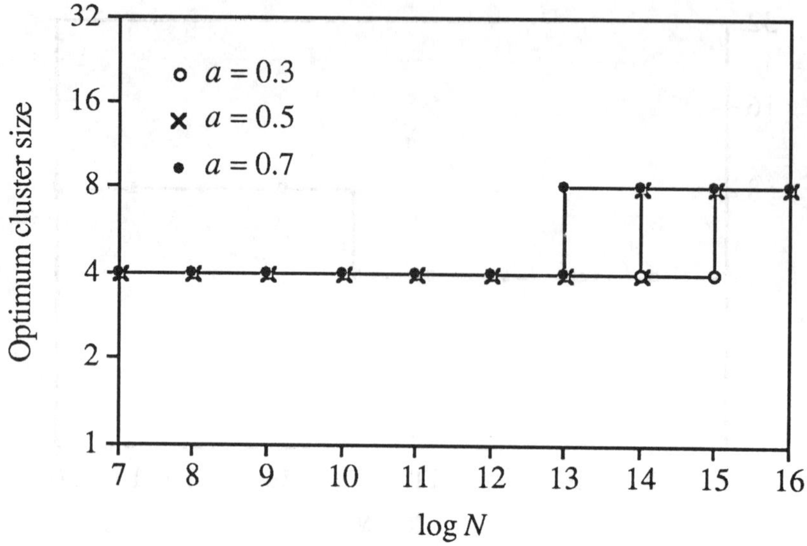

(a)

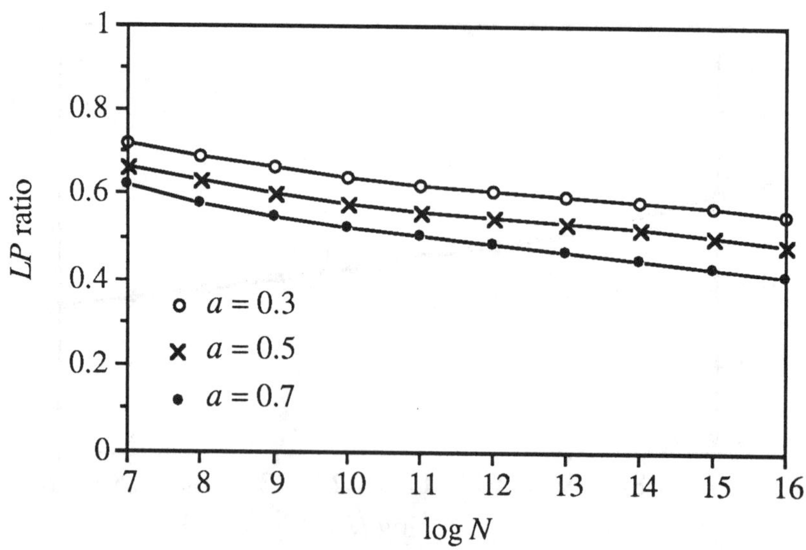

(b)

Figure 4.2 Optimum cluster size and the corresponding *LP* ratio for the BH/BH network (DPF)

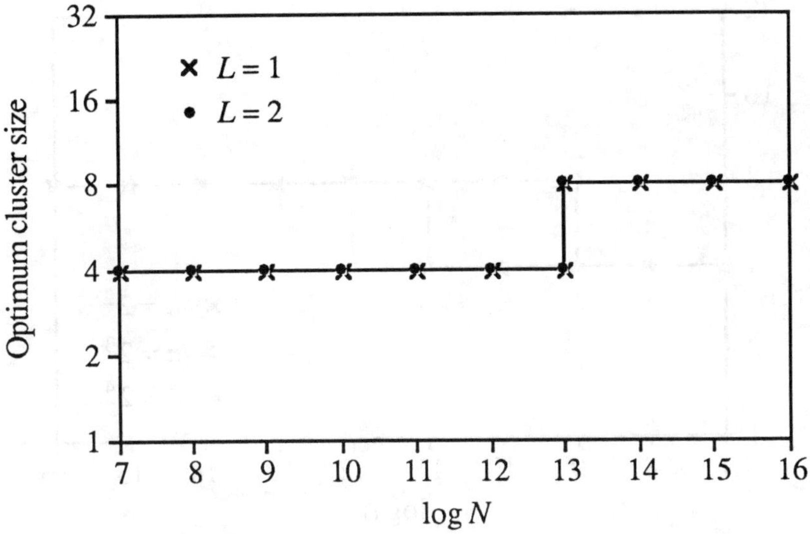

(a)

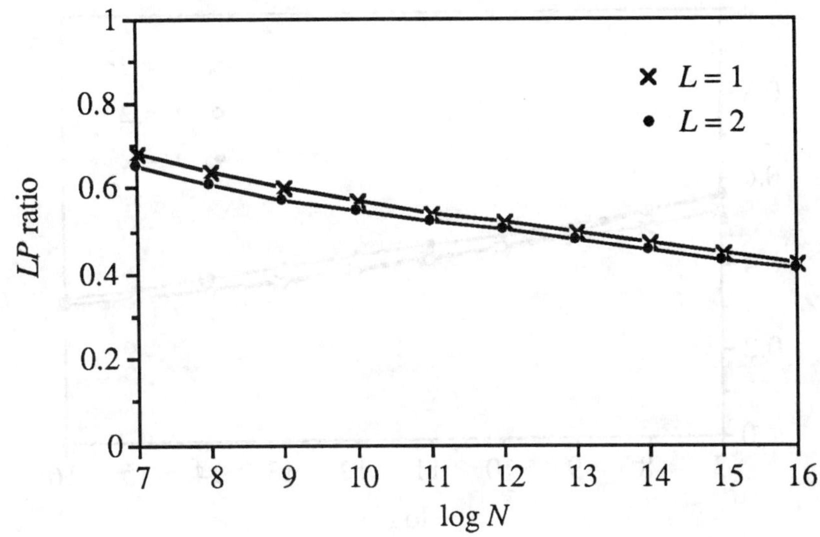

(b)

Figure 4.3 Optimum cluster size and the corresponding *LP* ratio for the BH/BH network (O-SOL with α = 0.75)

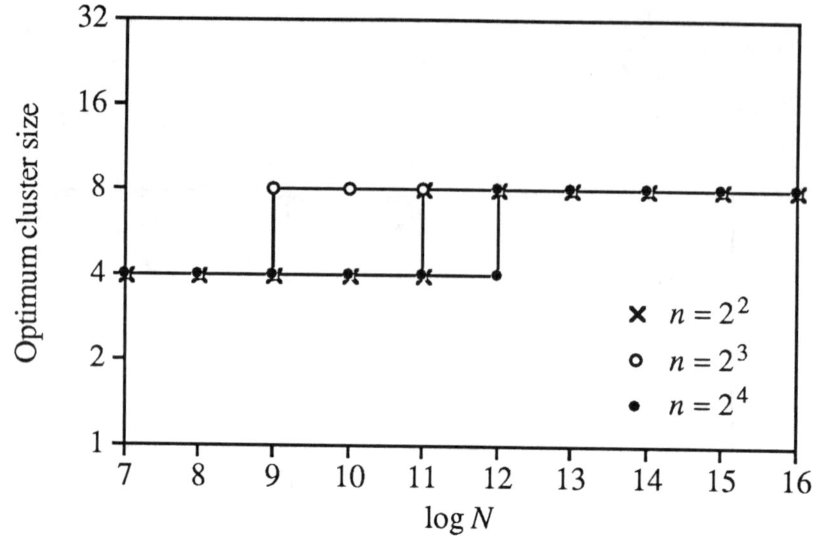

(a)

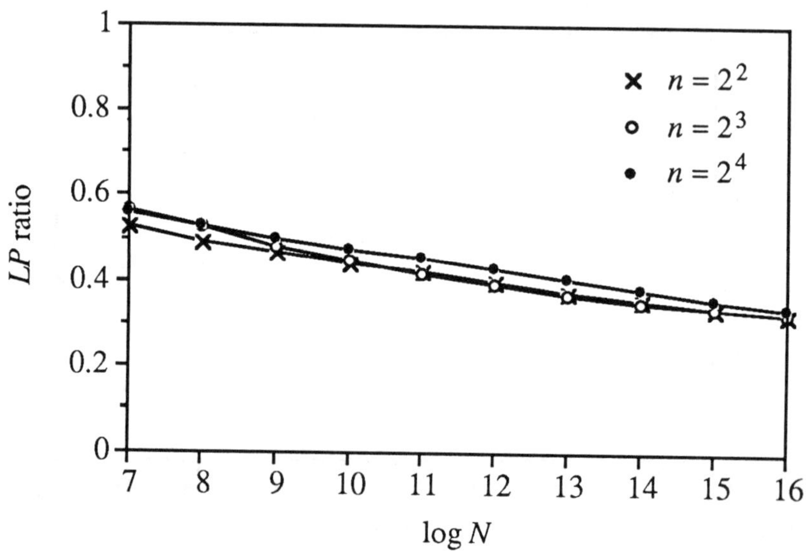

(b)

Figure 4.4 Optimum cluster size and the corresponding *LP* ratio for the BH/BH network (SOL with $\alpha = 0.75$)

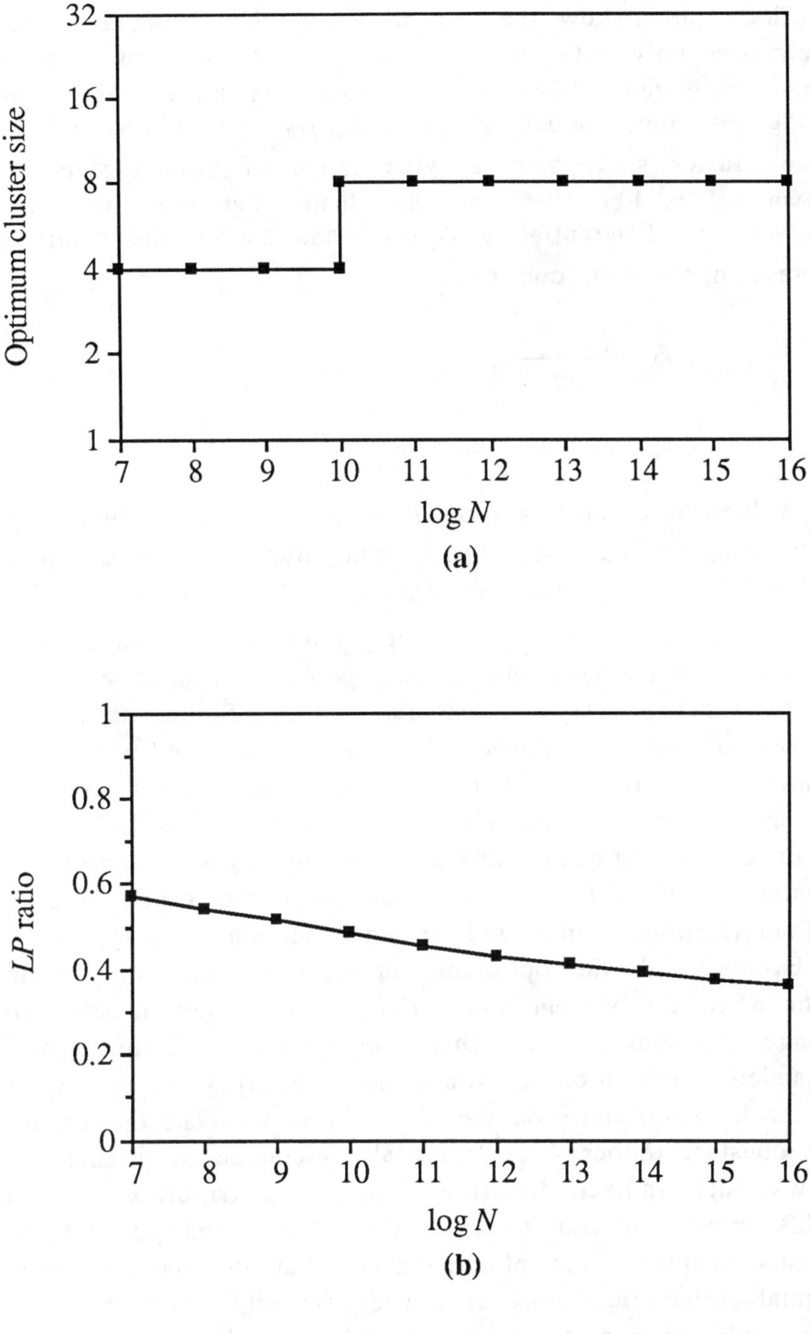

Figure 4.5 Optimum cluster size and the corresponding *LP* ratio for the BH/BH network (G-SOL for $F(i)$ values in Table 4.1)

These plots show that, in all cases, the optimum cluster size varies only between 4 and 8 over the range of network sizes considered. This small increase can be explained by noting that the number of links, $L_{BH/BH}$, is minimized for these cluster sizes over a wide range of system sizes as shown below. Let $2^{d_{opt}}$ be the cluster size that minimizes $L_{BH/BH}$. By differentiating $L_{BH/BH}$ and setting the resulting expression to zero, one obtains

$$d_{opt} = D + \frac{1 - 2^{d_{opt}}}{\log_e 2}$$

$$\approx D + 1.4423 - 1.4423 \times 2^{d_{opt}}$$

For values of D ranging from 7 to 9, d_{opt} (when constrained to be integral) is 2; for values ranging from 9 to 16, d_{opt} is 3. (When D is 9, d_{opt} has two possible values.) An implication of this is that even if the driving force to have an HIN is the cost, the optimum cluster size is either 4 or 8 over the range of network sizes considered. As the figures show, the impact of various types of locality characterizations is relatively minor in comparison to the impact of the number of links. These plots also show that the *LP* ratio obtained with uniform message routing gives a reasonable estimate of the *LP* ratio obtained with the other locality characterizations considered in this section.

Even though the optimum cluster size varies only from 4 to 8 as the system size increases it is not feasible to change the cluster size when the system is incrementally expanded. Therefore, it would be interesting to see what impact it would have on the *LP* ratio if we kept the cluster size constant (either 4 or 8 for all system sizes). Figure 4.6 shows this impact for the uniform distribution, which yields results similar to the other distributions considered in this chapter. This plot suggests that the use of near-optimal rather than optimal cluster size influences the *LP* ratio only marginally (the *LP* ratio deteriorates by less than 10% for most system sizes).

The queueing analysis in Chapter 3 has shown that the larger the cluster size in the BH/BH network, the larger the message transmission capacity that is required for the level 2 links. This would eliminate large cluster sizes from the set of feasible designs. Fortunately, the analysis done in this section suggests that the optimum cluster size in this network is 4 or 8, which is well within the range of feasible cluster sizes.

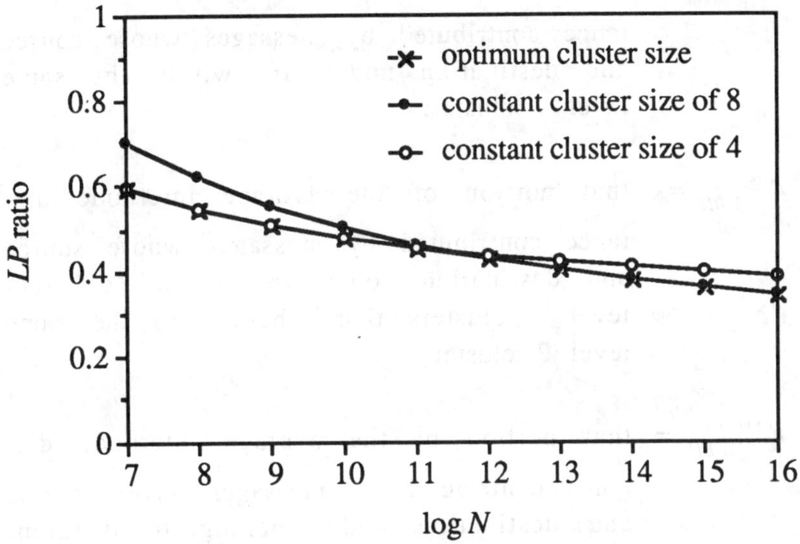

Figure 4.6 Impact of using a near-optimal rather than the optimal cluster size on the *LP* ratio (UNIF)

4.3. Increasing the Number of Hierarchy Levels

This section concerns the issue of the optimum number of levels in a binary hypercube-based HIN. Specifically, the impact of increasing the number of levels from two to three is investigated. Let 2^{d1} be the number of nodes in a level 1 cluster and 2^{d2} be the number of nodes in a level 2 cluster. In this case, the level 3 network contains 2^{d3} nodes, where $d3 = D - d1 - d2$. Then, the number of links in the BH/BH/BH (or 3BH for short) network is given by

$$L_{3BH} = d1\,2^{D-1} + d2\,2^{D-d1-1} + d3\,2^{d3-1}$$

P_{3BH} is given by

$$P_{3BH} = P'_{3BH} + P''_{3BH} + P'''_{3BH} \tag{4.7}$$

where

P'_{3BH} = that portion of the average internode distance contributed by messages whose source and destination nodes are within the same level 1 cluster;

P''_{3BH} = that portion of the average internode distance contributed by messages whose source and destination nodes are in two different level 1 clusters that belong to the same level 2 cluster;

P'''_{3BH} = that portion of the average internode distance contributed by messages whose source and destination nodes belong to different level 2 clusters.

The remainder of this section derives expressions for P_{3BH}, for each locality characterization.

4.3.1. Uniform Communication

With uniform communication, the probability that the source and destination nodes of a message are within the same level 1 cluster is $(2^{d1}-1)/(2^D-1)$ and the probability that the source and destination nodes of a message are in two different level 1 clusters that belong to the same level 2 cluster is $\frac{\left[2^{d2}-1\right]2^{d1}}{2^D-1}$.

It is straightforward then to derive the following:

$$P^{UNIF}_{3BH} = \left\{\frac{2^{d1}-1}{2^{D}-1}\right\}\left[\frac{d1\,2^{d1-1}}{2^{d1}-1}\right] + \left\{\frac{\left[2^{d2}-1\right]2^{d1}}{2^{D}-1}\right\}\left[d1 + \frac{d2\,2^{d2-1}}{2^{d2}-1}\right] +$$

$$\left\{1 - \left\{\frac{2^{d1}-1}{2^{D}-1}\right\} - \left\{\frac{\left[2^{d2}-1\right]2^{d1}}{2^{D}-1}\right\}\right\}\left[d1 + d2 + \frac{d3\,2^{d3-1}}{2^{d3}-1}\right]$$

4.3.2. Decreasing Probability and Overlapping Sphere of Locality

P'_{3BH} and P''_{3BH}, as defined above, are given by (from Eqs. (4.3) and (4.4))

$$P'_{3BH} = \sum_{l=1}^{d1}\binom{d1}{l} l\ \phi(l)$$

and

$$P''_{3BH} = \frac{1}{2^{d1}}\sum_{i=0}^{d1}\sum_{j=1}^{d2}\sum_{k=0}^{i}\sum_{m=0}^{d1-i}(i+j+k+m)\binom{d1}{i}\binom{d2}{j}\binom{i}{k}\binom{d1-i}{m}$$

$$\phi(j+k+m)$$

where $\phi(l)$ is given by Eq. (4.1) for DP, and by Eq. (4.5) for O-SOL. P'''_{3BH} can be derived through a similar argument as that used to derive $P''_{BH/BH}$, as

$$P'''_{3BH} = \frac{1}{2^{d1+d2}}\sum_{i=0}^{d1}\sum_{j=0}^{d2}\sum_{k=1}^{d3}\sum_{m=0}^{j}\sum_{n=0}^{d2-j}\sum_{x=0}^{i}\sum_{y=0}^{d1-i}$$

$$(i+j+k+m+n+x+y)\times$$

$$\times\binom{d1}{i}\binom{d2}{j}\binom{d3}{k}\binom{j}{m}\binom{d2-j}{n}\binom{i}{x}\binom{d1-i}{y}\times$$

$$\times\,\phi(k+m+n+x+y)$$

These component internode distances can be used in Eq. (4.7) to compute P^{DP}_{3BH} and $P^{O\text{-}SOL}_{3BH}$.

4.3.3. Sphere of Locality

For the 3BH network, the average internode distance P^{SOL}_{3BH} is given by Eq. (4.6). Consider the following three cases: (*i*) $s \le d1$ (*ii*) $d1 \le s \le d1{+}d2$, and (*iii*) $d1{+}d2 \le s \le D$. For each case, P_{iSOL} and P_{oSOL} are obtained as in Section 4.2.4.

Case (i): $s \le d1$

$$P_{iSOL} = \frac{s\,2^{s-1}}{2^{s}-1}$$

$$P_{oSOL} = \left[\frac{d1\,2^{d1-1} - s\,2^{s-1}}{2^{D}-2^{s}}\right] + \left[\frac{2^{d1+d2} - 2^{d1}}{2^{D}-2^{s}}\right]\left\{d1 + \frac{d2\,2^{d2-1}}{2^{d2}-1}\right\} + \left[\frac{2^{D} - 2^{d1+d2}}{2^{D}-2^{s}}\right]\left\{d1 + d2 + \frac{d3\,2^{d3-1}}{2^{d3}-1}\right\}$$

Case (ii): $d1 \le s \le d1{+}d2$

$$P_{iSOL} = \left[\frac{d1\,2^{d1-1}}{2^{s}-1}\right] + \left[\frac{2^{s} - 2^{d1}}{2^{s}-1}\right]\left\{d1 + \frac{(s-d1)\,2^{s-d1-1}}{2^{s-d1}-1}\right\}$$

$$P_{oSOL} = \left[\frac{2^{d1+d2} - 2^{s}}{2^{D}-2^{s}}\right]\left\{d1 + \frac{(d1+d2-s)\,2^{d1+d2-s-1}}{2^{d1+d2-s}-1}\right\} + \left[\frac{2^{D} - 2^{d1+d2}}{2^{D}-2^{s}}\right]\left\{d1 + d2 + \frac{d3\,2^{d3-1}}{2^{d3}-1}\right\}$$

Case (iii): $d1+d2 \leq s \leq D$

$$P_{iSOL} = \left[\frac{d1\,2^{d1-1}}{2^{s}-1}\right] + \left[\frac{2^{d1+d2} - 2^{d1}}{2^{s}-1}\right]\left\{d1 + \frac{d2\,2^{d2-1}}{2^{d2}-1}\right\} +$$

$$\left[\frac{2^{s} - 2^{d1+d2}}{2^{s}-1}\right]\left\{d1 + d2 + \frac{(s-d1-d2)2^{s-d1-d2-1}}{2^{s-d1-d2}-1}\right\}$$

$$P_{oSOL} = d1 + d2 + \frac{(D-s)\,2^{D-s-1}}{2^{D-s}-1}$$

4.3.4. Generalized Sphere of Locality

In this case, P'_{3BH} and P''_{3BH} are obtained (as in Section 4.2.5) as

$$P'_{3BH} = \sum_{i=1}^{d1} [F(i) - F(i-1)]\left[\frac{i+1}{2}\right]$$

and

$$P''_{3BH} = \sum_{i=d1+1}^{d1+d2} [F(i) - F(i-1)]\left[\frac{d1+i+1}{2}\right]$$

P'''_{3BH} is given by

$$P'''_{BH} = \sum_{i=d1+d2+1}^{D} [F(i) - F(i-1)]\, P'''_{avg}(i)$$

where $P'''_{avg}(i)$ is defined in a similar manner as $P_{avg}(i)$ was defined in Section 4.2.5, and can be derived as

$$P'''_{avg}(i) = \frac{\sum_{j=0}^{d1}\sum_{k=0}^{d2}\sum_{x=0}^{i-d1-d2-1}\sum_{y=0}^{d2}\sum_{z=0}^{d1}[z]}{2^{d1+d2}\,2^{i-d1-d2-1}\,2^{d1+d2}}$$

$$= \frac{d1 + d2 + i + 1}{2}$$

where

$$z = \binom{d1}{j}\binom{d2}{k}\binom{i-d1-d2-1}{x}\binom{d2}{y}\binom{d1}{z}(j + k + x + y + z + 1)$$

These component internode distances can be used in Eq. (4.7) to compute $P^{G\text{-}SOL}_{3BH}$.

4.3.5. Discussion of Results

Figures 4.7-4.11 show results concerning optimum cluster sizes and corresponding *LP* ratios for the 3BH network. The network size is varied from 2^7 to 2^{16} as in Section 4.2.6. Cluster sizes of 1 were not permitted in this study, since with a cluster size of 1 the resulting network is no longer three-level. The plots for UNIF, SOL and G-SOL suggest that using a three-level HIN may improve the *LP* ratio, but only moderately. For example, with UNIF distribution, when the network size is 2^7, the *LP* ratio improves from 0.6 to 0.5 when the optimum 3BH network is used. When the network size is 2^{16} the corresponding values are 0.34 and 0.25. In both the cases, the additional improvement in *LP* ratio is less than or equal to 10% (e.g., the *LP* ratio reduces from 1 associated with the BH network to 0.6 when the BH/BH network is used and from 1 to 0.5 with the 3BH network). For DPF and O-SOL, using a three-level network actually increases the *LP* ratio. (However, for smaller values of *a* in the DP distribution, and large networks, a three-level network does offer small improvements in the *LP* ratio.)

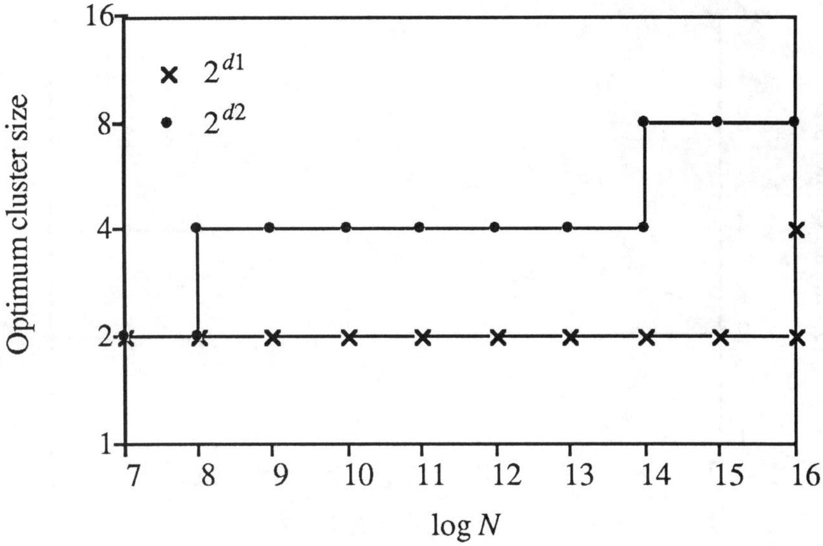

(a)

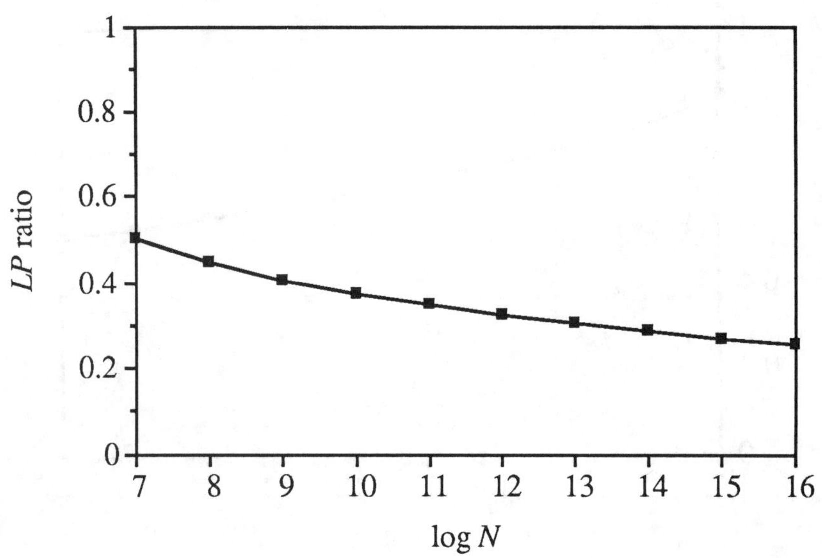

(b)

Figure 4.7 Optimum cluster size and the corresponding *LP* ratio for the BH/BH/BH network (UNIF)

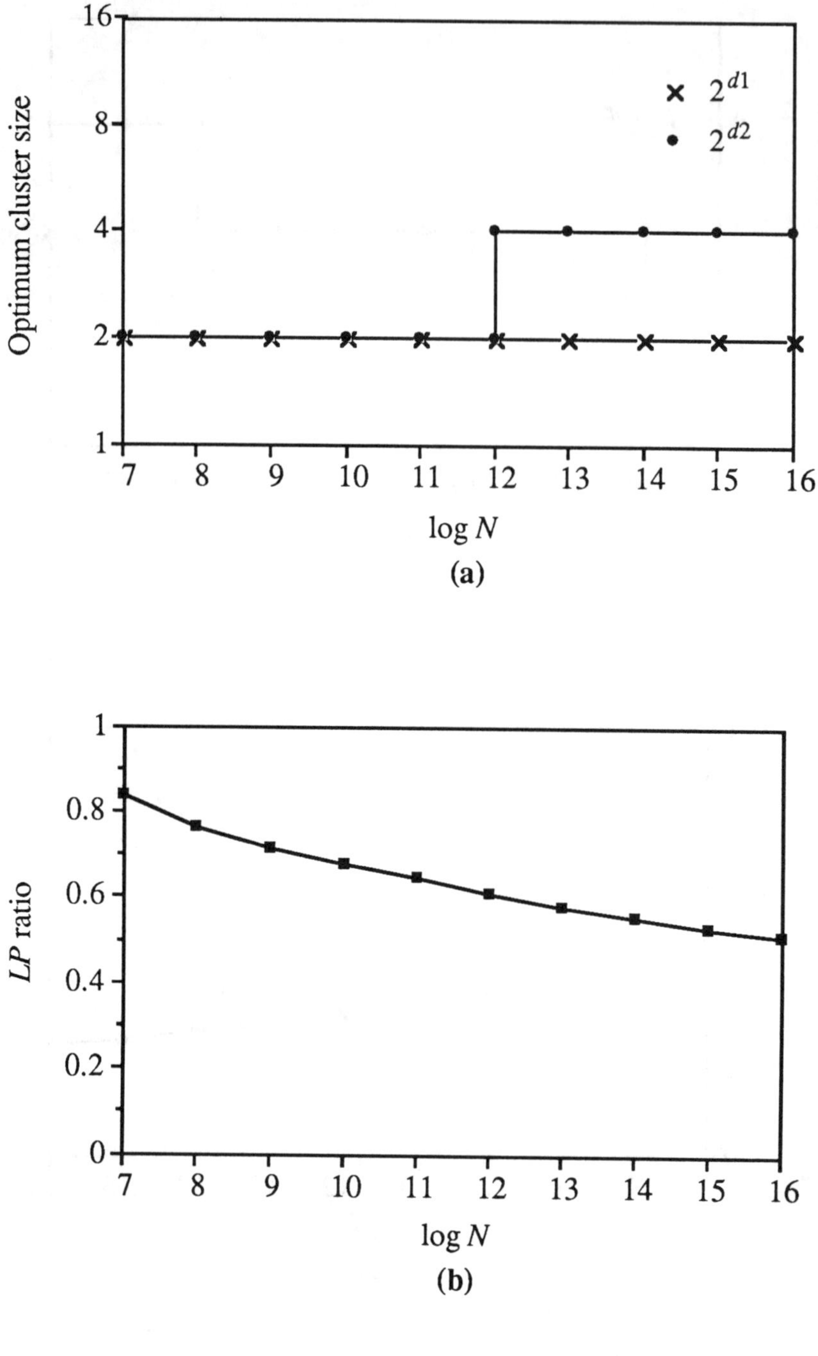

Figure 4.8 Optimum cluster size and the corresponding *LP* ratio for the BH/BH/BH network (DPF with a = 0.3)

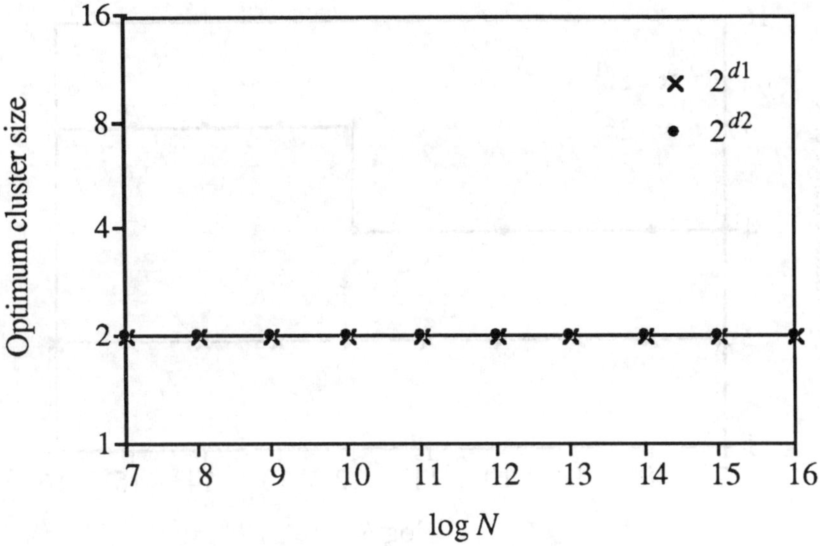

(a)

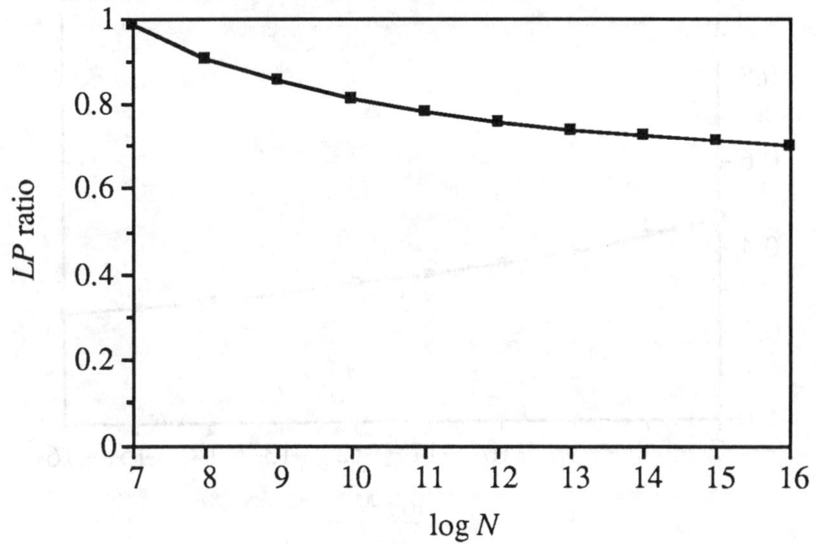

(b)

Figure 4.9 Optimum cluster size and the corresponding LP ratio for the BH/BH/BH network (O-SOL with $\alpha = 0.75$ and $L = 2$)

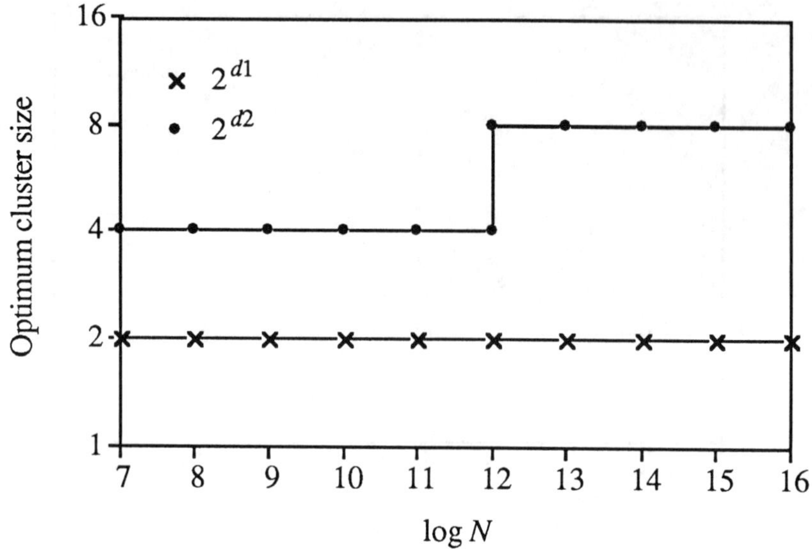

(a)

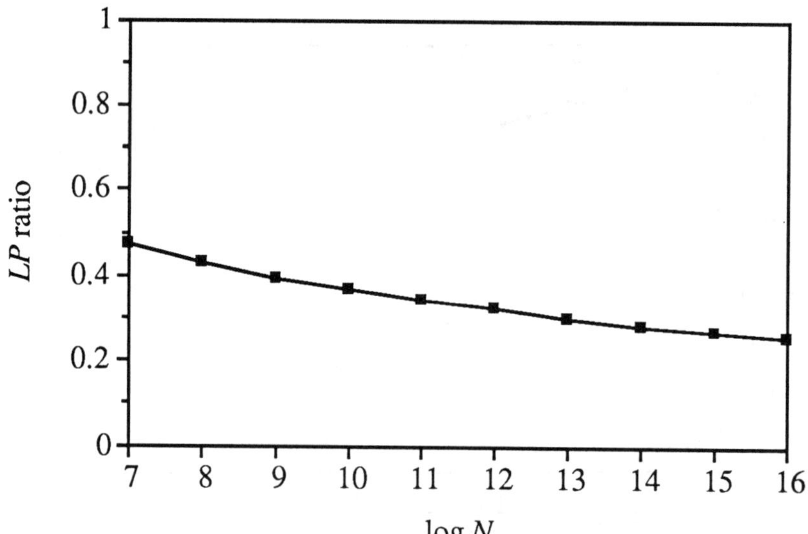

(b)

Figure 4.10 Optimum cluster size and the corresponding *LP* ratio for the BH/BH/BH network (SOL with $\alpha = 0.75$ and $n = 2^3$)

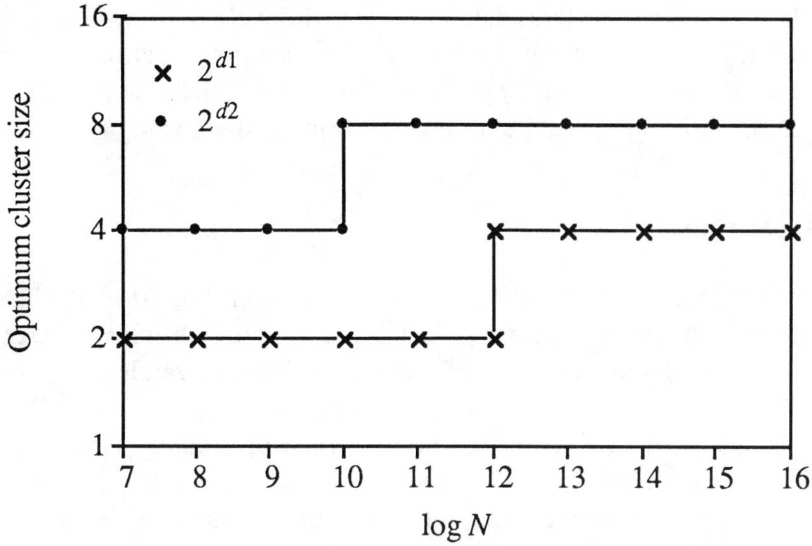

(a)

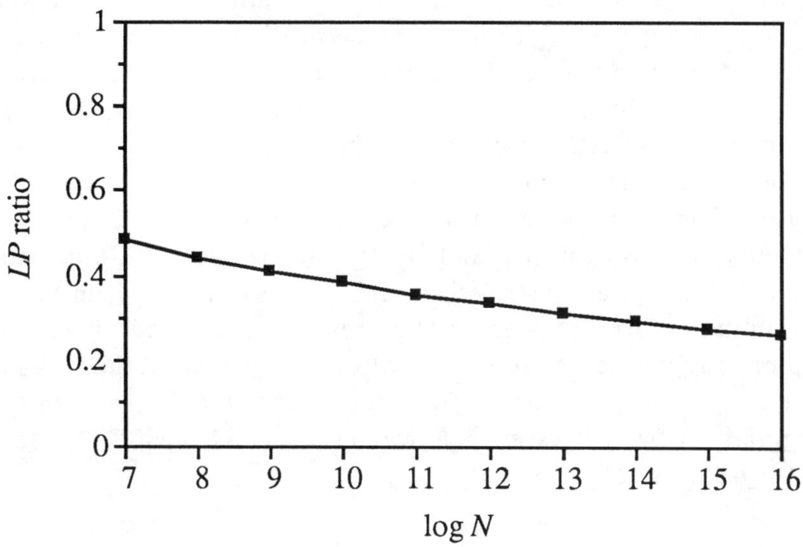

(b)

Figure 4.11 Optimum cluster size and the corresponding *LP* ratio for the BH/BH/BH network (G-SOL for $F(i)$ values in Table 4.1)

It appears from this data that a two-level HIN provides a reasonable compromise between the savings achieved in link cost with a hierarchical design and the penalty paid in terms of increased average internode distance.

4.4. Summary

This chapter considered two issues concerning the design of binary hypercube-based HINs – the optimum cluster size and the optimum number of levels in the hierarchy.

The optimum cluster size is dependent on the underlying degree of locality in communication. Five types of locality characterizations were considered. For all the locality characterizations, the optimum cluster size in a two-level binary hypercube-based HIN is shown to be either 4 or 8, over a wide range of network sizes. Further, increasing the number of levels to three yields at most a moderate improvement in the cost-benefit ratio, depending on the type of locality characterization considered. For some locality characterizations, the cost-benefit ratio deteriorates. Thus, an appropriate design for a binary hypercube-based HIN appears to be a two-level hierarchy, with a cluster size of either 4 or 8.

The change in optimum cluster size from 4 to 8 creates problems in system expandability. It would be nice to maintain the same cluster size and increase the system size by adding more clusters. The results presented in this chapter suggest that the use of near-optimal rather than optimal cluster size influences the *LP* ratio only marginally (the *LP* ratio deteriorates by less than 10% for most system sizes).

Further Reading

Abraham and Davidson [ABRA 86] consider optimum cluster size issues in two-level hierarchical interconnection networks for shared-memory multiprocessor systems. Their conclusions are somewhat different from the results presented here mainly because they obtain optimum cluster sizes that minimize the communication delay whereas here we are minimizing the *LP* ratio which represents a cost-benefit ratio. Optimum design issues are also considered in [WU 81].

Acknowledgement

Material presented in this chapter is partly based on [DAND 89].

References

[ABRA 86] S. G. Abraham and E. S. Davidson, "A Communication Model for Optimizing Hierarchical Multiprocessor Systems," *Proc. 1986 Int. Conf. Parallel Processing*, 1986, pp. 467-474.

[DAND 89] S. P. Dandamudi and D. L. Eager, "On Hypercube Based Hierarchical Interconnection Network Design," *Tech. Rep. SCR-TR-156*, Center for Parallel and Distributed Computing, School of Computer Science, Carleton University, Ottawa, Canada, 1989. (A version of this appears in *Int. J. Parallel and Distributed Computing*, 1991)

[HWAN 87] K. Hwang and J. Ghose, "Hypernet: A Communication-Efficient Architecture for Constructing Massively Parallel Computers," *IEEE Trans. Computers*, Vol. C-36, No. 12, December 1987, pp. 1450-1466.

[REED 83] D. A. Reed and H. D. Schwetman, "Cost-Performance Bounds for Multimicrocomputer Networks," *IEEE Trans. Computers*, Vol. C-32, No. 1, January 1983, pp.83-95.

[REED 87] D. A. Reed and D. C. Grunwald, "The Performance of Multicomputer Interconnection Networks," *IEEE Computer*, Vol. 20, No. 6, June 1987, pp. 63-73.

[WU 81] S. W. Wu and M. T. Liu, "A Cluster Structure as an Interconnection Network for Large Multimicrocomputer Systems," *IEEE Trans. Computers*, Vol. C-30,1981, pp. 254-264.

5

Hot-Spot Contention and Combining Schemes

Hot-spot contention refers to the situation where a large number of processors request access to the same data structure, or "service" by the same processor, at the same time. Such hot-spot contention creates congestion in the system. Hot-spot contention has been studied previously in the context of shared-memory multiprocessor systems that utilize multistage interconnection networks. This chapter considers the impact of hot-spot contention in multicomputer systems. Two hypercube-based static interconnection networks – BH and BH/BH – are treated. Section 5.2 gives details on the hot-spot and locality models used. Sections 5.3 and 5.4 discuss the impact of hot-spot contention on the performance of both these networks with unbounded and bounded buffering capacity, respectively.

In order to reduce the adverse effects of hot-spot contention on system performance, two techniques have been proposed for multiprocessor systems: *hardware combining* and *software combining*. The effectiveness of these two schemes in reducing the performance degradation due to hot-spot contention in multicomputer systems is also discussed. These results are presented in Sections 5.3 and 5.4 for networks with unbounded and bounded buffering capacity, respectively. Section 5.5 summarizes the results discussed in this chapter.

5.1. Introduction

In large parallel processing systems there is a possibility of many processors requesting access to the same data structure, or "service" by the same processor, at the same time. Such hot-spot contention creates congestion in the system, and this congestion becomes more serious as the number of processors involved increases. In multiprocessor systems, such behaviour saturates the memory module containing the "hot-spot" data structure. In multicomputer systems, hot-spot contention saturates the message links leading to the "hot-spot" processor, and hence degrades performance by substantially increasing message delivery times.

Hot-spot contention has been studied in the context of multiprocessor systems that utilize buffered multistage interconnection networks [PFIS 85a, LEE 86, YEW 87, HO 89]. It has been observed that hot-spots can produce effects that severely degrade all memory references, not just the references to hot-spot locations [PFIS 85a]. This unfortunate increase in the average memory access time of all memory references can be explained by a phenomenon called *tree saturation*. In tree saturation, a tree of switches rooted at the hot memory and extending to the switches connected to the processors becomes saturated; i.e., all the buffers in each queue in that tree become full. This degrades the performance of the whole system. It has been observed that the limitation on performance from this effect is quite significant for large systems. For example, in a system with 1000 processors, with only 0.125% hot-spot traffic (i.e., with only 0.125% of all memory references directed at the hot data structure) the potential speedup is reduced by half [PFIS 85a].

Two schemes have been proposed to reduce the adverse effects of hot-spot contention in multiprocessor systems – *hardware combining* and *software combining*. Both these schemes essentially use the same underlying principle of combining several hot-spot requests into a single request and forwarding this request to the hot-spot memory. These two schemes, however, differ in the way this combining is accomplished. In hardware combining, which is used in the IBM RP3 [PFIS 85b] and NYU Ultracomputer [GOTT 83], when several requests directed at the hot-spot location meet at a switch, they are combined by the switch into a single request, which is forwarded to the hot-spot location. When the response from memory returns, the switch hardware generates a response for each portion of the combined message. It is estimated [PFIS 85a] that the extra hardware to support combining increases the switch size and cost by factors of between 6 and 32, and this is only for combining networks consisting of 2×2 switches. For $k \times k$ switches ($k > 2$), the hardware cost will be even greater.

In software combining [YEW 87], a tree of hot-spots is created with the original hot-spot serving as the root of this tree. The total number of processors, N, is partitioned into l groups where l is the number of leaf nodes (i.e., hot-spots) in the tree. Each group of N/l processors operates on a hot-spot at the bottom of the tree. When a certain condition is satisfied by this leaf hot-spot, this fact is suitably reflected by one of the processors in the parent hot-spot. This process repeats until the root hot-spot is modified suitably. Communication may also proceed down the tree in the natural way (see Section 5.3.3). It has been shown that this technique is effective in decreasing memory contention and preventing tree saturation. Further details can be found in [YEW 87].

This chapter is concerned with hot-spot contention in distributed-memory multicomputer systems. Processors in such systems communicate by explicit message passing. It is easy to see that hot-spots can also exist in multicomputer systems. For example, consider database operations in a multicomputer system. In a shared-nothing database system each node consists of a processor, memory and a disk drive. To exploit the parallel I/O capability in such a system, relations are horizontally partitioned into disjoint subsets across all disk drives in the system (such an architecture is used in the Gamma database machine [SCHN 89]). Data from parallel paths need to be combined in order to compute the final result for each of the relational and scalar aggregation operations (e.g., max, min, sum etc.) [BARU 89]. In this situation, the processor coordinating the activity may become a "hot-spot" node.

Two hypercube-based static interconnection networks are considered in this study. One is a binary hypercube network (BH) and the other is a binary hypercube-based hierarchical interconnection network (BH/BH). These networks are different from multistage interconnection networks in several aspects:

(i) The two networks considered here are characterized by multiple paths between any pair of nodes. In contrast, the multistage interconnection networks used in previous hot-spot studies have only one path between any pair of communicating entities. Thus, this study provides an understanding of the impact of multiple paths on hot-spot contention. The results reported in this chapter indicate that improved routing algorithms provide substantial performance improvement.

(ii) The distance between communicating entities is not fixed in the hypercube-based interconnection networks. In contrast, multistage interconnection networks maintain a constant distance.

(iii) In multiprocessor systems, the messages are memory references. Therefore, message combining can be achieved relatively easily. In multicomputer systems, message combining may be more involved, depending on the complexity of the semantics of the "combinable" message types. Certainly, the transport mechanism must be given some knowledge of these semantics. For example, the Connection Machine CM-2 provides hardware support for *en route* combining of messages directed to the same destination for operations such as sum, max, min, logical OR etc. [TUCK 88].

The remainder of the chapter is organized as follows. Section 5.2 gives details on the hot-spot and locality models used in the study. Sections 5.3 and 5.4 present the results for unbounded and bounded buffering capacity, respectively. Section 5.5 concludes the chapter by summarizing the results.

5.2. The Model

The two characteristics of communication that are of interest in this study are the communication locality and the proportion of traffic that is directed towards a hot-spot. Each is modelled by a single parameter: α (as in SOL discussed in Chapter 4) is used to model locality in communication and a parameter h (defined below) is used to model the degree of hot-spot traffic.

Let $N=2^D$ be the total number of nodes in the network, $n=2^d$ the number of nodes in a cluster, and K the number of clusters, where $N = Kn$. Let α be the probability that both the source and the destination nodes of a message are in the same cluster. Therefore, $(1-\alpha)$ represents the probability that a message is destined for a node outside of the source node's cluster. It is further assumed that:

- intra-cluster (except hot-spot) communication is uniformly random (i.e., an intra-cluster message is destined for each node within the cluster with equal probability);
- inter-cluster (except hot-spot) communication is uniformly random (i.e., an inter-cluster message is destined for each cluster other than the source cluster with equal probability, and for each node within the destination cluster with equal probability).

The following assumptions are made about the network and its workload:

(i) Each node generates messages at rate λ and the time between successive message generations is exponentially distributed.

(ii) The node message generation processes are independent of each other.

(iii) Message service times are exponentially distributed; each cluster link processes these messages at rate μ_{CL} while each non-cluster link processes these messages at rate μ_{NCL}.

(iv) Packet-switching is used for message transmission.

(v) All messages are routed over a randomly chosen shortest path between the source and destination nodes. This assumption of random path selection is relaxed in Sections 5.3.4 and 5.4.

The assumptions (iii), (iv), and (v) hold for replies as well as messages. The links are assumed to be full-duplex. In the analysis that follows, each full-duplex link is conceptually replaced by two simplex links, each of which is modelled as an M/M/1 queueing centre [KLEI 75].

Hot-spots can be modelled in several ways [YEW 87]. In this study, we assume that there is only a single hot-spot and use the hot-spot model of Pfister and Norton [PFIS 85a]. In this model, each message has a probability h of being a *hot-spot* message (a combinable message destined for the hot-spot node) and a probability $(1-h)$ of being a *regular* message (assumed here to be a non-combinable). Here, the regular messages are further divided into *intra-cluster* and *inter-cluster* messages. When a message reaches its destination node, it is assumed that a reply is generated. Thus, there are hot-spot replies, intra-cluster replies, and inter-cluster replies. Message replies are included in this model, in contrast to the model used in Chapter 3, since they provide a natural and consistent way to model the expected traffic generated by a hot-spot node. When each non-hot-spot node generates messages at rate λ, it generates hot-spot messages at rate $h\lambda$, intra-cluster messages at rate $\alpha\lambda$, inter-cluster messages at rate $(1-\alpha-h)\lambda$, intra-cluster replies at rate $\alpha\lambda$, and inter-cluster replies at rate $(1-\alpha-h)\lambda$. The hot-spot node generates messages and replies at the same rates, except that it also generates hot-spot replies at rate $Nh\lambda$. (Allowing a node to send messages to itself is for convenience in analysis only; since we model only link congestion, such messages have no effect on performance.) Note that h must be less than or equal to $(1-\alpha)$.

5.3. Performance with Unbounded Buffering Capacity

In this section it is assumed that each node has unbounded buffering capacity. The impact of hot-spot contention on the average message delivery time or message "delay" R_{avg} is derived analytically in Section 5.3.1. Sections 5.3.2 and 5.3.3 provide details on the performance improvements possible with hardware combining and software combining schemes. These three sections assume a routing algorithm that selects randomly among shortest paths. The impact of an improved routing algorithm is presented in Section 5.3.4.

5.3.1. Analysis of Delay

A random routing algorithm is used in the analysis, in which, if more than one shortest path exists between a pair of nodes, one of these paths is randomly selected (i.e., each shortest path is selected with equal probability). Thus the routing scheme uses no information regarding the current state of the network. To facilitate the analysis, as in Section 3.5.2, Kleinrock's independence assumption [KLEI 76] is used. Further, although a reply is generated every time a message reaches its destination node, it is assumed that the replies are generated independently by each node at the rate at which the node receives messages. The results of the simulation experiments presented in Section 5.3.1.3 indicate that these assumptions are reasonable.

5.3.1.1. Analysis of the BH network

This section considers the BH network with $N = 2^D$ nodes. Each link is labelled with a number that depends on its distance from the hot-spot node. A link is labelled j (referred to as a j-level link) if the link connects nodes S and T such that node S is at distance $j-1$ from the hot-spot node and node T is at distance j. It is obvious from this definition that there is actually a set of links for each j value and that the value of j varies from 1 through D. The concept of j-level links is useful in the following analysis.

The assumptions stated in the previous section allow each (simplex) link to be modelled as an M/M/1 queueing centre [KLEI 75]. The links are divided into two groups: cluster (CL) links and non-cluster (NCL) links. The cluster links are those that connect only the nodes whose most significant $(D-d)$ bits are the same. The non-cluster links are those that connect only the nodes whose least significant d bits are the same.

Let $\lambda_{CL}(j)$ and $\lambda_{NCL}(j)$ be the effective arrival rates of messages and replies seen by a j-level cluster link and j-level non-cluster link, respectively. Once $\lambda_{CL}(j)$ and $\lambda_{NCL}(j)$ are known, it is straightforward to derive an expression for the following:

R_{reg}: average delay of a regular message or of a regular reply;

R_{hot}: average delay of a hot-spot message or of a hot-spot reply; and

R_{avg}: overall average delay.

Hot-spot traffic is not uniformly distributed over all cluster (or non-cluster) links. The total arrival rate of messages and replies at a j-level link is given by

$$\lambda_{CL}(j) = \lambda'_{CL}(j) + \lambda''_{CL}(j) + \lambda'''_{CL}(j) \qquad (5.1)$$

where

$\lambda'_{CL}(j)$ = arrival rate (at a j-level cluster link) due to regular intra-cluster messages or replies

$\lambda''_{CL}(j)$ = arrival rate (at a j-level cluster link) due to regular inter-cluster messages or replies; and

$\lambda'''_{CL}(j)$ = arrival rate (at a j-level cluster link) due to hot-spot messages or replies.

Note that the traffic due to intra-cluster and inter-cluster messages and replies is uniformly distributed over the cluster links. Thus, $\lambda'_{CL}(j)$ and $\lambda''_{CL}(j)$ are independent of j. An expression is now derived for each of these.

Consider a cluster of $n = 2^d$ nodes. These nodes generate intra-cluster messages at rate $\alpha\lambda$ and these messages travel an average distance of $d/2$ links. Similarly, intra-cluster replies are generated at rate $\alpha\lambda$ and they also travel an average distance of $d/2$ links. Therefore,

Total rate at which intra-cluster messages and their replies visit links = $n\alpha\lambda d$

Then, since there are $2d\ 2^{d-1}$ simplex links within a cluster, the effective arrival rate seen by a j-level cluster link is

$$\lambda'_{CL}(j) = \frac{2^d\ \alpha\lambda d}{2d\ 2^{d-1}} = \alpha\lambda \tag{5.2}$$

Similarly $\lambda''_{CL}(j)$ can be derived as

$$\lambda''_{CL}(j) = (1 - \alpha - h)\lambda \tag{5.3}$$

because inter-cluster messages (as well as their replies) are generated at rate $(1-\alpha-h)\lambda$.

In deriving $\lambda'''_{CL}(j)$, it should be noted that the links closer to the hot-spot node receive more hot-spot messages (and correspondingly more hot-spot replies) than those that are farther away. Let $p_1(j)$ be the probability that a hot-spot message (or a hot-spot reply) gets routed through a j-level link on its way to (or from) the hot-spot node. Then, $\lambda'''_{CL}(j)$ can be computed as

$$\begin{aligned} \lambda'''_{CL}(j) &= Nh\lambda p_1(j) \\ &= 2^D h\lambda p_1(j) \end{aligned} \tag{5.4}$$

where $p_1(j)$ is given by (see Section 3.5.2.2)

$$p_1(j) = \frac{\sum_{k=j}^{D} \binom{D}{k}}{(D-j+1)\binom{D}{j-1} 2^D}$$

Combining Eqs. (5.1), (5.2), (5.3) and (5.4) yields

$$\lambda_{CL}(j) = (1-h)\lambda + 2^D h\lambda p_1(j) \tag{5.5}$$

Now an expression for $\lambda_{NCL}(j)$ is derived. It can be expressed as

$$\lambda_{NCL}(j) = \lambda'_{NCL}(j) + \lambda''_{NCL}(j) \tag{5.6}$$

where

$\lambda'_{NCL}(j)$ = arrival rate (at a j-level non-cluster link) due to inter-cluster messages or replies, and

$\lambda''_{NCL}(j)$ = arrival rate (at a j-level non-cluster link) due to hot-spot messages or replies.

The traffic due to inter-cluster messages and replies is uniformly distributed over all the non-cluster links. Each inter-cluster message or reply travels, on average, P''_{BH} links, which is given by Eq. (3.5) as

$$P''_{BH} = \frac{D2^{D-1} - d\,2^{d-1}}{2^D - 2^d}$$

Therefore, the number of non-cluster links used by an inter-cluster message or reply, on average, is $(P''_{BH} - d/2)$. Since inter-cluster messages and their replies are each generated at rate $(1-\alpha-h)\lambda$ by each node and since there are $2\left[D\,2^{D-1} - 2^{D-d}\,d\,2^{d-1}\right] = 2(D-d)2^{D-1}$ non-cluster links, $\lambda'_{NCL}(j)$ is given as

$$\lambda'_{NCL}(j) = \frac{2(1-\alpha-h)\,\lambda 2^D\left[P''_{BH} - d/2\right]}{2(D-d)2^{D-1}}$$

$$= (1-\alpha-h)\lambda\frac{2^D}{2^D - 2^d} \tag{5.7}$$

Note that the derivation of $\lambda'''_{CL}(j)$ is independent of whether the j-level link is a cluster or non-cluster link. Therefore,

$$\lambda''_{NCL}(j) = \lambda'''_{CL}(j) \tag{5.8}$$

Eqs. (5.6), (5.7), and (5.8) yield

$$\lambda_{NCL}(j) = (1-\alpha-h)\lambda\frac{2^D}{2^D - 2^d} + 2^D h\lambda p_1(j) \tag{5.9}$$

Then, the average delays encountered by messages and replies at j-level cluster and non-cluster links are given by:

$$\Delta_{CL}(j) = \frac{1}{\mu_{CL} - \lambda_{CL}(j)}$$

and

$$\Delta_{NCL}(j) = \frac{1}{\mu_{NCL} - \lambda_{NCL}(j)}$$

where $\lambda_{CL}(j)$ and $\lambda_{NCL}(j)$ are given by Eqs. (5.5) and (5.9), respectively. The average total message and reply delays are given by:

$$R_{reg} = \frac{1}{(1-h)}\left[\alpha\left[\frac{d}{2}\right]\Delta_{CL}^{avg} + (1-\alpha-h)\times \left\{\left[\frac{d}{2}\right]\Delta_{CL}^{avg} + \left(P''_{BH} - \frac{d}{2}\right)\Delta_{NCL}^{avg}\right\}\right]$$

$$= \frac{1}{(1-h)}\left[\alpha\left[\frac{d}{2}\right]\Delta_{CL}^{avg} + (1-\alpha-h)\times \left\{\left[\frac{d}{2}\right]\Delta_{CL}^{avg} + \left(\frac{(D-d)2^{D-1}}{2^{D}-2^{d}}\right)\Delta_{NCL}^{avg}\right\}\right] \quad (5.10)$$

$$R_{hot} = \sum_{k=0}^{D-d}\left[\binom{D-d}{k}\left\{\sum_{l=1}^{d}(d-l+1)\binom{d}{l-1}\Delta_{CL}(k+l)\,p_1(k+l)\right\}\right]$$

$$+ \sum_{k=0}^{d}\left[\binom{d}{k}\left\{\sum_{l=1}^{D-d}(D-d-l+1)\binom{D-d}{l-1}\Delta_{NCL}(k+l)\,p_1(k+l)\right\}\right]$$

(5.11)

$$R_{avg} = (1-h)R_{reg} + h\,R_{hot} \quad (5.12)$$

where

Δ_{CL}^{avg} = average delay encountered on a cluster link

$$= \frac{1}{d\,2^{D-1}}\left[\sum_{k=0}^{D-d}\binom{D-d}{k}\left\{\sum_{l=1}^{d}(d-l+1)\binom{d}{l-1}\Delta_{CL}(k+l)\right\}\right]$$

Δ_{NCL}^{avg} = average delay encountered on a non-cluster link

$$= \frac{\left[\sum_{k=0}^{d}\binom{d}{k}\left\{\sum_{l=1}^{D-d}(D-d-l+1)\binom{D-d}{l-1}\Delta_{NCL}(k+l)\right\}\right]}{(D-d)\,2^{D-1}}$$

5.3.1.2. Analysis of the BH/BH network

In this network, one node from each cluster acts as an interface node. As in the analysis of the BH network, the links are divided into cluster and non-cluster links. The effective arrival rate for each group of links is derived. It is assumed that the hot-spot node is an interface node.

In deriving an expression for $\lambda_{CL}(j)$, it is necessary to consider only intra-cluster and non-intra-cluster message and reply traffic, where the non-intra-cluster traffic includes both inter-cluster and hot-spot messages and replies. (As will be seen there is no need to consider the hot-spot traffic separately.)

The effective arrival rate of messages and replies at a j-level cluster link is given by

$$\lambda_{CL}(j) = \lambda'_{CL}(j) + \lambda''_{CL}(j) \tag{5.13}$$

where

$\lambda'_{CL}(j)$ = arrival rate (at a j-level cluster link) due to intra-cluster messages or replies, and

$\lambda''_{CL}(j)$ = arrival rate (at a j-level cluster link) due to non-intra-cluster messages or replies.

It is easy to see that $\lambda'_{CL}(j)$ is given by Eq. (5.2). In deriving an expression for $\lambda''_{CL}(j)$, it should be noted that an interface node is very much like the hot-spot node in the BH network. Thus, since each cluster generates non-intra-cluster messages at rate $\lambda(1-\alpha)2^d$ and non-intra-cluster replies at rate $\lambda(1-\alpha-h)2^d$,

$$\lambda''_{CL}(j) = 2^d \lambda(2-2\alpha-h)p(j) \tag{5.14}$$

where $p(j)$ is the probability of an inter-cluster message or reply being routed through a j-level cluster link. $p(j)$ is given by (see Section 3.5.2.2)

$$p(j) = \frac{\sum_{k=j}^{d} \binom{d}{k}}{(d-j+1)\binom{d}{j-1}2^d}$$

Therefore, combining Eqs. (5.13), (5.2), and (5.14) yields

$$\lambda_{CL}(j) = \alpha\lambda + (2-2\alpha-h)2^d \lambda p(j) \tag{5.15}$$

$\lambda_{NCL}(j)$ can be expressed as follows:

$$\lambda_{NCL}(j) = \lambda'_{NCL}(j) + \lambda''_{NCL}(j) \tag{5.16}$$

where

$\lambda'_{NCL}(j)$ = arrival rate (at a j-level non-cluster link) due to inter-cluster messages or replies, and

$\lambda''_{NCL}(j)$ = arrival rate (at a j-level non-cluster link) due to hot-spot messages or replies.

In deriving $\lambda'_{NCL}(j)$ it should be noted that each inter-cluster message uses on average $\left\lceil \frac{(D-d)2^{D-d-1}}{2^{D-d}-1} \right\rceil$ non-cluster links and that each generates these messages and their replies at rate $\lambda(1-\alpha-h)2^d$ each. Therefore,

$$\lambda'_{NCL}(j) = \frac{2^{D-d}\, 2\, 2^d (1-\alpha-h)\,\lambda \left\lceil \frac{(D-d)2^{D-d-1}}{2^{D-d}-1} \right\rceil}{2(D-d)2^{D-d-1}}$$

$$= \frac{2^D(1-\alpha-h)\lambda}{2^{D-d}-1} \tag{5.17}$$

The derivation of $\lambda''_{NCL}(j)$ is similar to that of $\lambda'''_{CL}(j)$ for the BH network except that each node generates $2^d h\lambda$ hot-spot messages and there are 2^{D-d} nodes. Let $p_1(j)$ be the probability that a hot-spot message (or reply) gets routed through a j-level non-cluster link on its way to (or from) the hot-spot node. Then,

$$\lambda''_{NCL}(j) = 2^{D-d}\, 2^d\, h\lambda p_1(j)$$

$$= 2^D h\lambda p_1(j) \tag{5.18}$$

where

$$p_1(j) = \frac{\sum_{k=j}^{D-d} \binom{D-d}{k}}{(D-d-j+1)\binom{D-d}{j-1} 2^{D-d}}$$

Eqs. (5.16), (5.17), and (5.18) yield

$$\lambda_{NCL}(j) = \frac{2^D(1-\alpha-h)\lambda}{2^{D-d}-1} + 2^D h\lambda p_1(j) \tag{5.19}$$

Now, the delay encountered by messages at each cluster and non-cluster link can be computed as follows:

$$\Delta_{CL}(j) = \frac{1}{\mu_{CL} - \lambda_{CL}(j)}$$

$$\Delta_{NCL}(j) = \frac{1}{\mu_{NCL} - \lambda_{NCL}(j)}$$

where $\lambda_{CL}(j)$ and $\lambda_{NCL}(j)$ are given by Eqs. (5.13) and (5.16), respectively. Then the average message delays are given as follows:

$$R_{reg} = \frac{1}{(1-h)}\left[\alpha\left(\frac{d}{2}\right)\Delta_{avg} + (1-\alpha-h) \times \left\{2\Delta_{CL-avg} + \left(\frac{(D-d)2^{D-d-1}}{2^{D-d}-1}\right)\Delta^{reg}_{NCL-avg}\right\}\right] \quad (5.20)$$

$$R_{hot} = \Delta_{CL-avg} + \Delta^{hot}_{NCL-avg} \quad (5.21)$$

$$R_{avg} = (1-h)r_{reg} + h R_{hot} \quad (5.22)$$

where

Δ_{avg} = average delay encountered by intra-cluster messages on a cluster link

$$= \frac{1}{d\,2^{d-1}}\left[\sum_{j=1}^{d}\left\{(d-j+1)\binom{d}{j-1}\Delta_{CL}(j)\right\}\right]$$

Δ_{CL-avg} = average delay encountered by non-intra-cluster messages on a cluster link

$$= \sum_{j=1}^{d}\left\{(d-j+1)\binom{d}{j-1}\Delta_{CL}(j)\,p(j)\right\}$$

$\Delta_{NCL-avg}^{reg}$ = average delay encountered by an inter-cluster message on a level 2 network link

$$= \frac{\left[\sum_{j=1}^{D-d}\left\{(D-d-j+1)\binom{D-d}{j-1}\Delta_{NCL}(j)\right\}\right]}{(D-d)2^{D-d-1}}$$

$\Delta_{NCL-avg}^{hot}$ = average delay encountered by a hot-spot message on a level 2 network link

$$= \sum_{j=1}^{D-d}\left\{(D-d-j+1)\binom{D-d}{j-1}\Delta_{NCL}(j)\,p_1(j)\right\}$$

5.3.1.3. Validation of the analysis

Two assumptions were made in order to facilitate the analysis. It was assumed that whenever a message arrives at a link on its path to its destination, a new service time is generated from the exponential service time distribution. In a real system, of course, the messages would retain their service times, which reflect the lengths of the messages, from the times they are generated to the times they arrive at their destinations. The other assumption is that replies are generated independently by the same message generation process. In real systems, a reply is generated every time a message reaches its destination node. A simulation model was constructed in which these two assumptions were not made, and, therefore, allowed for the study of their effect on accuracy. In all other respects, the simulation model matched the analytic model.

Both the BH and BH/BH networks were used in the simulation experiments. For a network of each type, the two components of delay – R_{reg} and R_{hot} – are plotted as functions of α. The value of α is varied from 0.6 to 0.9 in steps of 0.1. The hot-spot proportion h is fixed at 8%. The

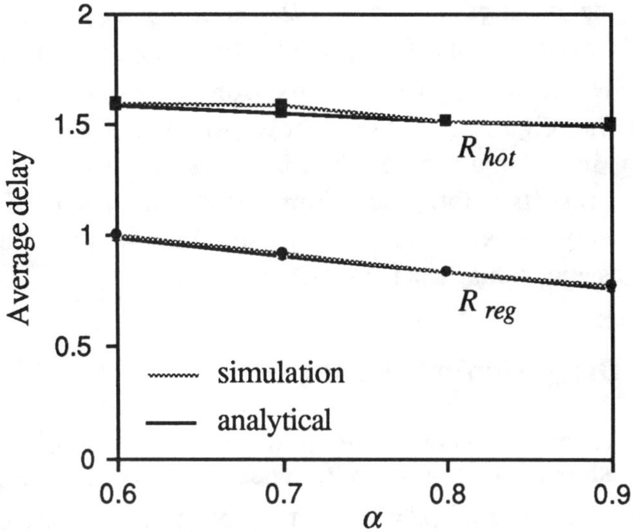

(a) BH network (d = 3, D = 6, λ = 1, $\mu_{CL} = \mu_{NCL}$ = 3, h = 8%)

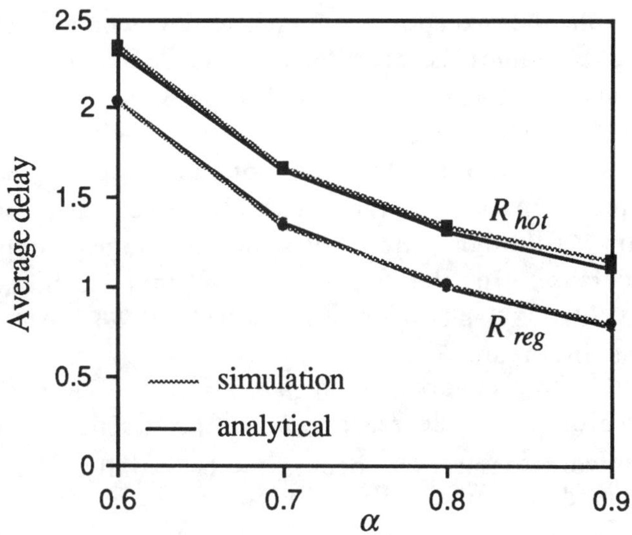

(b) BH/BH network (d = 3, D = 6, λ = 1, μ_{CL} = 3, μ_{NCL} = 6, h = 8 %)

Figure 5.1 Comparison of analytical and simulation results

other parameters used are: $d = 3$, $D = 6$, $\lambda = 1$, $\mu_{CL} = 3$, $\mu_{NCL} = 3$ for the BH network, and $d = 3$, $D = 6$, $\lambda = 1$, $\mu_{CL} = 3$, $\mu_{NCL} = 6$ for the BH/BH network. The results for the BH network are presented in Figure 5.1a and those for the BH/BH network are given in Figure 5.1b. It can be seen from these plots that the results obtained from the analytical formulas match closely those obtained by simulation, thus justifying the two assumptions used in the analysis.

5.3.1.4. Discussion of results

The impact of hot-spot contention on BH and BH/BH networks is shown in Figure 5.2. These graphs give R_{avg} for 256-node networks ($D=8$). The hot-spot proportion h is varied from 0% to 16%. The value of μ_{CL} is set at 1.4, for both cases, and μ_{NCL} to 1.4 for the BH network and to 1.4 and 2.8 for the BH/BH network. The other parameters used are d =3, and $\alpha = 0.75$. We have assumed $\alpha = 0.75$ throughout this chapter, with the exception of Figure 5.3 where the impact of varying α values is considered.

It should be noted that the delay presented in Figure 5.2 is the average delay R_{avg} experienced by all messages. If the delays encountered by hot-spot and regular messages are plotted separately, they exhibit essentially identical behaviour (although the hot-spot messages experience greater delays). In the remainder of this section, therefore, only the average delay R_{avg} over all messages is considered, as in Figure 5.2.

In both the networks, with $\mu_{NCL} = \mu_{CL}$, increasing the hot-spot proportion decreases λ_{sat} (the traffic intensity at which network saturation occurs) substantially. For all h values considered, the BH/BH network λ_{sat} values are less than the corresponding values for the BH network. This is a direct consequence of the reduction in the number of links (which is assumed to represent cost of the network) associated with the BH/BH network. (The BH network requires 1024 links whereas the BH/BH network requires only 464 links.) It can be seen from the structure of the BH/BH network that non-cluster (i.e., level 2 network)

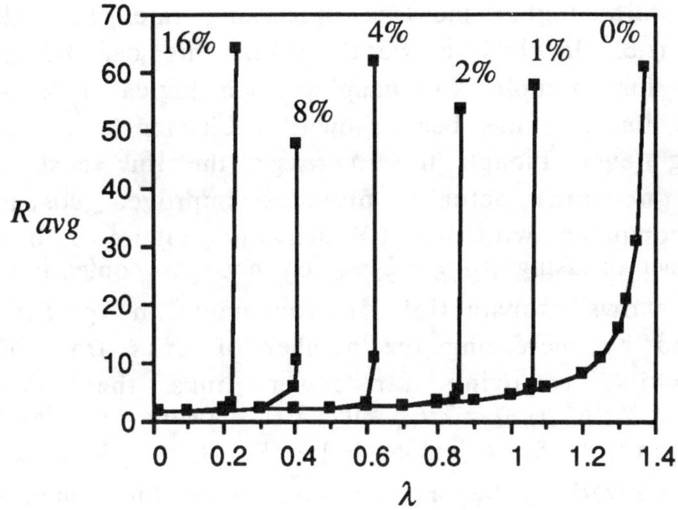

(a) BH network (d = 3, D = 8, $\mu_{CL} = \mu_{NCL}$ = 1.4, α = 0.75)

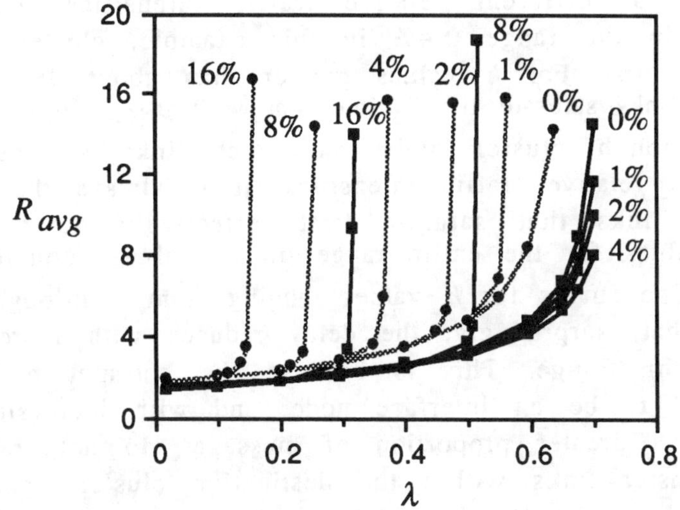

(b) BH/BH network (d = 3, D = 8, μ_{CL} = 1.4, α = 0.75, μ_{NCL} = 2.8 for solid lines, μ_{NCL} = 1.4 for dotted lines)

Figure 5.2 Impact of hot-spot contention on the BH and BH/BH networks (h is varied from 0% to 16%)

links require higher message processing rates than do the cluster (i.e., level 1 network) links. This can be accomplished, for example, by mapping each logical link to two physical links. It has been shown in Chapter 3 that such a mapping (even though this increases the link cost of the BH/BH network) actually provides improved cost-benefit ratios compared with the BH network. Figure 5.2b shows the impact of using $\mu_{NCL} = 2\mu_{CL}$ on hot-spot contention. This graph shows substantial improvement in performance (achieved by increasing the number of links from 464 to 544, whilst requiring far fewer links than the BH network). With $\mu_{NCL} = 2\mu_{CL}$, the BH network provides better λ_{sat} values only for h values 0-2%. For higher h values, the BH/BH network is better. For this reason, the remainder of the chapter uses $\mu_{NCL} = 2\mu_{CL} = 2.8$ for the BH/BH network.

With $\mu_{NCL} = 2\mu_{CL}$, the BH/BH network is less sensitive to the hot-spot proportion. In this case the BH/BH network behaves differently since cluster and non-cluster links saturate at different relative traffic intensities. For h values in the range 0-4% in this example, cluster links saturate first. For h values greater than about 4%, non-cluster links saturate first. (Note that with $\mu_{NCL} = \mu_{CL} = 1.4$, even though cluster and non-cluster links saturate at different relative traffic intensities, it is always the non-cluster links that saturate first, effectively determining λ_{sat} values for the entire range of h values considered here.) The curves for h values ranging from 0 through 4% show that, surprisingly, the delay reduces with increasing h in this range. This is because the hot-spot node is assumed to be an interface node, and with increasing h values, a greater proportion of messages do not traverse any cluster links within the destination cluster, reducing the load on the "bottleneck" network resources (the cluster links) and thus the average delay.

The impact of locality on hot-spot contention is shown in Figure 5.3. Here, the value of α is varied from 0.6 to 0.9 while keeping the value of h constant at 8%. As shown in the figure, the changes in α have negligible impact on the BH network. This is an expected result because the message traffic due to intra-cluster and inter-cluster messages is uniformly distributed over all the links within a conceptual cluster. In the BH/BH network, on the other hand, increasing α results in a significant improvement in performance. As the value of α is increased from 0.6 to 0.9, λ_{sat} increases from about 0.42 to 0.68. Note that, in this network, intra-cluster messages are uniformly distributed over all links within a cluster while the traffic due to inter-cluster messages tends to be highest on links that are closer to the interface node. Decreasing the proportion of inter-cluster messages decreases the load on these relatively heavily utilized links.

5.3.2. Hardware Combining

In hardware combining, the queues associated with links are partitioned into *forward queues* and *return queues*. A queue associated with link l that carries messages from node a to node b is termed a forward queue if node b is closer to the hot-spot node than node a, and a return queue if node a is closer to the hot-spot node than node b. A "wait buffer" must be associated with each node.

In hardware combining, when several hot-spot messages are queued in a forward queue, they are combined into a single hot-spot message, called a *combined message*, which is forwarded toward the hot-spot node. A record of all messages combined is kept in the wait buffer. When the reply from the hot-spot node returns, the node, using the information in the wait buffer, generates replies to all combined messages and places them in return queues. Note that a message may participate in many combinings before reaching the hot-spot node. In this section, unbounded buffering space for forward queues, return queues, and wait buffers is assumed.

The results of simulation experiments that were performed to assess the performance of hardware combining are shown in Figure 5.4. It is obvious from these graphs that hardware combining is effective in reducing the hot-spot contention. Interestingly, delays associated with regu-

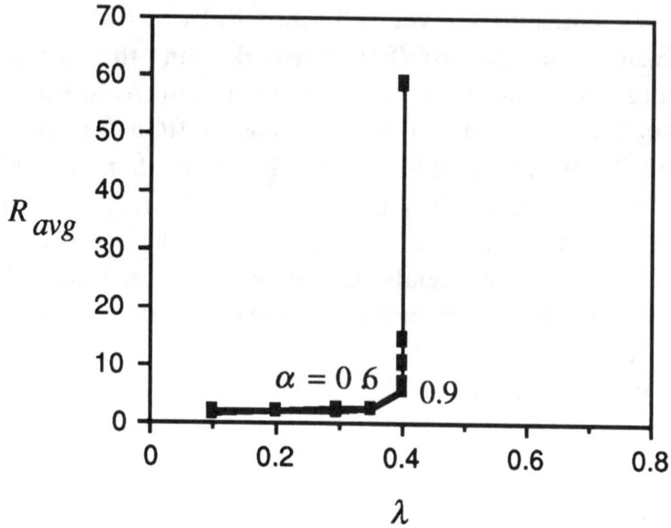

(a) BH network (d = 3, D = 8, $\mu_{CL} = \mu_{NCL}$ = 1.4, h = 8%)

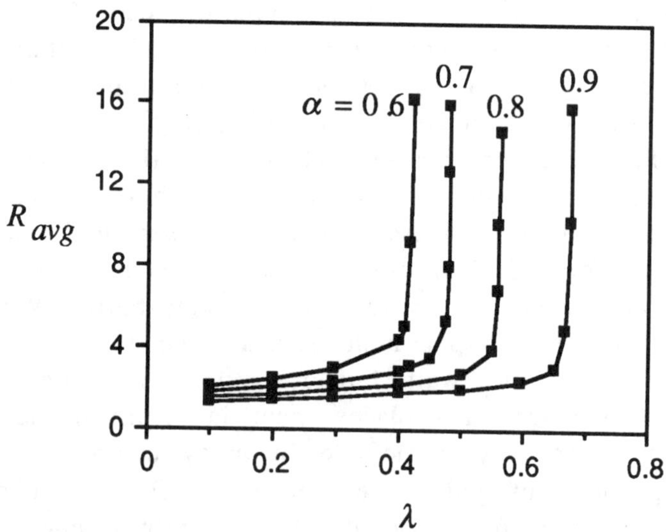

(b) BH/BH network (d = 3, D = 8, μ_{CL} = 1.4, μ_{NCL} = 2.8, h = 8%)

Figure 5.3 Impact of locality on hot-spot contention in the BH and BH/BH networks (α is varied from 0.6 to 0.9)

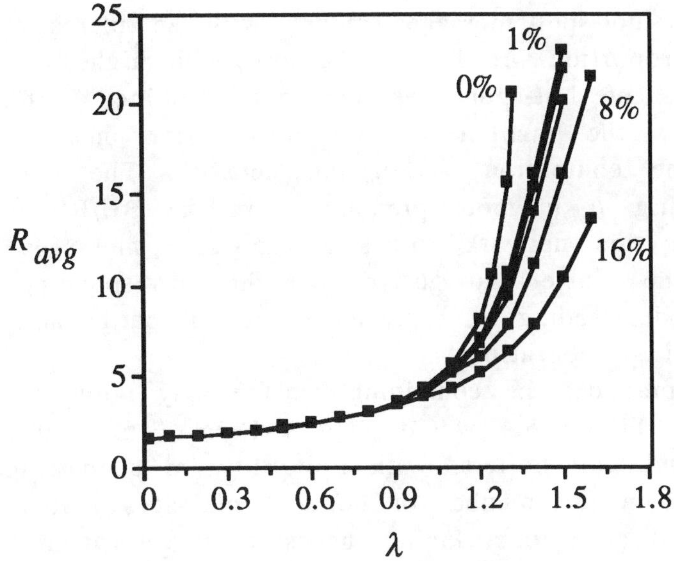

(a) BH network (d = 3, D = 8, $\mu_{CL} = \mu_{NCL}$ = 1.4, α = 0.75)

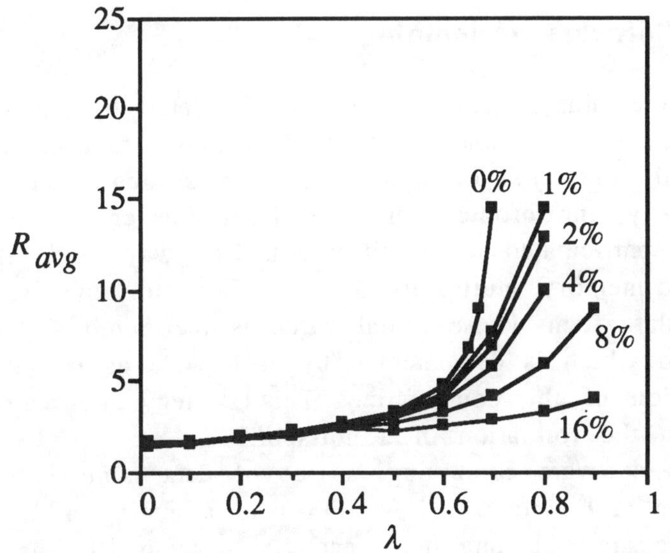

(b) BH/BH network (d = 3, D = 8, μ_{CL} = 1.4, μ_{NCL} = 2.8, α = 0.75)

Figure 5.4 Impact of hardware combining on hot-spot contention in the BH and BH/BH networks (h is varied from 0% to 16%)

lar and hot-spot messages reduce with an increasing hot-spot proportion h. This is because with higher h larger numbers of hot-spot messages get combined, effectively reducing the number of non-intra-cluster messages and thus the contention within the network. The impact of increasing h is more pronounced in the BH/BH network because this network forces all hot-spot messages (from the same cluster) to go through the corresponding interface node, leading to a greater chance of participating in a combining operation.

In practice, the combining scheme may not perform as well as Figure 5.4 would suggest because of finite queue sizes and wait buffers. With finite forward queues, there is a limit on the number of hot-spot messages that may be combined at a time. Finite queues are discussed in Section 5.4. Unbounded queues, however, provide an upper bound on the achievable performance improvements.

5.3.3. Software Combining

Software combining has been studied in detail by Yew *et al.* [YEW 87] in the context of shared-memory multiprocessors. Here only one type of application of this idea is described; specifically, the problem of recognizing the end of a computation participated in by all nodes. One way to do this in a shared-memory multiprocessor would be to have a single shared data item whose initial value is the number of nodes (N), and which is decremented by each node as it completes its portion of the computation. This strategy, however, will result in the formation of a hot-spot.

With software combining, a tree of data items is created as shown in Figure 5.5. If N=1000 and assuming a fan-in of 10, there are 111 data items each with value 10. The nodes are partitioned into 100 groups of ten, with each group sharing one of the data items corresponding to the leaves of the tree. When the last node in each group decrements its data item to zero, this node then decrements the parent data item. This process is repeated until the data item corresponding to the root of the tree is finally decremented to zero. Software combining reduces hot-spot contention in this example because there are 111 data items each being accessed by only 10 nodes instead of one data item being accessed by 1000 nodes.

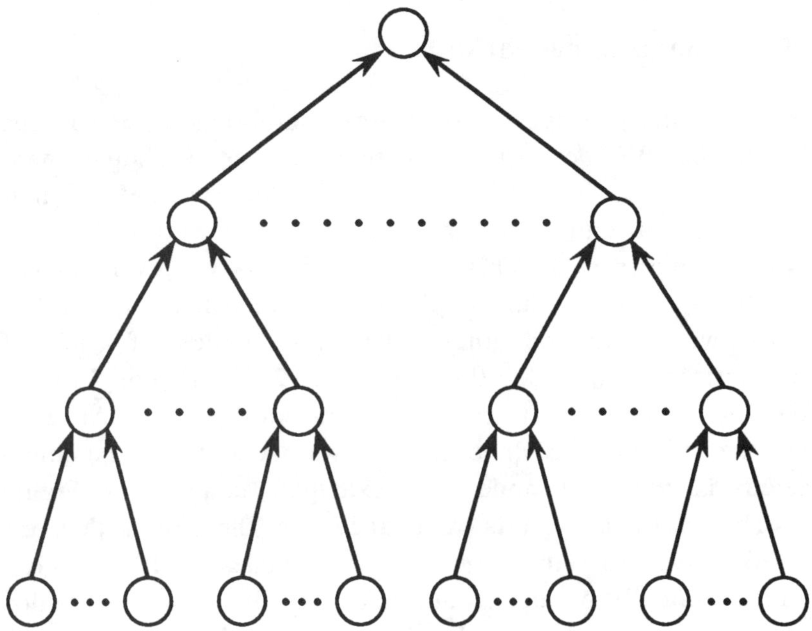

Figure 5.5 Software combining tree with a fan-in of 10

In a distributed-memory multicomputer, software combining can be applied to the problem of recognizing the end of a computation by logically constructing a tree of nodes that exchange messages so as to finally result in a "root" node being notified of the termination. This root node may then broadcast the fact that the computation has terminated back down the tree. As an example, consider a shared-nothing database machine such as the Gamma system [SCHN 89]. Database operations such as aggregate operations (e.g., min, max, sum, etc.) could be implemented by propagating partially valid results towards the root of the tree. The final valid result is computed by the root node, which may then be broadcast to all nodes back down the tree. Another example database operation that can effectively use software combining is the project operation. With this operation, duplicate elimination can be carried out in parallel at each internal node of the tree.

5.3.3.1. The BH network

There are many ways a software combining tree can be built on the BH network. This section uses a simple mapping scheme that is applicable to both BH and BH/BH networks. The structure of the software combining tree is shown in Figure 5.6. This structure is a two-level, unbalanced tree. Nodes within a cluster are linked by a level 1 tree (shown in dashed lines). The root nodes of each of these subtrees (i.e., nodes 0, 8, 16, and 24 in Figure 5.6) are linked by a level 2 tree (shown in solid lines). At each level, the mapping is done as follows. A node is randomly selected as the root node (for example, node 8 in Figure 5.6). The children of this root node are the nodes that are one link away from the root node (i.e., nodes 9, 10, and 12), the grandchildren of this root node are all those nodes that are two links away (i.e., nodes 11, 14, and 13), and so on. In any part of the tree, the addresses of a node and its child differ in one coordinate. Therefore, there is exactly one link that connects these two nodes and this link is used as the *tree link*. For example, there is only one link that provides a direct communication channel between nodes 8 and 12. The set of children nodes is distributed over the set of parent nodes as uniformly as possible. For example, the children nodes 11, 14, and 13 are attached one each to the parent nodes 9, 10 and 12. Further, if there is a choice of parent node to which a node can be attached in building the software combining tree, a parent node is randomly selected. In the example shown in Figure 5.6, node 15 could also be attached to either node 13 or node 14, instead of node 11. It should be noted that, irrespective of the degree of a node, all links in the tree process hot-spot messages at rate $h\lambda$.

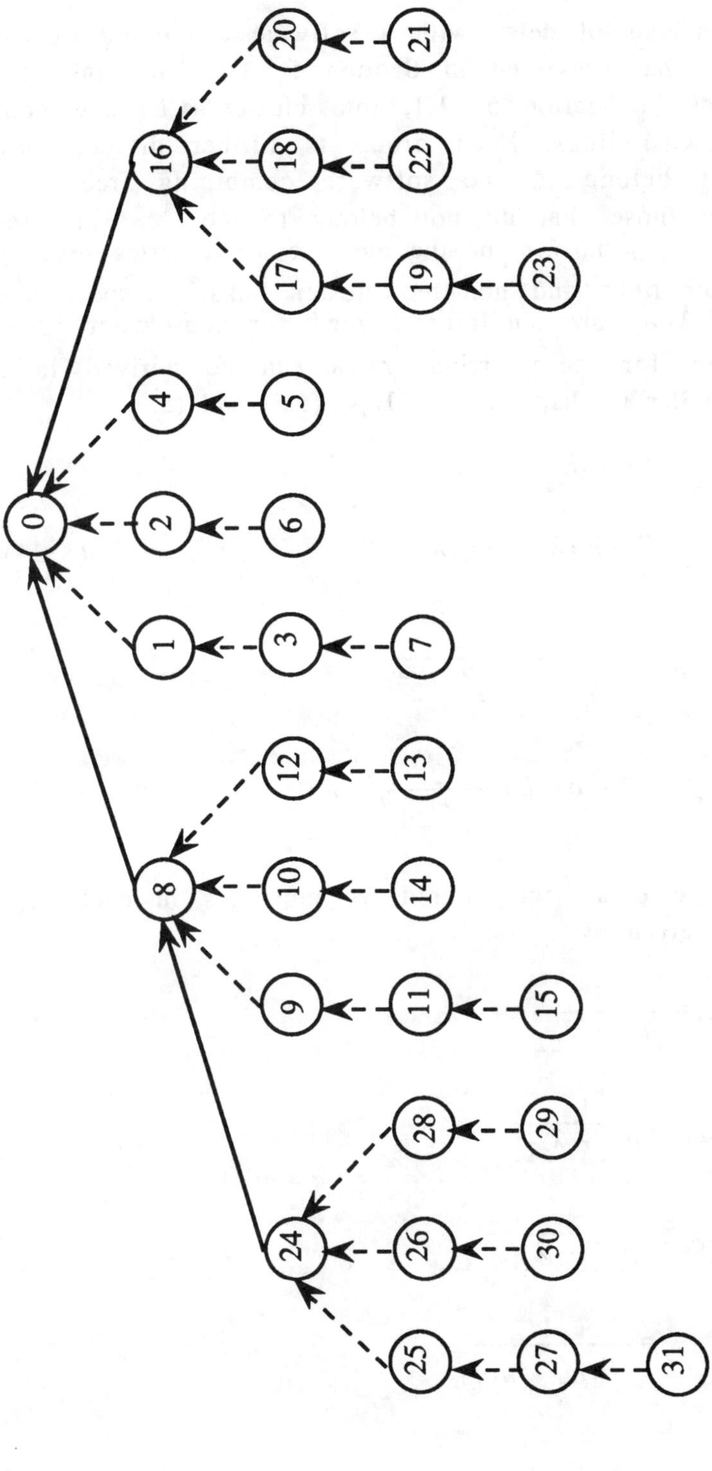

Figure 5.6 Software combining tree for the BH and BH/BH networks ($D = 5$ and $d = 3$)

The analysis of delay with a software combining tree is similar to that presented in Section 5.3.1.1. The links are divided, as in Section 5.3.1.1, into cluster (CL) and non-cluster (NCL) links. Each group is further divided into links that belong to the software combining tree (tree links) and those that do not belong to the tree (non-tree links). Let λ_{CLt} and λ_{CL} be the message arrival rates seen by tree cluster links and non-tree cluster links, respectively. λ_{NCLt} and λ_{NCL} are similarly defined for non-cluster links. Expressions for these arrival rates can be derived in a manner similar to that used for Eqs. (5.5) and (5.9).

$$\lambda_{CL} = (1 - h)\lambda \tag{5.23}$$

$$\lambda_{CLt} = (1 - h)\lambda + h\lambda = \lambda \tag{5.24}$$

$$\lambda_{NCL} = (1 - \alpha - h)\lambda \frac{2^D}{2^D - 2^d} \tag{5.25}$$

$$\lambda_{NCLt} = (1 - \alpha - h)\lambda \frac{2^D}{2^D - 2^d} + h\lambda \tag{5.26}$$

The average delay encountered by messages in each type of link is given by

$$\Delta_{CL} = \frac{1}{\mu_{CL} - \lambda_{CL}}$$

$$\Delta_{CLt} = \frac{1}{\mu_{CL} - \lambda_{CLt}}$$

$$\Delta_{NCL} = \frac{1}{\mu_{NCL} - \lambda_{NCL}}$$

$$\Delta_{NCLt} = \frac{1}{\mu_{NCL} - \lambda_{NCLt}}$$

The average message delays are given by Eqs. (5.10), (5.11), and (5.12) where Δ_{CL}^{avg}, Δ_{NCL}^{avg} are given by the following.

$$\Delta_{CL}^{avg} = \frac{1}{d2^{d-1}}\left[\left(2^{d} - 1\right)\Delta_{CLt} + \left(d2^{d-1} - 2^{d} + 1\right)\Delta_{CL}\right]$$

because there are $(2^d - 1)$ links in a tree of 2^d nodes. Similarly,

$$\Delta_{NCL}^{avg} = \frac{\left(2^{D-d} - 1\right)\Delta_{NCLt} + \left((D-d)2^{D-1} - 2^{D-d} + 1\right)\Delta_{NCL}}{(D-d)2^{D-1}}$$

In computing R_{hot} note that each hot-spot message is going to at most one neighbouring node in the tree. However, a hot-spot "reply" must be propagated all the way down the tree from the root node. Here, an expression is given for R_{hot} that represents in this case the average delay encountered by a hot-spot reply.

It is easy to see that the average number of tree cluster links traversed by hot-spot replies is given by

$$\frac{\sum_{i=1}^{d} i\binom{d}{i}}{2^{d}} = \frac{d}{2}$$

Similarly, the average number of tree non-cluster links travelled by hot-spot replies is $(D-d)/2$. Therefore,

$$R_{hot} = \frac{d}{2}\Delta_{CLt} + \frac{D-d}{2}\Delta_{NCLt}$$

The impact of utilizing a software combining tree is presented in Figure 5.7a for a 256-node BH network. All parameters remain the same as those used in Figure 5.2. The graph shows that the software combining scheme is effective in reducing the adverse effect of hot-spot contention. For all values of h, λ_{sat} remains constant. This is because λ_{CLt} is independent of h and these tree cluster links saturate first, for the parameter values considered here.

It is easy to show that this simple mapping scheme works for any network size. In order to prove this, it is necessary to show that, when $h>0$, the use of a software combining tree results in a λ_{sat} that is greater than or equal to the λ_{sat} obtainable without the use of a software combining tree when no hot-spot traffic exists (i.e., when $h = 0$). It follows from Eqs. (5.5) and (5.9) that cluster links saturate at $\lambda_{sat} = \mu_{CL}$ and non-cluster links at $\lambda_{sat} = \mu_{NCL} \dfrac{2^D - 2^d}{2^D\,(1-\alpha)}$ when $h = 0$. It can be seen from Eqs. (5.23) and (5.24) that both tree and non-tree cluster links process messages at a rate less than or equal to the message generation rate λ (i.e., these links saturate at message generation rates greater than or equal to μ_{CL}). Similarly, it is straightforward to see from Eqs. (5.25) and (5.26) that tree and non-tree non-cluster links saturate at message generation rates greater than or equal to $\mu_{NCL} \dfrac{2^D - 2^d}{2^D\,(1-\alpha)}$. This proves that this mapping scheme is suitable for any network size.

5.3.3.2. The BH/BH network

In this network, each interface node acts as an intermediate hot-spot node. The same mapping scheme is used in this network as in the BH network. The analysis is similar to that presented in the last section. As in the last section, let λ_{CLt} and λ_{CL} be the message arrival rates seen by tree cluster links and non-tree cluster links, respectively. λ_{NCLt} and λ_{NCL} are similarly defined for non-cluster links. Analogous to the derivations of Eqs. (5.15) and (5.19), the arrival rates can be obtained as

$$\lambda_{CL} = \alpha\lambda + 2(1 - \alpha - h)\,\lambda 2^{d}\, p_o(j)$$

$$= \alpha\lambda + (1 - \alpha - h)\,\lambda 2^{d+1}\, p_o(j)$$

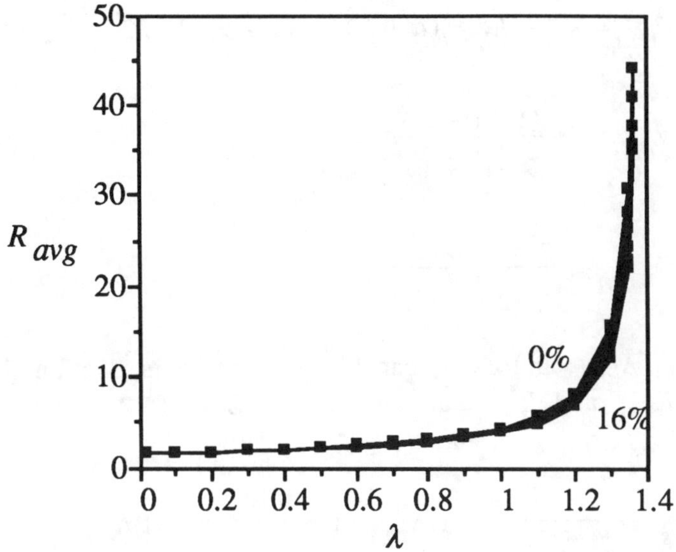

(a) BH network (d = 3, D = 8, $\mu_{CL} = \mu_{NCL}$ = 1.4, α = 0.75)

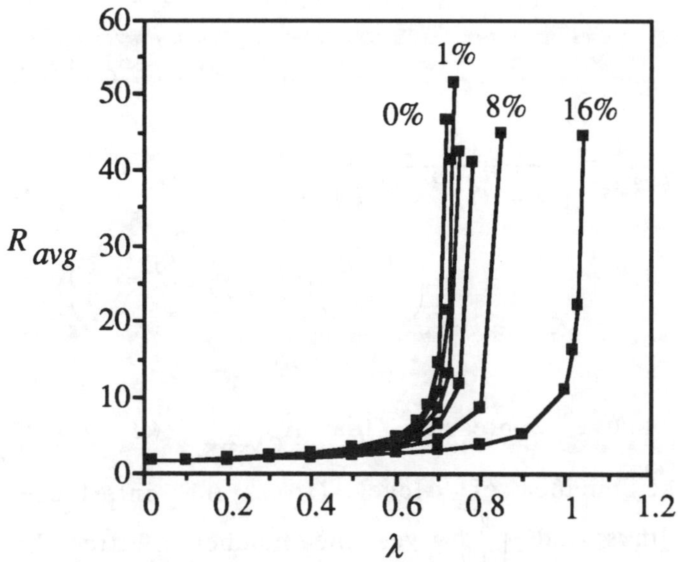

(b) BH/BH network (d = 3, D = 8, μ_{CL} = 1.4, μ_{NCL} = 2.8, α = 0.75)

Figure 5.7 Impact of software combining on hot-spot contention in the BH and BH/BH networks (h is varied from 0% to 16%)

$$\lambda_{CLt} = \lambda_{CL} + h\lambda = (\alpha + h)\lambda + (1 - \alpha - h)\lambda 2^{d+1} p_o(j)$$

$$\lambda_{NCL} = \frac{2^D (1 - \alpha - h)\lambda}{2^{D-d} - 1}$$

and,

$$\lambda_{NCLt} = \frac{2^D (1 - \alpha - h)\lambda}{2^{D-d} - 1} + h\lambda$$

Δ_{CL}, Δ_{CLt}, Δ_{NCL}, and Δ_{NCLt} can be obtained as in Section 5.3.3.1. Then, R_{reg} and R_{avg} are given by Eqs. (5.20) and (5.23) where Δ_{avg}, $\Delta_{CL\text{-}avg}$, and $\Delta_{NCL\text{-}avg}$ are given by:

$$\Delta_{avg} = \frac{1}{d 2^{d-1}}\left[(2^d - 1)\Delta_{CLt} + (d\, 2^{d-1} - 2^d + 1)\Delta_{CL}\right]$$

$$\Delta_{CL-avg} = \sum_{j=1}^{d}\left\{\left[(d - j + 1)\binom{d}{j-1} - \binom{d}{j}\right]\Delta_{CL}(j)\, p_o(j) + \binom{d}{j}\Delta_{CLt}(j)\, p_o(j)\right\}$$

$$\Delta^{reg}_{NCL-avg} = \frac{1}{(D - d)2^{D-d-1}}\sum_{j=1}^{D-d}\left\{\left[(D - d - j + 1)\binom{D-d}{j-1} - \binom{D-d}{j}\right]\Delta_{NCL}(j) + \binom{D-d}{j}\Delta_{NCLt}(j)\right\}$$

In the above expression for Δ_{CL-avg}, $(d - j + 1)\binom{d}{j-1}$ gives the number of j-level (from the interface node) cluster links and $\binom{d}{j}$ gives the number of tree links in that group. R_{hot} is given by

$$R_{hot} = \left[\frac{D - d}{2}\right]\Delta_{NCLt}(j) + \frac{1}{2^d}\sum_{j=1}^{d}\left[\sum_{k=j}^{d}\binom{d}{k}\right]\Delta_{CLt}(j)$$

The delay encountered by hot-spot messages in the level 2 network is given by, as in Section 5.3.3.1, $\frac{(D-d)}{2}\Delta_{NCLt}$. Since the delay incurred at the tree cluster links depends on how close they are to the interface node, the average delay encountered by hot-spot messages in the level 1 network is given as shown in the second term in the above expression.

A plot of R_{avg} is shown in Figure 5.7b. The network parameters are the same as those used in Figure 5.2. Again, as for the BH network, software combining with this simple mapping works well. As with hardware combining, λ_{sat} increases with an increasing proportion of hot-spot traffic h.

Comparing Figures 5.4 and 5.7, we note that hardware combining and software combining provide performance that is comparable to each other in terms of λ_{sat} values. Limited buffer space, however, may reduce the effectiveness of hardware combining because of the more limited opportunities for combining messages. This effect is demonstrated in Section 5.4, which discusses the effectiveness of both these schemes with bounded buffering capacity.

5.3.4. Impact of Improved Routing Algorithms

The analysis and the simulation experiments described in Sections 5.3.1 through 5.3.3 used a random routing algorithm in which each of the shortest paths between the source and destination nodes is selected with equal probability. However, the links that are used by hot-spot messages tend to saturate much earlier than the other links. Thus, if the routing algorithm can be improved such that it chooses that shortest path with the least traffic, the adverse impact of hot-spot contention on system performance can be reduced.

Several simulation experiments were conducted on the BH and BH/BH networks using an improved algorithm that works as follows. At each node, if a message can take one of

l links (on shortest path), it is routed over the link that has the shortest queue of messages waiting to be forwarded. The results of these experiments are shown in Figures 5.8 and 5.9. (The network parameters are identical to those used in Figure 5.2.) With this improved routing algorithm, regular messages can be directed away from links that saturate because of hot-spot traffic, thus lessening the impact of hot-spot contention on regular traffic. For this reason, the delays of regular and hot-spot messages are shown separately in these graphs. These graphs show that the improved routing algorithm reduces the hot-spot contention considerably. More specifically, regular message throughput is not affected as is the case with the random routing algorithm. As shown in Section 5.4, however, these messages will experience increased delays because of hot-spot message interference in the case of bounded buffering capacity.

5.4. Performance with Bounded Buffering Capacity

This section presents simulation results for the case of bounded buffering capacity. When the number of buffers is finite, there is a possibility of store-and-forward deadlock [MERL 80]. Store-and-forward deadlock refers to the situation in which there is a set of buffers, all of which hold messages waiting to be forwarded, and in which these messages can be forwarded only to other buffers of the set. The result is a deadlock. It can be shown that store-and-forward deadlock implies a cycle of buffer requests [COFF 71, HOLT 72].

The simulation experiments implemented a scheme for deadlock avoidance proposed by Merlin and Schweitzer [MERL 80]. Let M be the maximum number of hops a message can make in the network. At each node, suppose that there are $M+1$ buffers, say $[B_0, B_1, ..., B_M]$. When a message is generated, it is placed in buffer B_0 at the source node. For a given message, let t denote the total number of hops from source to destination. When a message has made $s<t$

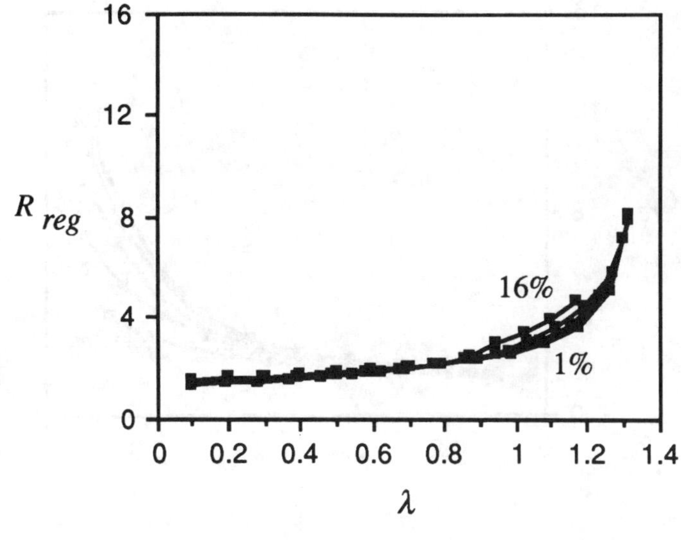

(a)

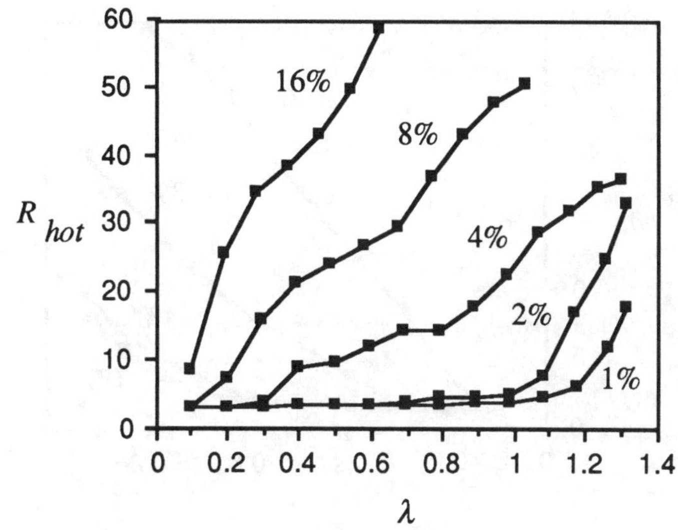

(b)

Figure 5.8 Impact of improved routing algorithm on hot-spot contention in the BH network (h is varied from 0% to 16%, $d = 3$, $D = 8$, $\mu_{CL} = \mu_{NCL} = 1.4$, $\alpha = 0.75$)

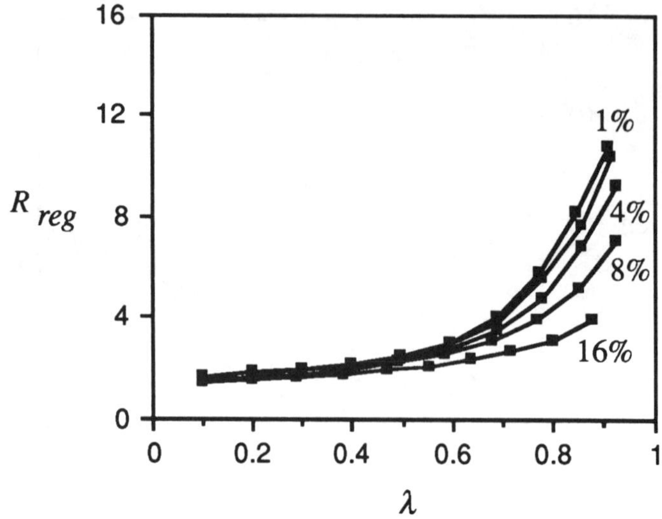

(a)

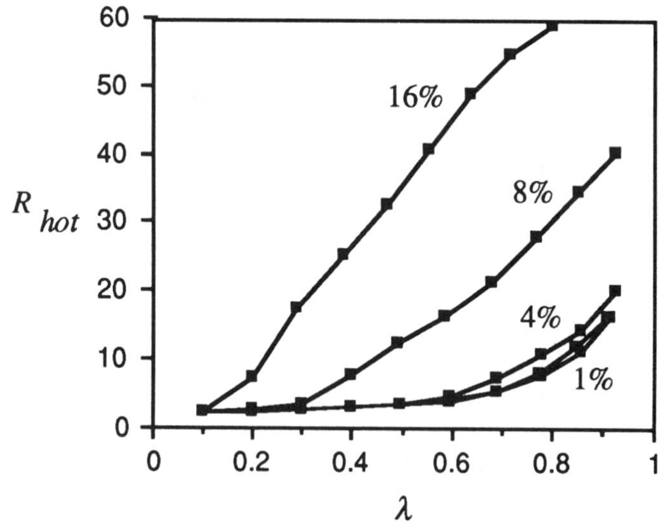

(b)

Figure 5.9 Impact of improved routing algorithm on hot-spot contention in the BH/BH network (h is varied from 0% to 16%, $d = 3$, $D = 8$, $\mu_{CL} = 1.4$, $\mu_{NCL} = 2.8$, $\alpha = 0.75$)

hops, it can be placed in any buffer B_g at an adjacent node (lying on the message route) such that

$$0 \leq g \leq M - (t - s) + 1.$$

It can be shown that if this rule is followed, there will not be store-and-forward deadlocks. For the BH network, $M = D$ and each node should have at least $(D+1)$ buffers. For the BH/BH network, $M = D + d$ and each node should have a minimum of $(D+d+1)$ buffers. If the actual number of buffers C is greater than M, the message can be placed in any buffer B_g at an adjacent node such that

$$0 \leq g \leq C - (t - s) + 1. \tag{5.27}$$

The simulation experiments were conducted on a 256-node network with a cluster size of 8 (d=3). Thus, each node should have a minimum of 12 buffers. In the simulation, when a message is available for transmission, the buffer space at an adjacent node along a shortest path to the destination is checked for a free buffer B_g that satisfies Eq. (5.27). If there is such a buffer, the message transmission commences. On the other hand, when an empty buffer becomes available at a node, a node that has a message to be transmitted to this node is randomly selected from among the neighbouring nodes.

The simulation results reported in the remainder of this chapter were obtained from a single run of simulation because of the amount of time involved in running these experiments. A typical simulation run may take about 48 hours to run on a SUN-3/50. The run length, which was constant for all simulations, was selected after several initial runs with various input parameter values.

Several simulation experiments were done with different numbers of buffers. Figure 5.10 presents selected results that illustrate well the effect of this parameter. Two performance measures are used – the average delay R_{avg} and throughput. For the BH network, the parameters used are: $\mu_{CL} = \mu_{NCL} = 1.4$, $\lambda = 1.3$, $\alpha = 0.75$ and $h = 0\%$, and for the BH/BH network, the parameters used are: $\mu_{CL} = 1.4$, $\mu_{NCL} = 2.8$,

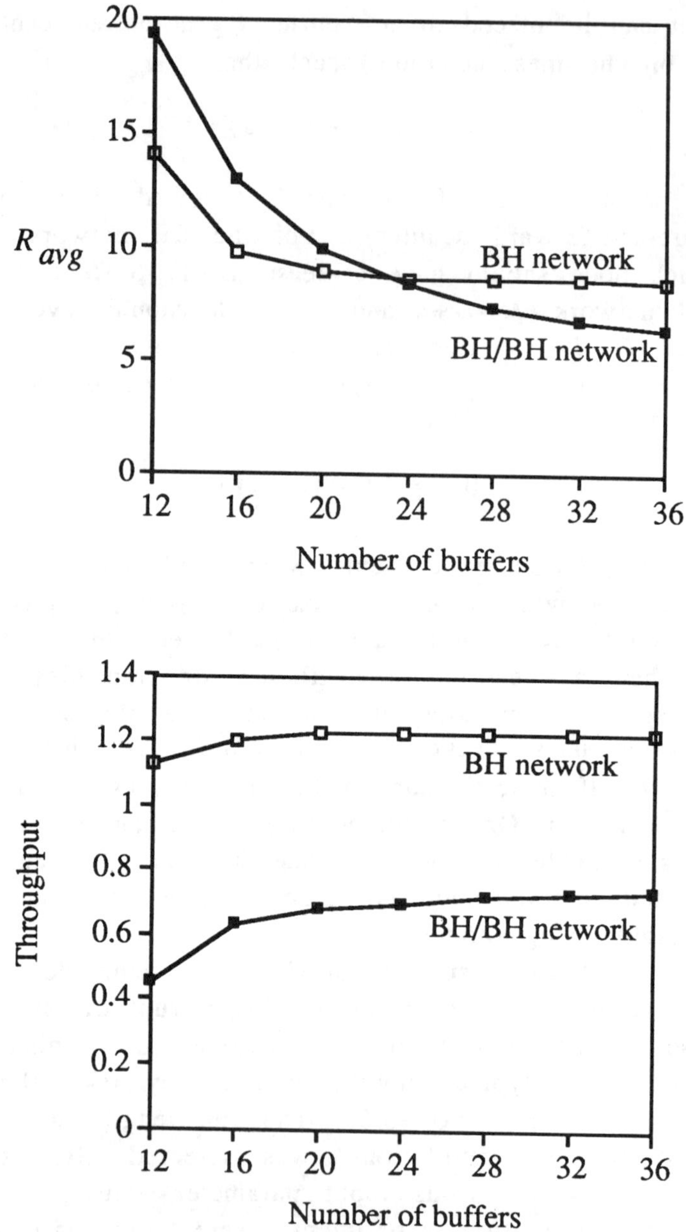

Figure 5.10 Impact of finite buffering capacity on performance of the BH and BH/BH networks: BH network (d = 3, D = 8, $\mu_{CL} = \mu_{NCL}$ = 1.4, λ = 1.3, α = 0.75, h = 0%); BH/BH network (d = 3, D = 8, μ_{CL} = 1.4, μ_{NCL} = 2.8, λ = 0.8, α = 0.75, h = 0%)

$\lambda = 0.8$, $\alpha = 0.75$, and $h = 0\%$. These results show that the BH/BH network is more sensitive to the number of buffers.

In the remainder of this section, a buffer capacity of 32 is assumed. Results for the BH network are shown in Figure 5.11. Note that these graphs use throughput rather than the message generation rate λ on the x-axis, and that the throughput may be less than the message generation rate because of buffer limitations. The results are somewhat different from those shown in Figure 5.8, which assumed unbounded buffering capacity. With finite buffering capacity, the hot-spot proportion greatly affects the performance of the regular messages, even with the improved routing algorithm. The hot-spot messages as well experience substantially more delay than in the case of unbounded buffering capacity.

Figure 5.12 shows the results for the BH/BH network. These plots show a distinctive "fold-back" characteristic in the sense that increasing the message generation rate beyond the saturation point results not only in increased delays but also in *decreased* throughput. This effect is most pronounced in Figure 5.12a for h values of 8% and 16%. A possible explanation for this effect is that increasing the message generation rate results in more contention for buffer space, and may result in intra-cluster messages "hogging" the buffer space in interface nodes, causing the hot-spot and inter-cluster message throughput to drastically decrease. This results in a drastic decrease in overall throughput. Such behaviour is not observed with the BH network because there are more alternative paths in the network.

The impact of hardware combining on both the average delays of hot-spot (R_{hot}) and non-hot-spot (R_{reg}) messages and replies is shown in Figures 5.13 and 5.14. These graphs show that hardware combining is still effective in reducing the adverse effects of hot-spot contention. For the BH network, using hardware combining practically eliminates the interference of hot-spot messages on regular message transmission. As shown in Figure 5.13a, the impact of varying the hot-spot proportion h on regular

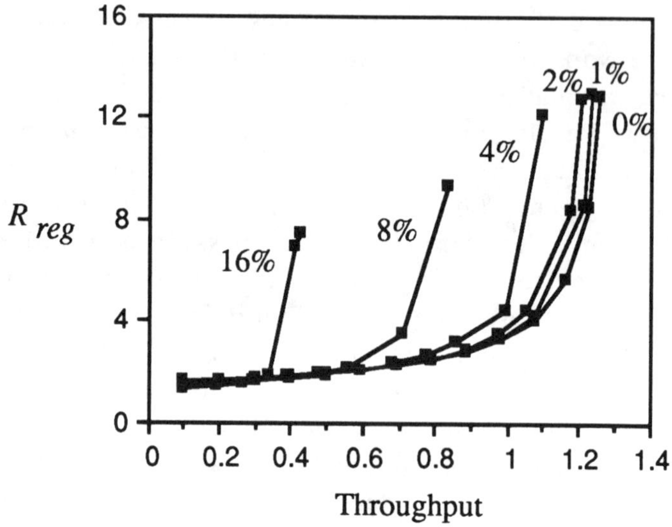

(a)

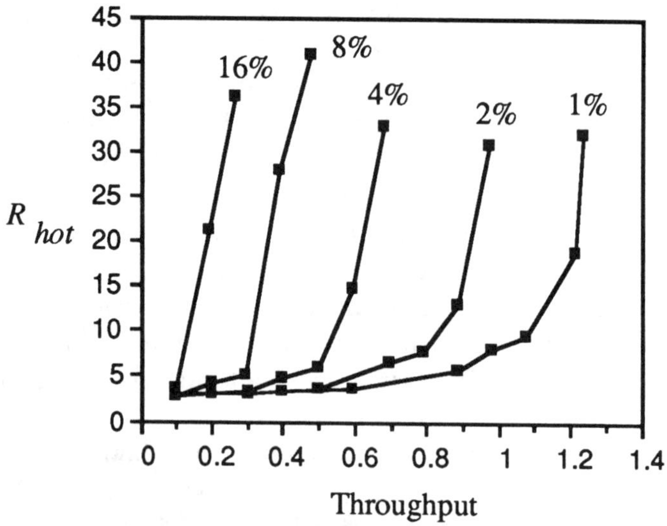

(b)

Figure 5.11 Impact of hot-spot contention in the BH network - the case of finite buffering capacity (h is varied from 0% to 16%, $d = 3$, $D = 8$, $\mu_{CL} = \mu_{NCL} = 1.4$, $\alpha = 0.75$, number of buffers = 32)

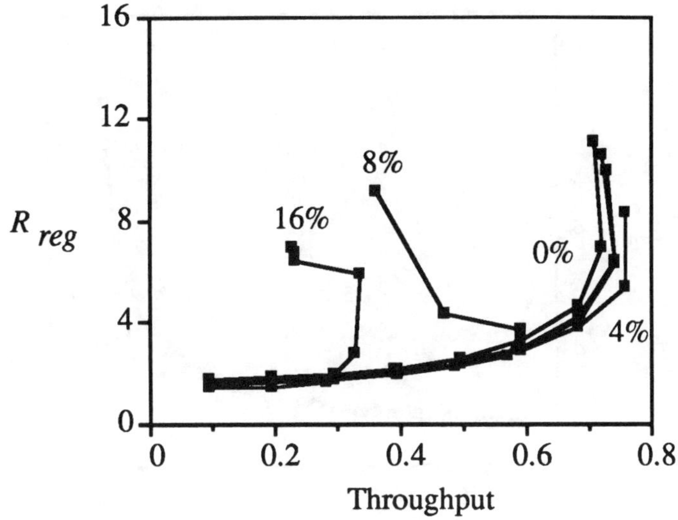

(a)

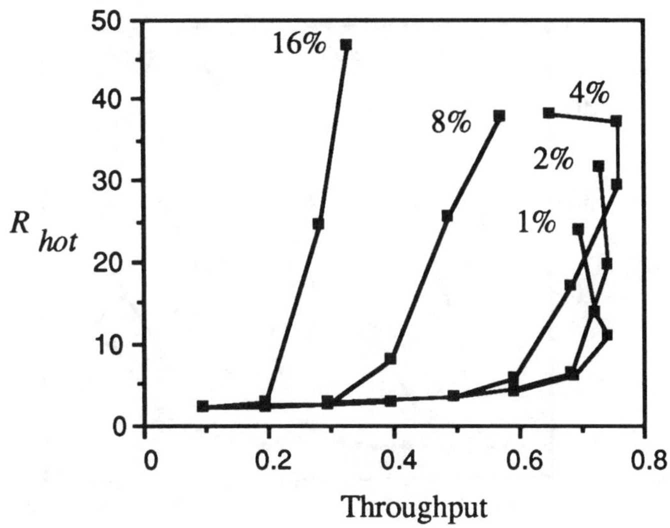

(b)

Figure 5.12 Impact of hot-spot contention in the BH/BH network - the case of finite buffering capacity (h is varied from 0% to 16%, $d = 3$, $D = 8$, $\mu_{CL} = 1.4$, $\mu_{NCL} = 2.8$, $\alpha = 0.75$, number of buffers = 32)

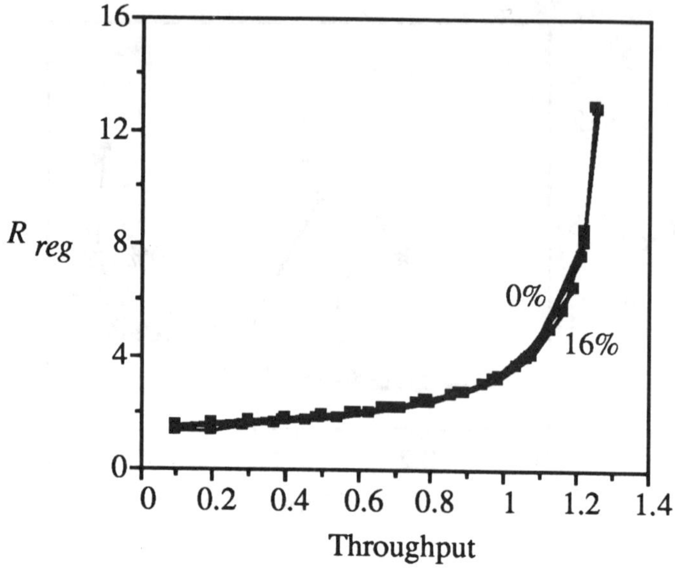

(a)

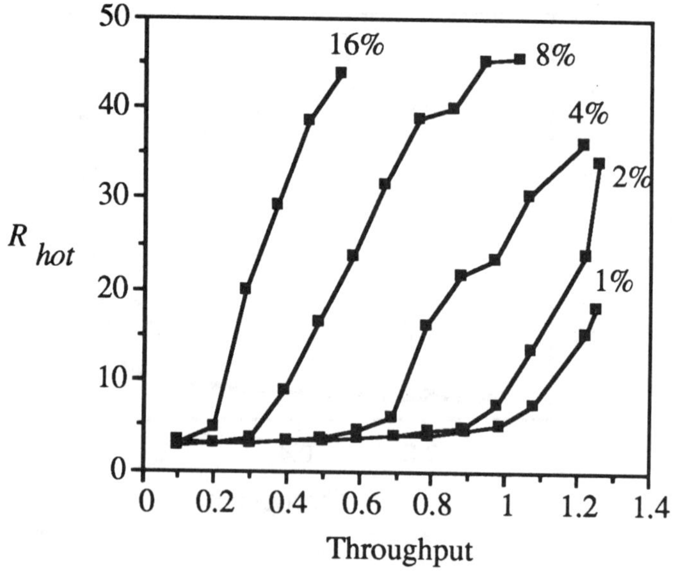

(b)

Figure 5.13 Impact of hardware combining on hot-spot contention in the BH network - the case of finite buffering capacity (h is varied from 0% to 16%, d = 3, D = 8, $\mu_{CL} = \mu_{NCL}$ = 1.4, α = 0.75, number of buffers = 32)

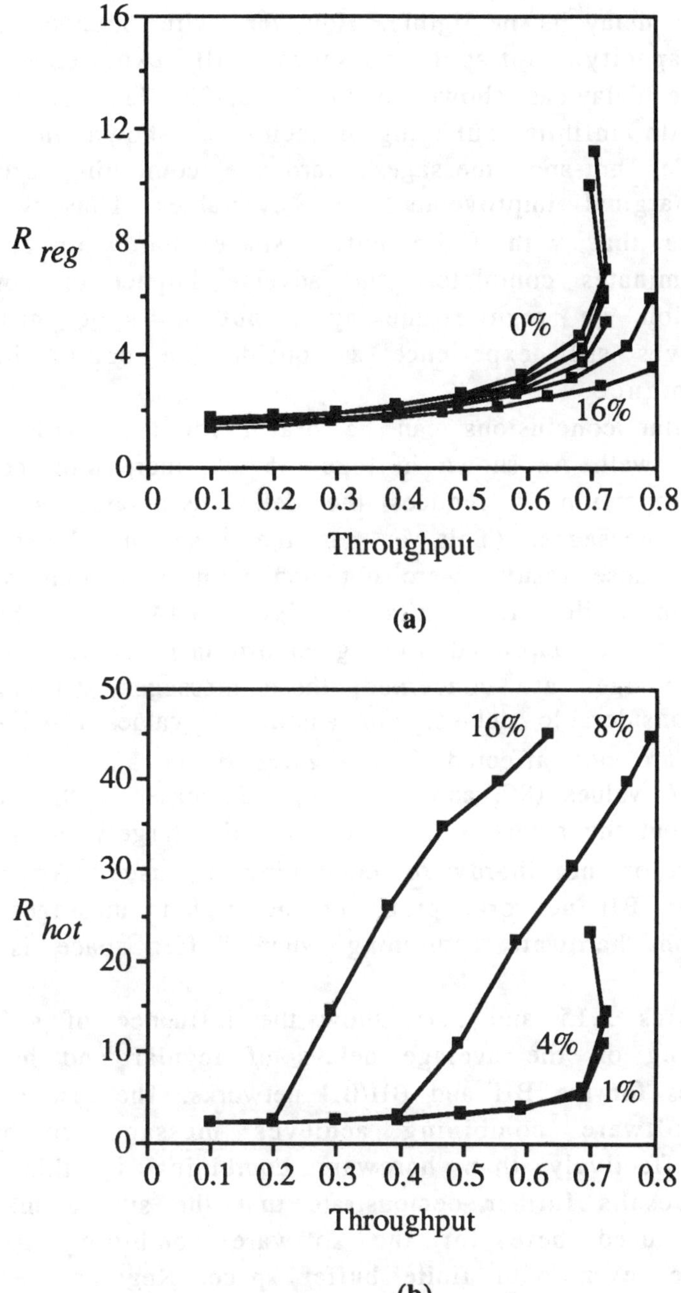

Figure 5.14 Impact of hardware combining on hot-spot contention in the BH/BH network - the case of finite buffering capacity (h is varied from 0% to 16%, d = 3, D = 8, μ_{CL} = 1.4, μ_{NCL} = 2.8, α = 0.75, number of buffers = 32)

message delay is negligible. However, with bounded buffering capacity, hot-spot messages still experience considerable delay as shown in Figure 5.13b. This is not the case with infinite buffering capacity as shown in Figure 5.4a. For hot-spot messages, hardware combining provides only marginal improvement in λ_{sat} values. Thus we may conclude that with finite buffer space, hardware combining eliminates completely the adverse impact of hot-spot contention on regular messages, but hot-spot messages themselves still experience a considerable degradation in performance.

Similar conclusions can be drawn for the BH/BH network as well. As shown in Figure 5.14a, increasing the hot-spot proportion h reduces the delay associated with the regular messages. (This is not the case in Figure 5.2b because those results were obtained with a random routing algorithm while the results in Figure 5.14 were obtained by using the improved routing algorithm.) As far as hot-spot messages are concerned, these messages still experience considerable delays. For smaller h values (1-4%) λ_{sat} values are not affected (see Figures 5.14a and 5.2b). For higher h values (8% and 16%), λ_{sat} decreases with increasing h, but the actual λ_{sat} values remain largely unaffected whether or not hardware combining is used. Again, as with the BH network, primarily the regular messages benefit from hardware combining when buffer space is limited.

Figures 5.15 and 5.16 show the influence of software combining on the average delays of regular and hot-spot messages for the BH and BH/BH networks. The results show that software combining achieves message combining more effectively than hardware combining in this case. These results further demonstrate that the simple mapping scheme used here for the software combining tree is adequate, even with finite buffer space. Regular messages experience similar delays with both hardware combining and software combining schemes (compare Figures 5.15a and 5.16a with Figures 5.13a and 5.14a). However, for both networks, the hot-spot message delays with software com-

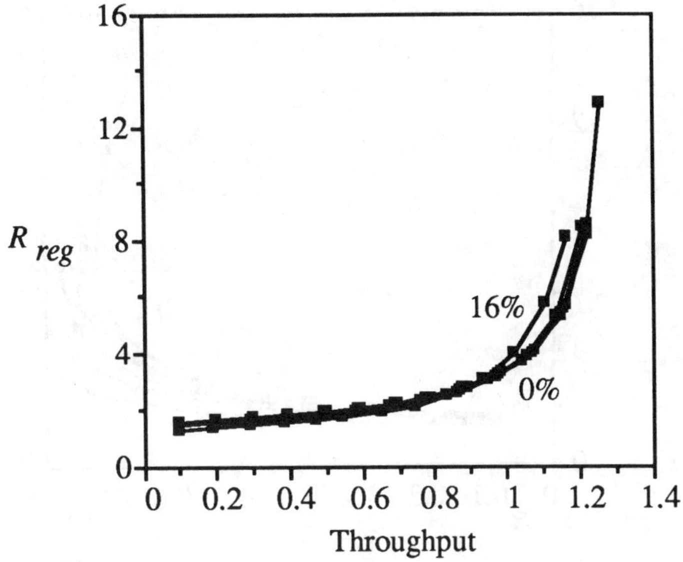

(a)

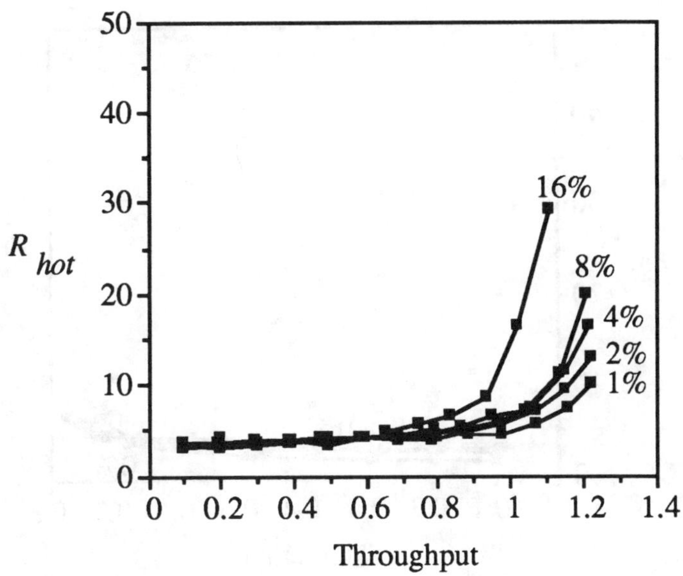

(b)

Figure 5.15 Impact of software combining on hot-spot contention in the BH network - the case of finite buffering capacity (h is varied from 0% to 16%, d = 3, D = 8, $\mu_{CL} = \mu_{NCL}$ = 1.4, α = 0.75, number of buffers = 32)

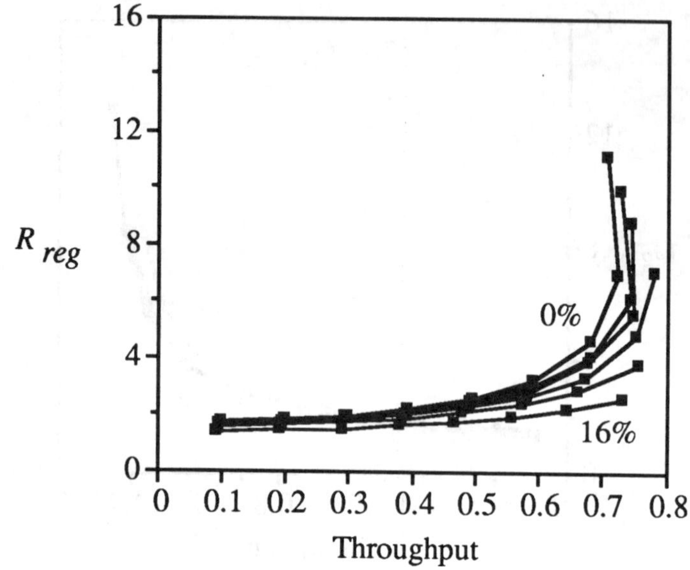

(a)

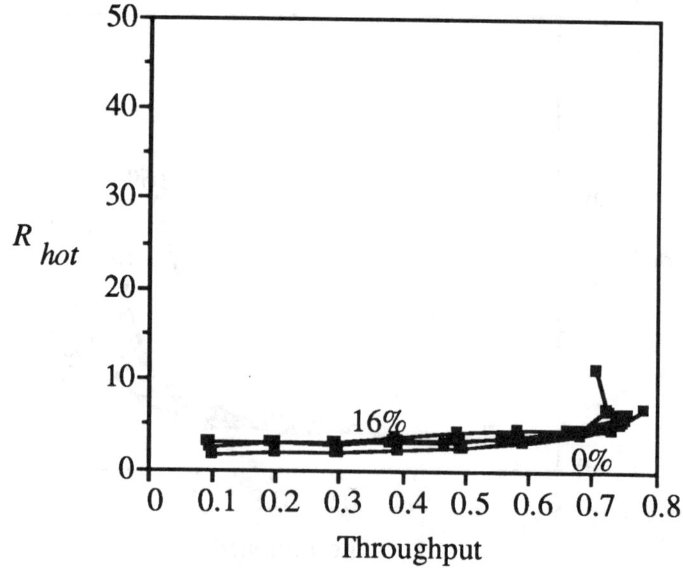

(b)

Figure 5.16 Impact of software combining on hot-spot contention in the BH/BH network - the case of finite buffering capacity (h is varied from 0% to 16%, d = 3, D = 8, μ_{CL} = 1.4, μ_{NCL} = 2.8, α = 0.75, number of buffers = 32)

bining are substantially less compared with the delays with hardware combining.

5.5. Summary

This chapter has studied the impact of hot-spot contention in two static interconnection networks. One is a standard BH network and the other is an HIN – the BH/BH network.

An analysis for average delays was done, assuming unbounded buffering capacity. With unbounded buffering capacity, the use of a routing algorithm in which each of the shortest paths between the source and destination nodes is randomly selected with equal probability resulted in extreme sensitivity to the hot-spot proportion h of traffic. With the random routing algorithm, increasing h reduced the message generation rate at which saturation occurs substantially.

The impact of improved routing algorithms was also studied, through simulations of a "shortest queue" routing algorithm. This improved routing algorithm resulted in much less sensitivity in the delays of regular messages to the proportion of hot-spot traffic, as regular messages could avoid links congested by hot-spot traffic.

Even with the improved routing algorithm, however, limitations on buffering capacity were found to induce significantly restricted network capacity as the hot-spot proportion was increased. The BH/BH network was found to exhibit a "fold-back" characteristic in the sense that increasing the message generation rate beyond the saturation point resulted not only in increased delays but also in decreased throughput. Such behaviour was not observed with the BH network because there are more alternative paths in the network.

The impacts of two schemes – hardware combining and software combining – that have been proposed for multiprocessor systems to reduce hot-spot contention are also studied in this chapter.

With unbounded buffering capacity at each node, both schemes tend to provide similar performance improvements and completely eliminate the adverse effects of hot-spot contention on both the regular (non-hot-spot) messages and hot-spot messages.

With bounded buffering capacity, however, hardware combining could eliminate only the influence of hot-spot contention on regular messages; the hot-spot messages experience degraded performance whether or not hardware combining is used. With bounded buffering capacity, software combining is more effective than hardware combining. Although regular messages experience similar delays with both hardware combining and software combining, only the software combining scheme provides substantial improvements in the throughput capacity and in the delays associated with hot-spot messages. However, as the number of buffers is increased, hardware combining tends to improve its performance for hot-spot messages as well. But this may require an infeasibly large number of buffers.

It should be noted that the results for the finite buffer case (in particular, the ability to eliminate the interference of hot-spot contention on regular messages) are also dependent on using a good (adaptive) routing algorithm.

Further Reading

As stated at the beginning of this chapter hot-spot contention has been studied extensively in the context of buffered multistage interconnection networks for shared-memory multiprocessor systems. In addition to the references cited in the text, the following references provide additional information on the impact of hot-spot contention on the performance of multistage interconnection networks [KUMA 86, THOM 86, RETT 86, PATE 88, LANG 88, GUPT 89, TZEN 89, LEE 89]. Also see [ALMA 89] for a brief and informative summary of the research done on hot-spot contention in multistage interconnection networks.

The author is not aware of any references that deal with hot-spot contention in static interconnection networks for multicomputer systems, except [DAND 90, DAND

91]. Note that part of this chapter is based on these two references. Abraham and Padmanabhan [ABRA 89] discuss the performance of the binary hypercube as an interconnect for multiprocessor systems.

Acknowledgement

Material presented in this chapter is partly based on [DAND 90] and [DAND 91].

References

[ABRA 89] S. Abraham and K. Padmanabhan, "Performance of the Direct Binary n-Cube Network for Multiprocessors," *IEEE Trans. Computers,* Vol. C-38, No. 7, July 1989, pp. 1000-1011.

[ALMA 89] G. S. Almasi and A. Gottlieb, *Highly Parallel Computing,* Benjamin/Cummings, Redwood City, California, 1989, pp. 445-459.

[BARU 89] C. K. Baru and O. Frieder, "Database Operations in a Cube-Connected Multicomputer System," *IEEE Trans. Computers,* Vol. C-38, No. 6, June 1989, pp. 920-927.

[COFF 71] E. G. Coffman, Jr., M. J. Elphick, and A. Shoshani, "System Deadlocks," *ACM Comput. Surveys,* Vol. 3, No. 2, June 1971, pp. 67-78.

[DAND 90] S. P. Dandamudi and D. L. Eager, "The Effectiveness of Combining in Reducing Hot-Spot Contention in Hypercube Multicomputers," *Proc. 1990 Int. Conf. Parallel Processing,* 1990, Vol. 1, pp. 291-295.

[DAND 91] S. P. Dandamudi and D. L. Eager, "Hot-Spot Contention in Binary Hypercube Networks," *IEEE Trans. Computers,* Vol. C-40, 1991.

[GOTT 83] A. Gottlieb et al., "The NYU Ultracomputer – Designing a MIMD, Shared Memory Parallel Machine," *IEEE Trans. Computers,* Vol. C-32, No. 2, February 1983, pp. 175-189.

[GUPT 89] R. Gupta and C. R. Hill, "A Scalable Implementation of Barrier Synchronization using an Adaptive Combining

Tree," *Int'l J. Parallel Programming*, Vol. 18, No. 3, June 1989, pp. 161-180.

[HO 89] W. S. Ho and D. L. Eager, "A Novel Strategy for Controlling Hot Spot Congestion," *Proc. 1989 Int. Conf. Parallel Processing*, 1989, Vol. 1, pp. 14-18.

[HOLT 72] R. C. Holt, "Some Deadlock Properties of Computer Systems," *ACM Comput. Surveys*, Vol. 4, No. 3, September 1972, pp. 179-196.

[KLEI 75] L. Kleinrock, *Queueing Systems: Volume 1*, Wiley, New York, 1975.

[KLEI 76] L. Kleinrock, *Queueing Systems: Volume 2*, Wiley, New York, 1976.

[KUMA 86] M. Kumar and G. F. Pfister, "The Onset of Hot-Spot Contention," *Proc. 1986 Int. Conf. Parallel Processing*, 1986, pp. 28-34.

[LANG 88] T. Lang and L. Kurisaki, "Nonuniform Traffic Spots (NUTS) in Multistage Interconnection Networks," *Proc. 1988 Int. Conf. Parallel Processing*, 1988, pp. 191-195.

[LEE 86] G. Lee, C. Kruskal, and D. J. Kuck, "The Effectiveness of Combining in Shared Memory Parallel Computers in the Presence of 'Hot Spots'," *Proc. 1986 Int. Conf. Parallel Processing*, 1986, pp. 35-41.

[LEE 89] G. Lee, "A Performance Bound of Multistage Combining Networks," *IEEE Trans. Computers*, Vol. C-38, No. 10, October 1989, pp. 1387-1395.

[MERL 80] P. M. Merlin and P. J. Schweitzer, "Deadlock Avoidance in Store-and-Forward Networks – I: Store-and-Forward Deadlock," *IEEE Trans. Communications*, Vol. COM-28, No. 3, March 1980, pp. 345-354.

[PATE 88] N. M. Patel and P. G. Harrison, "On Hot-spot Contention in Interconnection Networks," *Proc. 1988 ACM SIGMETRICS Conf.*, May 1988, pp. 114-123.

[PFIS 85a] G. F. Pfister, W. C. Brantley, D. A. George, S. L. Harvey, K. P. Kleinfelder, E. A. Melton, V. A. Norton, and J. Wiess, "The IBM Research Parallel Processor Prototype (RP3): Introduction and Architecture," *Proc. 1985 Int. Conf. Parallel Processing*, 1985, pp. 764-771.

[PFIS 85b] G. F. Pfister and V. A. Norton, " 'Hot Spot' Contention and Combining in Multistage Interconnection Networks," *IEEE Trans. Computers*, Vol. C-34, No. 10, October 1985, pp. 943-948.

[RETT 86] R. Rettberg and R. Thomas, "Contention is No Obstacle to Shared Memory Multiprocessing," *Comm. ACM*, Vol. 29, No. 12, December 1986, pp. 1202-1212.

[SCHN 89] D. A. Schneider and D. J. DeWitt, "A Performance Evaluation of Four Parallel Join Algorithms in a Shared-Nothing Multiprocessor Environment," *Proc. 1989 SIGMOD Conf.*, Portland, Oregon, 1989, pp. 110-121.

[THOM 86] R. H. Thomas, "Behavior of the Butterfly Parallel Processor in the Presence of Memory Hot Spots,"," *Proc. 1986 Int. Conf. Parallel Processing*, 1986, pp. 46-50.

[TUCK 88] L. W. Tucker and G. G. Robertson, "Architecture and Applications of the Connection Machine," *IEEE Computer*, Vol. 21, No. 8, August 1988, pp. 26-38.

[TZEN 89] N.-F. Tzeng, "Design of a Novel Combining Structure for Shared-Memory Multiprocessors," *Proc. 1989 Int. Conf. Parallel Processing*, 1989, Vol. 1, pp. 1-8.

[YEW 87] P. -C. Yew, N. -F. Tzeng, and D. H. Lawrie, "Distributing Hot-Spot Addressing in Large-Scale Multiprocessors," *IEEE Trans. Computers*, Vol. C-36, No. 4, April 1987, pp. 388-395.

6

Fault-Tolerance and Reliability

It has been shown in Chapter 3 that HINs provide better cost-benefit ratios than the corresponding non-hierarchical interconnection networks. This is achieved mainly by reducing the number of links needed to construct an HIN. However, the structure of the HIN does not seem to provide good fault-tolerance and reliability. Since HINs are aimed at connecting large numbers of processors it is important to ensure that this reduction in the number of links does not compromise fault-tolerance and reliability properties of the network. This chapter presents two schemes to improve fault-tolerance of binary hypercube-based HINs.

Both these schemes, described in Section 6.2, use hardware redundancy. In one, a standby spare node is provided to reduce the impact of the interface node failures on network reliability; in the other, the level 2 network is duplicated. This chapter compares their fault-tolerance (Section 6.3) and reliability (Section 6.4) with that of the other non-hierarchical networks discussed in Chapter 2, including the standard binary hypercube network.

This chapter also considers the impact of these two fault-tolerance schemes on performance. The analysis is presented in Section 6.5. In this analysis, we use the random routing algorithm of Chapter 3. The impact of other routing algorithms on network performance is the topic of the next chapter. A summary of the chapter is given in Section 6.6.

6.1. Introduction

The fault-tolerance of an interconnection network (IN) is its ability to provide (at least a degraded level of) service, even in the presence of faults in the components that constitute the IN. In static interconnection networks, there are two network components: communication links or simply *links* and processors or *nodes*. A fault in either of these components can be permanent or transient. In the rest of this chapter, faults are assumed to be permanent.

The reliability $R(t)$ of an IN is a function of time, defined as the conditional probability that the IN will operate correctly throughout the interval $[t_0, t]$, given that the IN was operating correctly at time t_0. In other words, the reliability is the probability that the IN will operate correctly throughout a complete interval of time.

Typically, reliability is used to characterize a non-repairable system. Repairable system is best characterized by its availability. System availability at time t is the probability that the system is operational at time t [DAS 90]. It is clear from this definition that the system can go through the fail-repair cycle a number of times during the interval.

Fault-tolerance is a technique that can improve reliability, but a fault-tolerant system does not necessarily have to have a high reliability. The reliability of a system also depends on individual component reliabilities. If we use the same "quality" components, fault-tolerance schemes increase overall system reliability. On the other hand, we can build a very simple system with extremely "good" components such that the probability of system failure is very low. In other words, a system can achieve a high reliability but not possess the attribute of fault-tolerance.

The notion of fault-tolerance is closely related to the fault-tolerance model, which consists of the following two components [ADAM 87].

- *Fault Model:* This component of fault-tolerance model specifies what type of faults are anticipated. The fault model does not have to correspond exactly to the real world problems that could develop in the components. The model may be chosen to simplify reliability analysis [ADAM 87].

  In the context of static interconnection networks, we consider two types of faults: *link failures* and *node failures*. For the results reported in this chapter, the nodes and links are assumed to have identical and exponential distribution of failure time.

- *Fault-tolerance criterion:* This is just a statement about the minimal service that is to be expected from the IN which is known to have certain faults. In other words, this is the basis by which we judge whether the IN in question has tolerated the faults in a reasonable manner. The more stringent the criterion becomes, the more elaborate the design of the IN becomes.

  The ideal fault-tolerance criterion is that the network perform exactly the same functions it performed before the faults were developed. Of course, it can be seen that this ideal criterion cannot be met without investing a lot in extra hardware and/or software. In practice, a criterion weaker than this is usually specified.

Fault-tolerance can be achieved by many techniques. One approach that is often used in the context of interconnection networks is to detect and locate the fault that has occurred and reconfigure the network to remove the faulty component. This implies that the network should have some form of redundancy. This redundancy can take one of several forms.

- ***Hardware Redundancy*** is the addition of extra hardware to tolerate faults. For example, we might add extra links in a tree network to tolerate link failures. Note, however, that some interconnection networks such as the binary hypercubes do not require additional links to tolerate link failures.

- ***Software Redundancy*** is the addition of software to detect and possibly tolerate faults. For example, in static interconnection networks, this might take the form of an improved routing algorithm that dynamically reroutes a message if a link failure has occurred.

- ***Information Redundancy*** is the addition of extra information beyond that required to implement a given function. For example, error detecting codes use a form of information redundancy.

In general, the fault-tolerance techniques applicable to static interconnection networks can be grouped into two classes, based on whether or not they alter the underlying topology. There are basically two kinds of techniques that do not alter the network topology: *link duplication* and *node duplication*. In this technique, spare links (or nodes) are provided for "critical" links (or nodes) in the network. In both cases, the network topology is not altered. The standby-spare interface node scheme discussed in the next section belongs to this category.

In practice, however, it is not common to provide spare links; instead, these additional links are added to the network such that they not only improve fault-tolerance but, when there are no faults in the network, they tend to improve some other performance measure such as the average internode distance. These methods typically alter network topology. The majority of the fault-tolerant networks described in Chapter 2 belong to this category.

6.2. Fault-Tolerant HINs

Since HINs are aimed at connecting large numbers of processors it is important to ensure that the fault-tolerance and reliability of the network is not compromised. From the structure of HINs, shown in Figure 3.3, it is straightforward to see that they provide good fault-tolerance to link failures but not to node failures. The interface nodes in this structure play a critical role in the sense that an interface node failure leaves the entire cluster of nodes disconnected from the network; thus reducing the number of available nodes in the network. This section presents some modifications to the structure of the HIN to improve fault-tolerance to node failures as well.

Two schemes are considered. Both these schemes use hardware redundancy. In one, the level 2 network is duplicated; in the other, a standby spare interface node is provided to reduce the impact of interface node failures on network reliability.

(i) *Replication Scheme*: In this scheme, each cluster uses two nodes as interface nodes. The level 2 network is duplicated for each interface node. From a performance point of view, it is advantageous to keep the two interface nodes belonging to a level 1 cluster as far apart as possible. For the BH/BH HIN under consideration, the distance between the two interface nodes is d when the cluster size is 2^d. An example HIN incorporating this fault-tolerance scheme is shown in Figure 6.1. This network is referred to as the BH/BH-RS network.

(ii) *Standby-Spare Interface Node Scheme*: Since the interface nodes are the weak components compromising network reliability, we introduce hardware redundancy by providing standby-spare interface nodes. In this scheme, one interface node is operational and the other serves as a spare. If a fault is detected and located, the faulty node is removed from the operation and replaced with the spare. The reconfiguration operation can be viewed conceptually as a switch whose output is selected from one, and one only, of the nodes providing the input to the switch [JOHN 89]. This network is referred to as the BH/BH-SI network.

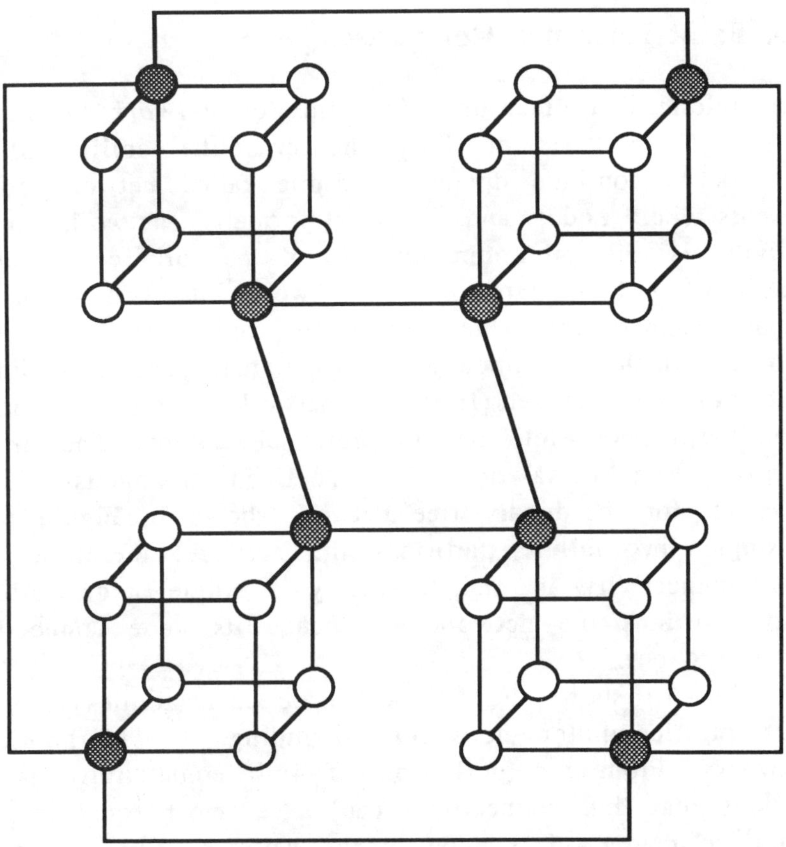

Figure 6.1 An example BH/BH-RS hierarchical interconnection network with a cluster size of 8

Each of these two schemes increases the complexity of the network. The BH/BH-SI network requires a fault detection scheme to identify the faulty node (for details on fault detection and location, see [JOHN 89]). The BH/BH-RS network increases link cost. It should, however, be noted that even with this increased number of links the BH/BH-RS network requires far fewer links than does the BH network. However, it will be shown later that the performance of the BH/BH-RS network is substantially better than the BH/BH-SI network justifying the increase in link cost.

6.3. Fault-Tolerance Comparison

Fault-tolerance is measured in terms of *network connectivity*. Network connectivity measures the ability of a network to continue operation despite failed network components (i.e., nodes and links). Informally, network connectivity is the minimum number of network components that must fail to partition the network into two or more disjoint subnetworks. This leads us to *link connectivity* of a network which is defined as the minimum number of links that must be removed from the network in order to partition the network into two or more subnetworks. The *node connectivity* of a network is defined analogously. For example, for the binary tree network shown in Figure 6.2, a single link failure partitions the network; therefore, its link connectivity is one. Similarly a single node failure also partitions the network and hence its node connectivity is also one.

Table 6.1 shows the link and node connectivities of various multicomputer networks, including the hierarchical networks. From the definition of link connectivity it is obvious that link connectivity can be at most equal to the minimum degree of a node in the network. The link connectivities of ring- and tree-based networks along with the cube-connected cycles have a fixed value independent

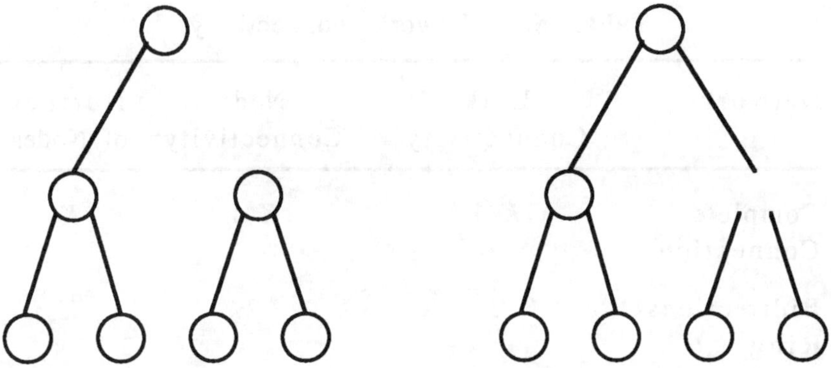

A single link failure   A single node failure

Figure 6.2 Link and node failures in a binary tree

of the network size. The cube-connected networks exhibit link connectivities that are dependent on the network size and dependent on a particular design. The complete connection, obviously, provides the maximum link connectivity.

Compared with link connectivities, fewer networks exhibit better node connectivities as shown in Table 6.1. Most networks, including the hierarchical hypercube networks, exhibit fixed node connectivities independent of the network size. Only the binary hypercube, torus, and the R-ary N-cube networks are more resilient to node failures. However, for torus and R-ary N-cube networks if *D* and *R* are fixed then they provide node connectivities that are independent of network size. For example, a 2-ary N-cube provides a node connectivity of 4. So does a two-dimensional torus. It should be noted that, while the binary hypercube provides a node connectivity that is logarithmically proportional to the network size, the number of node connections per node is technology-limited.

Table 6.1 Network connectivity

Network	Link Connectivity	Node Connectivity	Number of Nodes
Complete Connection	K-1	K-1	K
Bidirectional Ring	2	2	K
Chordal Ring	3	3	K
Binary Tree	1	1	$2^n - 1$
X-Tree	2	2	$2^n - 1$
Hypertree	2	2	$2^n - 1$
Binary Hypercube	D	D	2^D
Cube-connected Cycles	3	3	$D\,2^D$
Torus	$2D$	$2D$	W^D
R-ary N-cube	$2R$	$2R$	$N\,R^N$
BH/BH	min $\{d, (D-d)\}$	1	2^D
BH/BH-RS	min $\{d, 2(D-d)\}$	2	2^D
BH/BH-SI	min $\{d, (D-d)\}$	2	2^D

K : total number of nodes in the network
n : number of levels in a tree network (the root node is at level 0)
D : number of dimensions
W : width of a torus network
d : $\log_2$(cluster size of a hierarchical network)

6.4. Reliability Evaluation of HINs

Reliability of parallel and distributed systems is generally evaluated using either terminal reliability or task-based reliability. In terminal reliability definition, a system is considered to be working as long as any node is connected to any other node in the system. With task-based reliability measure, a system is considered to be working as long as some minimum number of nodes I are available for the execution of a task [INGL 77]. Since task-based reliability is more appropriate for parallel processing systems, we use this definition of reliability in this study. This reliability measure is often used to evaluate reliability of multi-computer interconnection networks [BHUY 86, KIM 89, DAS 90].

This section provides reliability evaluation of HINs. Section 6.4.1 gives details on the simulation experiment. The results are discussed in Section 6.4.2.

6.4.1. The Simulation Experiment

The simulation model that we have used is similar to the one reported in [BHUY 86]. The nodes and links are assumed to have identical and exponential distribution of failure time. Although we use exponential distribution in the simulation experiments, the simulation model is valid for other distributions such as Weibull. Let λ_n and λ_l denote node and link failure rates, respectively. The reliabilities of nodes and links are then given by $R_n(t) = e^{-\lambda_n t}$ and $R_l(t) = e^{-\lambda_l t}$. The node and link failure rates of the network are then given by $N_a\lambda_n$ and $L_a\lambda_l$, respectively, where N_a and L_a are the number of active nodes and links in the network.

The given interconnection network is represented by its adjacency matrix. The adjacency matrix of an interconnection network with N nodes is an $N \times N$ symmetric binary matrix $A = [a_{ij}]$ such that $a_{ij} = 1$ if there is a link between ith and jth nodes, and $a_{ij} = 0$ if there is no link between them

[DEO 74]. A non-failed node i, $1 \le i \le N$, is represented by making the diagonal element $a_{ii} = 1$.

The network connectivity is shown by using the reachability matrix. This matrix specifies whether or not there exists a path between two nodes that are not necessarily adjacent. The reachability matrix can be obtained from the adjacency matrix using any standard algorithm [DEO 74, TANE 81]. The adjacency matrix is modified depending on the type of fault (i.e., node failure or link failure). The failure of a link connecting nodes i and j is represented by making $a_{ij} = a_{ji} = 0$. The failure of node i is represented by making all entries of ith row and ith column of the adjacency matrix '0'. This modification of the adjacency matrix is then reflected in the reachability matrix, which is used to determine whether the system is up or down (i.e., whether or not at least I nodes are connected together).

We also consider on-line repair of the nodes and links with exponential distribution of repair times given by $1/\mu_n$ and $1/\mu_l$ respectively. We assume a single repair facility for both nodes and links. The failed component is put in a FIFO queue waiting for the repair facility. When the component is repaired, the corresponding entries in the adjacency matrix are updated. When the repaired component is a node, updating the adjacency matrix requires care. In this case, we not only have to make the diagonal element $a_{ii} = 1$ but also have to make selected (not all) entries of ith row and ith column of the adjacency matrix '1' representing those links that were deemed failed (but not actually failed) due to the node failure.

6.4.2. Results and Discussion

This section presents the results obtained from the simulation experiments. The majority of the results reported here are for a network of 64 nodes (because of the length of time needed to run these experiments). However, some results are reported for a network of 128 nodes to assess the impact of network size on the results. Most of the results presented here assume a node failure rate of λ_n = 100 per 10^6 hours and a link failure rate of λ_l = 20 per 10^6 hours. The impact of varying these failure rates is also presented. Since it has been shown in Chapter 4 that the optimum cluster size for the BH/BH network is either 4 or 8 for a wide range of network sizes, in the following discussion, the BH/BH network and its fault-tolerant versions use a cluster size of either 4 or 8.

Figure 6.3a shows reliabilities of various networks with N = 64 and I =48. The HINs use a cluster size of 8. For comparison purposes, reliabilities of the bidirectional ring (BR) and the complete connection (CC) networks are included. It can be seen from this figure that the BH network reliabilities are as good as the complete connection. This confirms an earlier finding by Bhuyan and Das [BHUY 86] for a smaller network size (N =16). As can be expected, the BR network reliabilities are at the other extreme. The BH/BH network provides reliabilities which are intermediate between these two extremes. Note, however, the BH/BH network uses substantially fewer links than the BH (and the CC) network.

The impact of the two fault-tolerant schemes discussed in Section 6.2 is also shown in Figure 6.3a. Both these schemes provide similar reliabilities (the RS scheme is marginally better). Both these schemes provide substantial improvement in reliability compared to that of the BH/BH network.

The effect of smaller cluster size on network reliabilities of the BH/BH network is shown in Figure 6.3b. This figure gives reliability values when a cluster size of 4 is used. In general, all three networks – the BH/BH, BH/BH-RS and the BH/BH-SI networks – show marginal improvement when cluster size is reduced from 8 to 4. This is mainly due to the fact that the penalty associated with an interface node failure decreases as the cluster size reduces. Further, the reliability of the BH/BH-RS network is uniformly better than that of the BH/BH-SI network. This is due to the fact that the BH/BH-RS uses more links at level 2

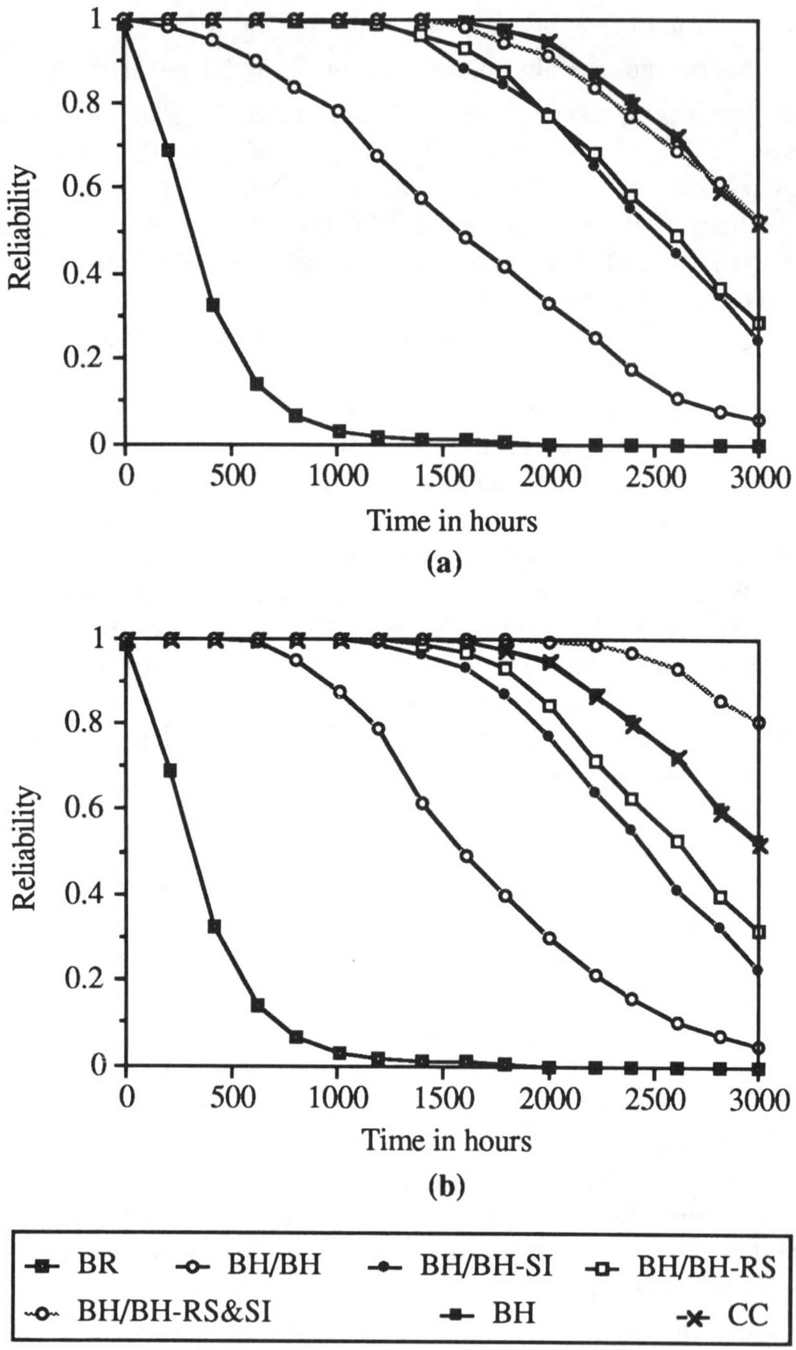

Figure 6.3 Reliability comparison of various interconnection networks (N = 64, I = 48) (**a**) cluster size = 8; (**b**) cluster size = 4

network than does the BH/BH-SI network. The number of these additional links increases as the cluster size reduces (for a given network size). From a reliability point of view, this increase in link cost associated with the BH/BH-RS network does not result in commensurate improvement in network reliability. However, it is shown in Section 6.5 that adding these additional links improves performance (by reducing the average message delay substantially) of the network (in most cases) compensating for the increase in link cost. Therefore, from a reliability point of view, the BH/BH-SI network may be preferred but when both reliability and performance are considered the BH/BH-RS network may be the network of the choice.

A weakness of both the BH/BH-RS and the BH/BH-SI networks is that their reliability is uniformly poorer than the BH network. This drawback can be remedied by combining the two fault-tolerant schemes. This is achieved by adding standby-spare interface nodes to the BH/BH-RS network (we refer to this network as BH/BH-RS&SI network). This, of course, increases the network cost but this increase (over that of the BH/BH-RS network) is a one-time design cost and can easily be amortized without significantly affecting the overall system cost. It should be noted that, in designing large multiprocessor systems, it is not the VLSI logic cost that is of major concern in system expansion but the link cost. For example, as discussed in Section 3.1, for the NCUBE/ten, which uses 640 wires to provide inter-PCB connections, the link cost creates major problems in system expansion. Thus, from overall system design point of view, the penalty associated with the BH/BH-RS&SI network may not be significant. This, however, improves the network reliability substantially as shown in Figure 6.3. With a cluster size of 8, the BH/BH-RS&SI network reliabilities are as good as the BH network. When the cluster size is reduced to 4, the reliability of the BH/BH-RS&SI network is much better than that of the BH network. Thus, the increase in network cost is justified from the reliability point of view. Note, however, the performance of this network remains the same as that of the BH/BH-RS network.

The impact of increasing the network size from 64 to 128 is shown in Figure 6.4. In order to see whether the results are scalable for a larger network we have maintained $I = 0.75\ N$ (i.e., 96 nodes are assumed to be required for task execution). It is clear by comparing Figures 6.3 and 6.4, that the conclusions obtained from the 64-node network generally hold for this network too.

The results presented so far assumed an I value that is equal to 75% of the total nodes N. The effect of changing the I value is shown in Figure 6.5. This figure gives reliabilities of various networks (with $N = 64$ and cluster size = 8) when a task requires $I = 56$ nodes for its execution. Interestingly, the reliabilities of both the BH/BH-RS and the BH/BH-SI networks are very close to the reliabilities of the BH and CC networks. The reason for this is that, as the I value approaches N, the node failures basically determine the network reliability (for the failure rates considered here); the link failures play a relatively minor role. Similar results were obtained when the cluster size is reduced from 8 to 4 and are not presented. The BH/BH-RS&SI network provides reliabilities similar to the BH network when the cluster size is 8. With a cluster size of 4 this network provides better reliabilities than the BH network (not shown) as is the case with $I = 48$ and $I = 96$ in Figures 6.3 and 6.4.

Figure 6.6 shows reliabilities of various networks when the node failure rate is increased from 0.0001 to 0.0002 (for $N = 64$, $I = 48$ and the cluster size = 8). The effect of doubling the node failure rate can be seen by comparing Figures 6.3a and 6.6. Even with the increased node failure rate, the conclusions drawn from Figure 6.3 are still valid. This is further demonstrated in Figure 6.7, which gives network reliabilities at $t = 1000$ for various node failure rates. Even though the networks providing better reliabilities tend to be more costly (they either require more links or nodes or both), they can be built with less reliable nodes, which may affect the overall network cost.

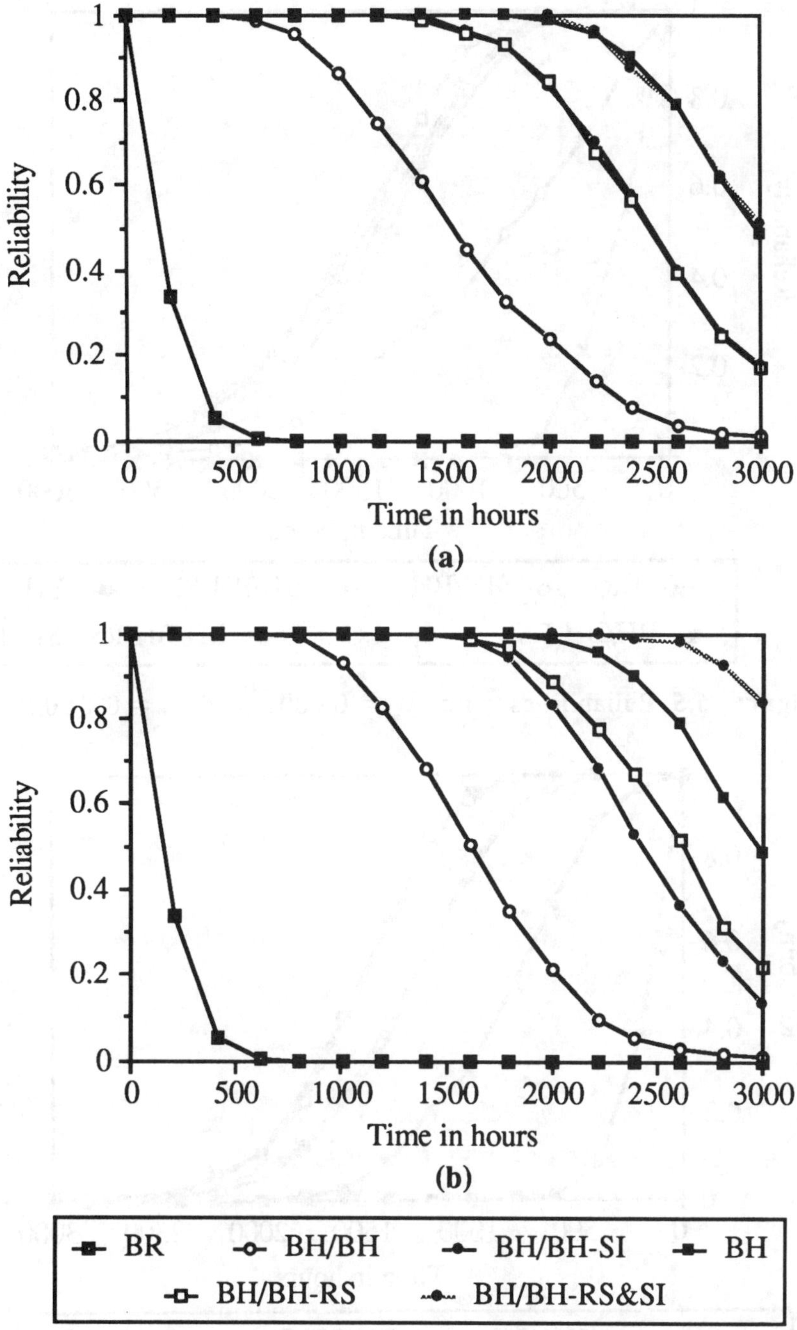

Figure 6.4 Reliability comparison of various interconnection networks (N = 128, I = 96) (**a**) cluster size = 8; (**b**) cluster size = 4

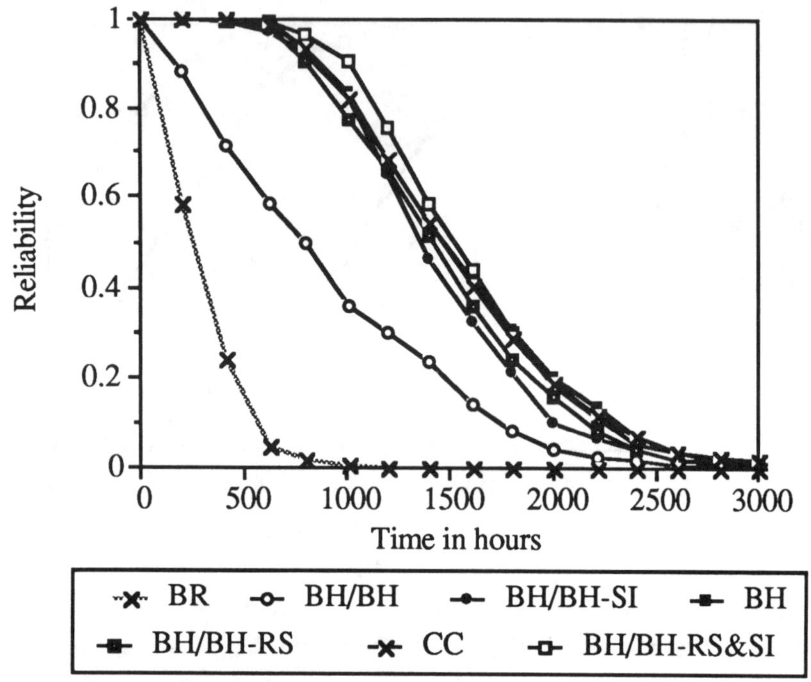

Figure 6.5 Reliabilities with $\lambda_n = 0.0001$ and $\lambda_l = 0.00002$

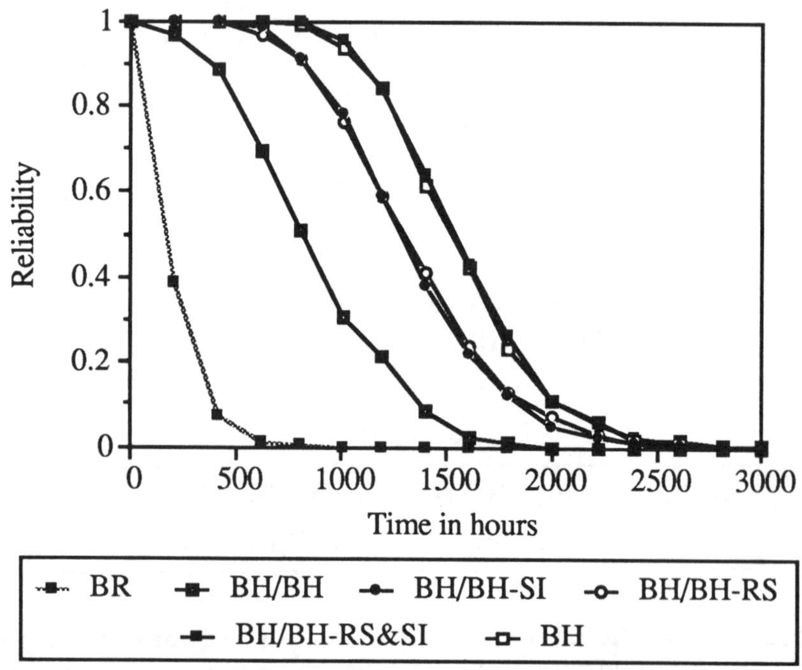

Figure 6.6 Reliabilities with $\lambda_n = 0.0002$ and $\lambda_l = 0.00002$

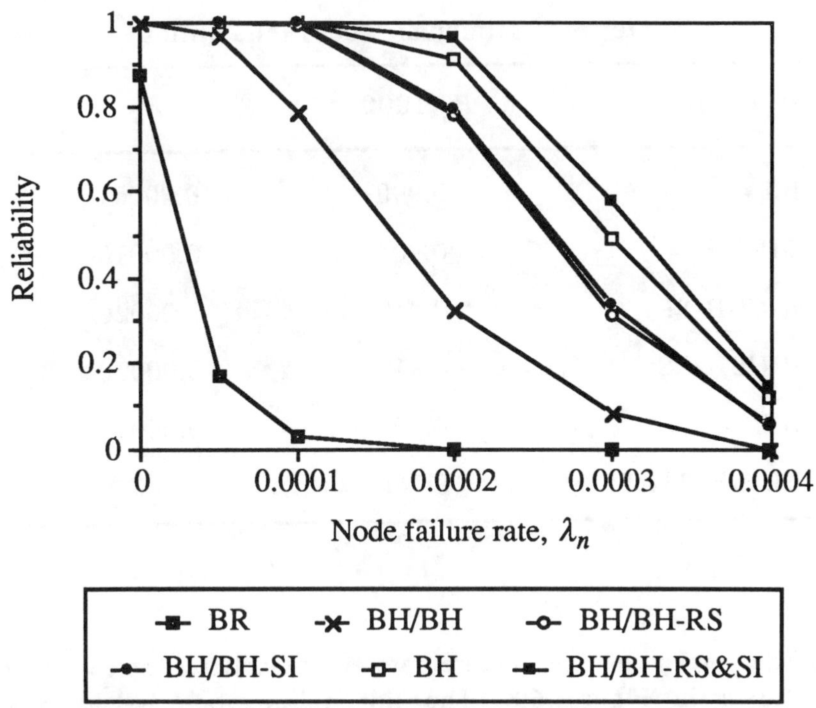

Figure 6.7 Effect of node failure rates on network reliabilities (N= 64, l= 48, λ_l = 0.00002 and cluster size = 8)

For example, consider an application that requires unmaintained system level reliability $R_s(1000) \geq 0.8$. The minimum node reliability $R_n(1000)$ of various networks is shown in Table 6.2. It can be seen from this table that the bidirectional ring network requires node reliabilities $R_n(1000)$ to be greater than or equal to 0.99. On the hand, the binary hypercube network requires node reliabilities $R_n(1000) \geq 0.79$. The BH/BH-RS&SI network requires even smaller values.

Table 6.2 also gives the maximum node failure rates λ_n (recall that $R_n(t) = e^{-\lambda_n t}$). The binary ring network can tolerate a maximum node failure rate of 0.00001. The binary hypercube network and the fault-tolerant versions of the BH/BH network can tolerate twice this node failure rate.

Table 6.2 Minimum node reliabilities

Network	$R_n(1000)$	λ_n
BR	0.990	0.00001
BH/BH	0.905	0.00010
BH/BH-SI	0.819	0.00020
BH/BH-RS	0.819	0.00020
BH	0.790	0.00024
BH/BH-RS&SI	0.768	0.00026

The impact of link failure rate on reliabilities at $t = 1800$ is shown in Figure 6.8. The link failure rate has a relatively minor effect on network reliabilities compared to that of the node failure rate. It is clear from this graph that, as the number of links used by the network increases, it becomes less sensitive to link failure rate. The BH network, which uses the maximum number of links among the networks considered in Figure 6.8, shows little sensitivity to link failure rate. At the other extreme we have the BH/BH and BH/BH-SI networks, which use the minimum number of links and exhibit increased sensitivity to link failure rate. The other two networks fall in between these two extremes.

Figure 6.9 shows availabilities assuming $1/\mu_n = 10$ hours and $1/\mu_l = 2$ hours. Note that availability evaluation does not require continuous operation during the interval under consideration. The system can go through several fail-repair cycles during this interval. Figure 6.9a gives the availabilities for $N = 64$, $I = 48$ and cluster size = 8. It can be seen that, with single repair facility, all but the BR network provide perfect availability for the length of time considered here. With repair, the BR network provides substantially better availability. However, because of the

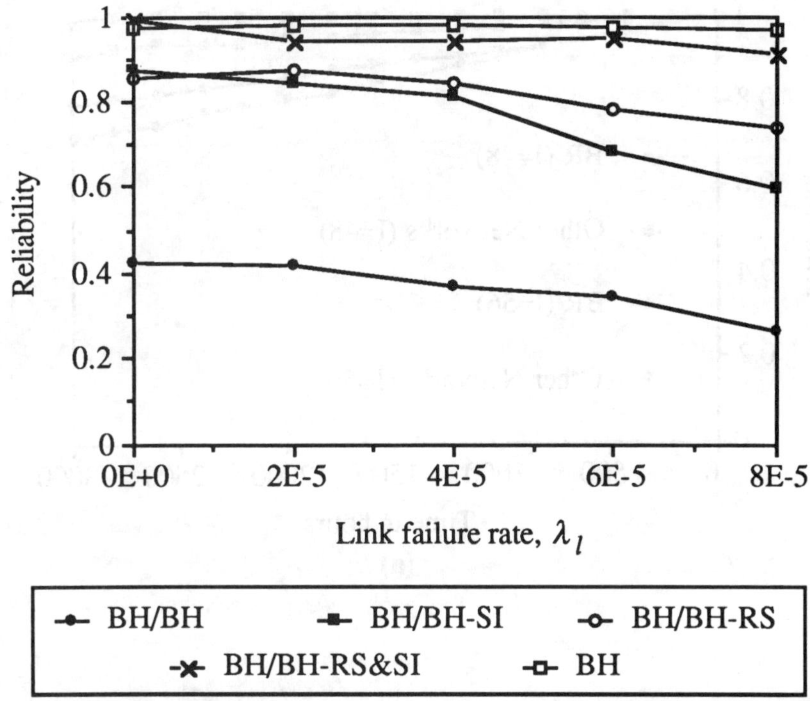

Figure 6.8 Effect of link failure rates on network reliabilities (N= 64, I= 48, λ_n = 0.0002 and cluster size = 8)

minimal redundancy in the network, this is not as good as that provided by the other networks. The impact of increasing I from 48 to 56 is also shown in Figure 6.9a. It is straightforward to see that, when $I = N$, repair will have no impact on the reliabilities of the networks. In order to see the effect of repair on larger systems, we have conducted simulation experiments on a network of size N = 128. The results are shown in Figure 6.9b for I = 96. Note that, with a single repair facility, as the network size increases it takes more time for a failed component to be repaired. This is reflected in availabilities provided by the BR network as shown in Figure 6.9b. However, all the remaining networks are not affected.

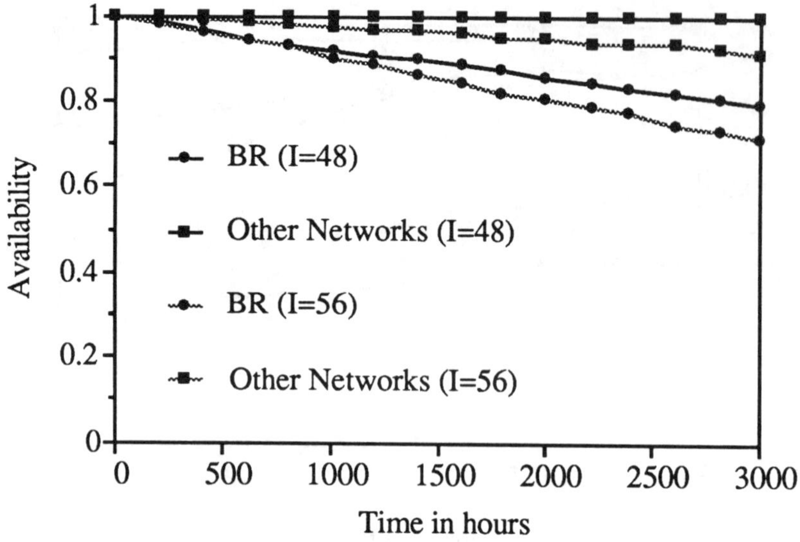

(a)

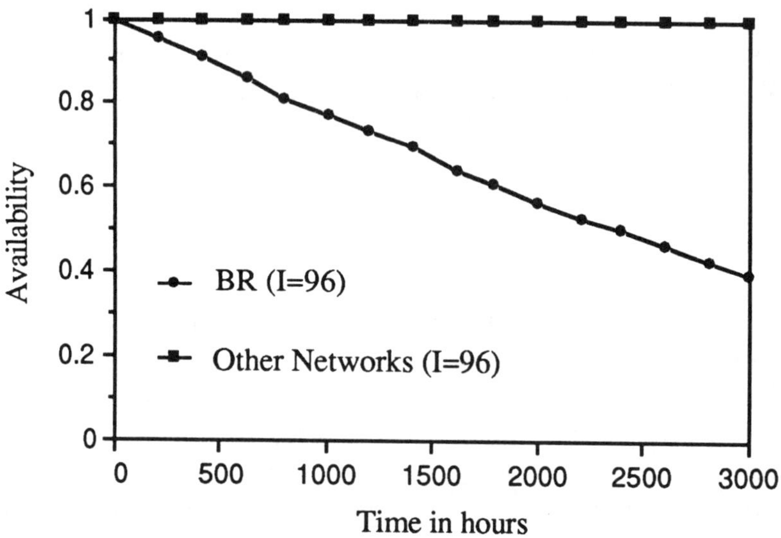

(b)

Figure 6.9 Availabilities with cluster size = 8, $\lambda_n = 0.0002$, $\lambda_l = 0.00002$, $\mu_n = 0.1$ and $\mu_l = 0.5$ **(a)** $N = 64$ and $I = 48$ and 56 **(b)** $N = 128$ and $I = 96$

6.5. Performance Analysis of Fault-Tolerant HINs

This section discusses the impact of these two fault-tolerance schemes on performance. Their performance is compared against the corresponding non-hierarchical BH network. As in Chapter 3, the link cost L is used to measure the network cost. The number of links is used to represent the link cost. The performance of the network is measured by the average message delay R. Since Chapter 3 gives the average message delay analysis of the BH/BH network (which is the same as the BH/BH-SI network from a performance point of view) and the BH network, Section 6.5.1 presents the analysis of the BH/BH-RS network.

6.5.1. Performance Analysis of BH/BH-RS Network

This network has two interface nodes per cluster (see Figure 6.1). When an inter-cluster message is generated, the routing algorithm passes the message to the closest interface node in the source cluster. If more than one interface node is at the same distance, one of them is randomly selected. Thus, the analysis assumes that both the interface nodes are equally utilized.

The analysis is done under the assumptions made about the network and its workload given in Section 3.5.2. Again, as in Section 3.5.2, to facilitate the analysis, Kleinrock's independence assumption [KLEI 76] is used. The results of the simulation experiments in Section 6.5.2 indicate that the error introduced by this assumption is negligible.

The links are divided into two groups: cluster (CL) links and non-cluster (NCL) links. Cluster links are those that connect only the nodes within a cluster and non-cluster links are those that connect two nodes that are in two different clusters. Let μ_{CL} and μ_{NCL} be the message processing rates of cluster and non-cluster links, respectively. Further, let $\lambda_{link,CL}$ and $\lambda_{link,NCL}$ be the effective message arrival rates at cluster and non-cluster links, respectively. The effective arrival rate for each group of links is derived.

The message load of inter-cluster messages is uniformly distributed over the non-cluster links. It is straightforward to derive $\lambda_{link,NCL}$ as (similar to the derivation of $\lambda_{link,NCL}$ for the BH/BH network in Section 3.5.2.2)

$$\lambda_{link,\,NCL} = \frac{2^{D-d}\,2^{d}(1-\alpha)\,\lambda\left[\dfrac{(D-d)\,2^{D-d-1}}{2^{D-d}-1}\right]}{4(D-d)\,2^{D-d-1}}$$

$$= \frac{2^{D-2}(1-\alpha)\,\lambda}{2^{D-d}-1} \qquad (6.1)$$

The message load of intra-cluster messages is uniformly distributed over the cluster links. However, the message load due to inter-cluster messages is not distributed equally among the links in a cluster. The cluster links closer to the interface nodes receive more inter-cluster messages than those that are farther away. Thus $\lambda_{link,CL}$ is dependent on how close a link is to the interface nodes. To indicate this distance, we label the cluster links by their distance to an interface node. A j-level link is defined as a cluster link that connects two nodes that are at distance j and j-1 form the interface node under consideration. Then the arrival rate of messages at a j-level link in the source cluster $\lambda_{link,CLs}$ is given by

$$\lambda_{link,\,CLs}(j) = \lambda'_s(j) + \lambda''_s(j)$$

where

$\lambda'_s(j)$ = arrival rate (at a j-level link in the source cluster) due to intra-cluster messages, and

$\lambda''_s(j)$ = arrival rate (at a j-level link in the source cluster) due to inter-cluster messages.

Since intra-cluster message load is uniformly distributed over the links within a cluster, $\lambda'_s(j)$ is given by

$$\lambda'_s(j) = \frac{\alpha \lambda 2^{d-1}}{2^d - 1} \quad \text{for all } j$$

However, $\lambda''_s(j)$ is not the same for all j. It is given by

$$\lambda''_s(j) = 2^{d-1}\lambda(1-\alpha)\, p_1(j) + 2^{d-1}\lambda(1-\alpha)\, p_2(d-j+1)$$

where $p_1(j)$ is the probability that an inter-cluster message generated in the source cluster gets routed through a given j-level link on its way out of the cluster (through one interface node, say, i_0) and $p_2(j)$ is the probability that an inter-cluster message (destined to a node within the source cluster under consideration) that gets routed through a given j-level link on its way to the destination node through the other interface node i_1.

We now derive an expression for $p_1(j)$. First consider the case where d is odd. A set of links J, all of whose element links are j-level links (just the "out" direction), act as intermediate links for all inter-cluster messages generated by any source node within the cluster that is a distance at least j but less than $(d+1)/2$ from the interface node. Therefore, the number of source nodes for which an element of J acts as an intermediate link is $2^{d-1} - \sum_{k=0}^{j-1} \binom{d}{k}$.

Since there are $(d-j+1)\binom{d}{j-1}$ such links (i.e., the number of elements in J)

$$p_1(j) = \frac{2^{d-1} - \sum_{k=0}^{j-1} \binom{d}{k}}{(d-j+1)\binom{d}{j-1} 2^{d-1}} \qquad \text{if } d \text{ is odd}$$

Similarly, when d is even, $p_1(j)$ is given by

$$p_1(j) = \frac{\left(\sum_{i=0}^{\frac{d}{2}-1}\binom{d}{i} + \frac{\binom{d}{d/2}}{2}\right) - \sum_{k=0}^{j-1}\binom{d}{k}}{(d-j+1)\binom{d}{j-1}\left(\sum_{i=0}^{\frac{d}{2}-1}\binom{d}{i} + \frac{\binom{d}{d/2}}{2}\right)} \qquad \text{if } d \text{ is even}$$

Note that $p_2(j)$ is given by $p_1(j)$ in Section 3.5.2.2.

$$p_2(j) = \frac{\sum_{k=j}^{d}\binom{d}{k}}{(d-j+1)\binom{d}{j-1}2^d}$$

Therefore, $\lambda_{link,\,CLs}$ is given by

$$\lambda_{link,\,CLs}(j) = \frac{\alpha\lambda 2^{d-1}}{2^d - 1} + 2^{d-1}\lambda(1-\alpha)[\,p_1(j) + p_2(d-j+1)]$$

The final component of the delay is accounted for by the delay encountered by an inter-cluster message in the destination cluster (i.e., the cluster containing the destination node of the inter-cluster message). The effective message arrival rate in the destination cluster $\lambda_{link,CLd}$ can be derived as

$$\lambda_{link,\,CLd}(j) = \lambda'_d(j) + \lambda''_d(j)$$

where

$\lambda'_d(j) =$ arrival rate (at a j-level link in the destination cluster) due to intra-cluster messages;

$$= \frac{\alpha\lambda 2^{d-1}}{2^d - 1} \quad \text{for all } j$$

and

$\lambda''_d(j) =$ arrival rate (at a j-level link in the destination cluster) due to inter-cluster messages.

$$= \begin{cases} 2^{d-1}\lambda(1-\alpha)\,p_2(j) & \text{if } j \le \left\lceil \frac{d}{2} \right\rceil \\ 2^{d-1}\lambda(1-\alpha)\,[p_2(j) + p_1(d-j+1)] & \text{if } j > \left\lceil \frac{d}{2} \right\rceil \end{cases}$$

Then, the average message delay is given by

$$R^{RS}_{BH/BH} = \alpha\left[\frac{d\,2^{d-1}}{2^{d}-1}\right]\Delta_{Avg} + (1-\alpha)\times$$

$$\left\{\Delta_{CLs-Avg} + \Delta_{CLd-Avg} + \left(\frac{(D-d)\,2^{D-d-1}}{2^{D-d}-1}\right)\Delta_{NCL-Avg}\right\}$$

where

$\Delta_{NCL-Avg} =$ average delay, at a link, of an inter-cluster message in the level 2 network

$$= \frac{1}{\mu_{NCL} - \lambda_{link,\,NCL}}$$

$\Delta_{CLs-Avg} =$ average delay encountered by an inter-cluster message in the source cluster

$$= \sum_{j=1}^{\left\lfloor \frac{d}{2} \right\rfloor} \left\{ (d-j+1)\binom{d}{j-1} p_1(j)\,\Delta_s(j) \right\}$$

$\Delta_{CLd-Avg} =$ average delay encountered by an inter-cluster message in the destination cluster

$$= \sum_{j=1}^{d} \left\{ (d-j+1)\binom{d}{j-1} p_2(j)\,\Delta_d(j) \right\}$$

and

Δ_{Avg} = average delay, at a link, of an intra-cluster message

$$= \begin{cases} \dfrac{1}{d\,2^{d-1}} \left[\sum_{j=1}^{\frac{d}{2}} \left\{ (d-j+1) \binom{d}{j-1} \Delta_d(j) \right\} + \sum_{j=1}^{\frac{d}{2}} \left\{ (d-j+1) \binom{d}{j-1} \Delta_s(j) \right\} \right] & \text{if } d \text{ is even} \\[2ex] \dfrac{1}{d\,2^{d-1}} \left[\sum_{j=1}^{\frac{d+1}{2}} \left\{ (d-j+1) \binom{d}{j-1} \Delta_d(j) \right\} + \sum_{j=1}^{\frac{d-1}{2}} \left\{ (d-j+1) \binom{d}{j-1} \Delta_s(j) \right\} \right] & \text{if } d \text{ is odd} \end{cases}$$

Cluster link delays in source and destination clusters $\Delta_s(j)$ and $\Delta_d(j)$ are given by

$$\Delta_s(j) = \frac{1}{\mu_{CL} - \lambda_{link,\,CLs}(j)}$$

$$\Delta_d(j) = \frac{1}{\mu_{CL} - \lambda_{link,\,CLd}(j)}$$

6.5.2. Validation of the Analysis

To facilitate the queueing analysis, it was assumed that whenever a message arrives at a link on its path to its destination, a new service time is generated from the exponential service time distribution. In a real system, of course, the messages would retain their service times, which reflect the lengths of the messages, from the times they are generated to the times they arrive at their destinations. A simulation model was constructed that reflected this reality, and, therefore, allowed validation of the independence assumption used in the analysis (and to verify the analysis itself). In all other respects, the simulation model matched the analytic model.

We have conducted simulation experiments with different parameters. Selected results are presented in Figure 6.10 that illustrate well the results of these experiments. Figure 6.10a gives the average message delay as a function of α and Figure 6.10b gives the average message delay as a function of network size N. The value of α is varied from 0.5 to 1.0 in steps of 0.1 and N is varied from 32 to 256 nodes. It can be seen from these plots that the results obtained from the analytical formulas match closely those obtained by simulation, thus justifying the use of Kleinrock's independence assumption.

6.5.3. Performance Comparison

This section compares the performance of the two fault-tolerant BH/BH networks: the BH/BH-SI network and the BH/BH-RS network. In addition, as stated in Chapter 3, the standard binary hypercube (BH) network is used as a reference network against which the performance of these two networks is compared.

We consider two different scenarios in doing this performance comparison. First, we assume that both the cluster (CL) and non-cluster (NCL) links have the same message processing rates (i.e., $\mu_{CL} = \mu_{NCL}$). For fair performance comparison, these rates are assumed to be equal to those of the reference BH network. Therefore, the BH/BH-RS network, which also uses $\mu_{CL} = \mu_{NCL}$ condition, increases the network cost by doubling the number of links in the level 2 network. To account for this difference in the cost factor, we use a cost-benefit ratio, called the LR ratio, which is defined in Chapter 3 as

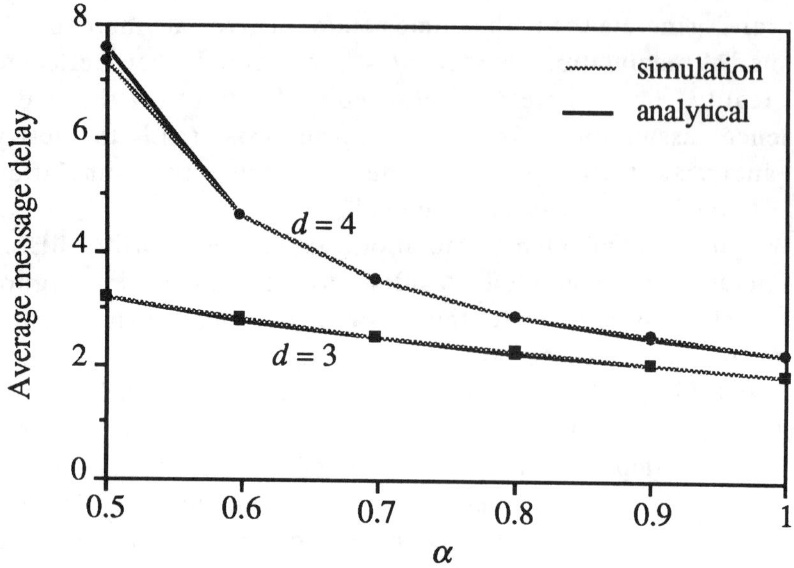

(a)

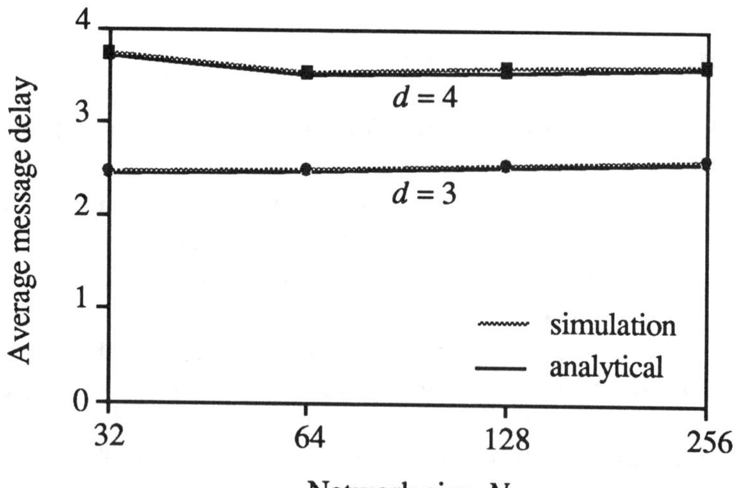

(b)

Figure 6.10 Comparison of analytical and simulation results for the BH/BH-RS network (**a**) $D = 6$, $\lambda = 1$, $\mu_{CL} = 1.5$, $\mu_{NCL} = 3$; (**b**) $\lambda = 1$, $\mu_{CL} = 1.5$, $\mu_{NCL} = 3$, $\alpha = 0.7$

$$LR \text{ ratio} = \frac{L_{HIN} \times R_{HIN}}{L_{REF} \times R_{REF}}$$

where L_{HIN} and L_{REF} are the link costs of the HIN and the reference network, respectively. Similarly, R_{HIN} and R_{REF} refers to the average message delays of the HIN and the reference network, respectively. As stated earlier, we use the BH network as the reference network in our comparisons. Smaller *LR* ratio values (smaller than 1) are preferred. A value of 1 for the *LR* ratio indicates that the HIN under consideration has the same cost-benefit ratio (as measured by the *LR* ratio).

In the other scenario, discussed in Section 6.5.3.4, we assume that $\mu_{NCL} = 2\mu_{CL}$ for the BH/BH-SI network. This means that each logical link in the level 2 network is mapped to two physical links. It has been shown in Chapter 3 (Section 3.6.1) that the cost-benefit ratio tends to improve with this mapping (when compared to the situation with $\mu_{CL} = \mu_{NCL}$). However, in BH/BH-RS network, we use $\mu_{CL} = \mu_{NCL}$. Thus, in this case, the BH/BH-RS network can be thought of as redistributing the total number of physical links in the level 2 network of the BH/BH-SI network. Thus, both the BH/BH-SI and the BH/BH-RS networks use the same number of physical links. Hence the link cost remains the same for both these fault-tolerant HINs. Thus any increase in performance should be reflected in a similar improvement in cost-benefit ratio.

6.5.3.1. Impact of Communication Locality

Figure 6.11a depicts the average message delays associated with the BH, BH/BH-SI, and BH/BH-RS networks for the following parameters: $\lambda = 1$, $\mu_{CL} = \mu_{NCL} = 3$, $d = 3$, and $D = 9$ (i.e., network size $N = 512$). The value of α is increased from 0.5 to 1 in steps of 0.1. Since HINs are cost-effective when there is communication locality, we do not consider α values less than 0.5. Figure 6.11b shows the corresponding *LR* ratio values for the two fault-tolerant BH/BH networks.

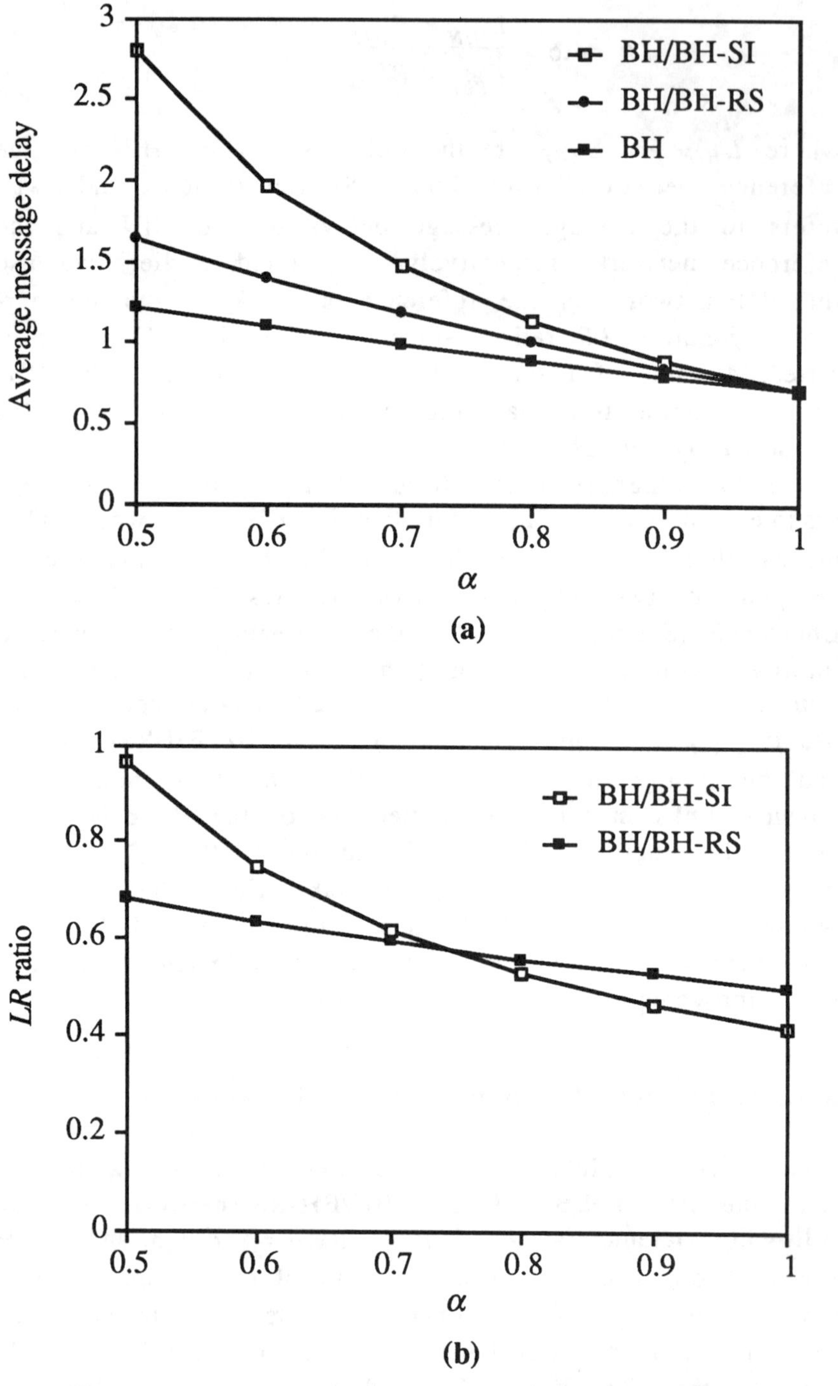

Figure 6.11 Average message delivery time and the corresponding *LR* ratio (N = 512 and cluster size = 8)

The delays associated with the BH/BH-RS networks are substantially smaller than those of the BH/BH-SI network for smaller values of α. This improvement in performance is, however, associated with an increase in network cost. From Figure 6.11b it can be concluded that for smaller values of α the reduction in the average message delay more than compensates for the increase in link cost of the BH/BH-RS network. The situation is different for α values greater than around 0.75. For these higher α values, since there are fewer inter-cluster messages, the replication of the level 2 network does not justify the increase in cost. It should, however, be noted that the BH/BH-RS network degrades gracefully when α values decrease (as is clear from the less steep *LR* ratio and message delay curves). This is important in a general-purpose multicomputer system that supports a wide range of workloads. Behaviour under low communication locality is important even if typical applications have higher α values (say, $\alpha \geq 0.8$). As illustrated in Figure 6.11, the BH/BH-RS network handles low communication locality applications better than the BH/BH-SI network.

These observations are valid even for larger networks. Figure 6.12, which depicts the results for a network of size 2^{13}, is presented to support this observation. (Other parameters are fixed as in Figure 6.11.) As the network size increases, the difference between the average message delays associated with the three networks increases. However, the *LR* ratio difference between the two fault-tolerant BH/BH networks tends to decrease because, as network size increases (for a fixed cluster size) there are correspondingly more links in the level 2 network of the BH/BH-RS network. Still, the BH/BH-RS network has the better cost-benefit ratio for α values below 0.7 (the cross-over point is not substantially different from that in a network of size 2^9).

6.5.3.2. Impact of Network Size

Figures 6.13a and 6.13b show the average message delay and the corresponding *LR* ratios, respectively, versus the

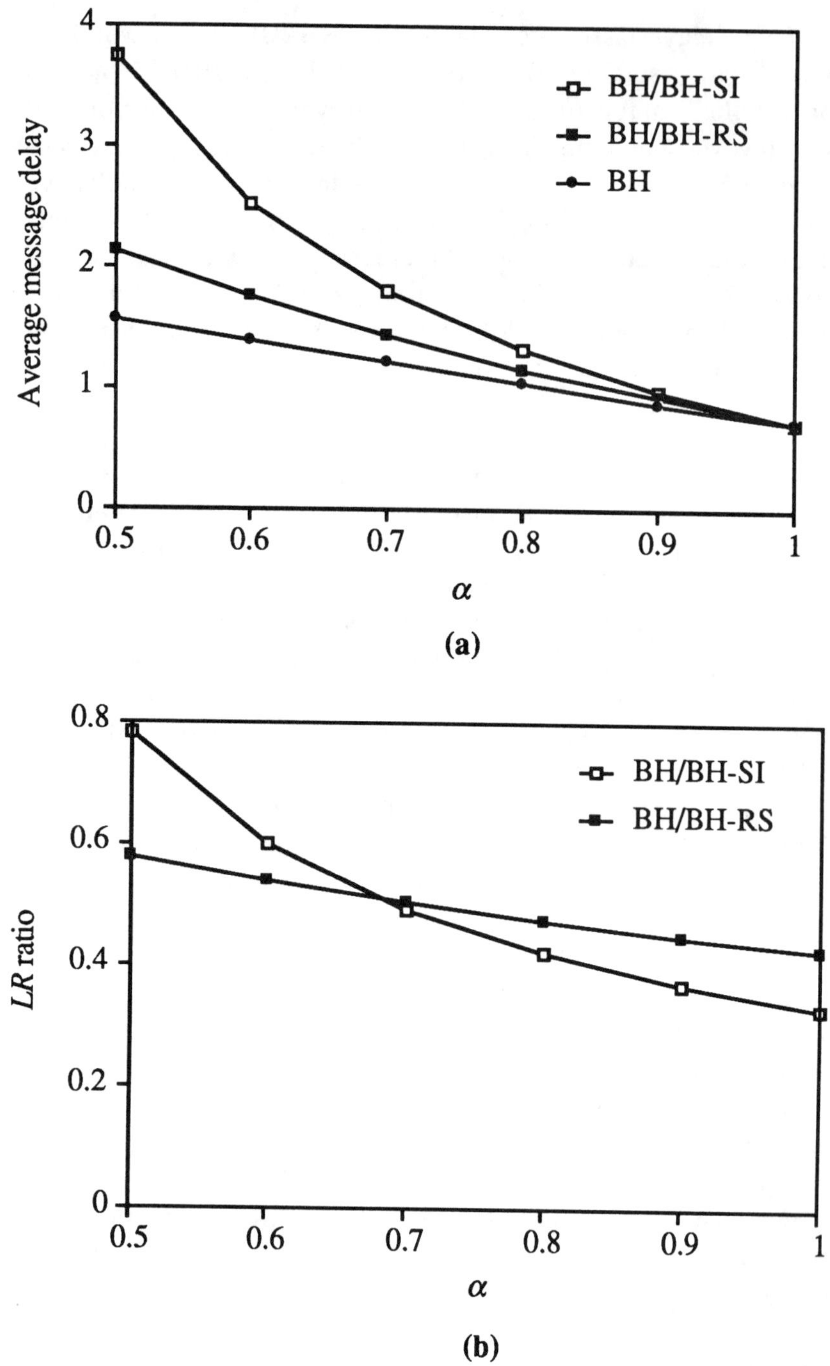

Figure 6.12 Average message delay and the corresponding LR ratio (N = 8192 and cluster size = 8)

network size. The network size is increased from 2^7 through 2^{15}. Each graph is plotted for two α values (0.5 and 0.8). The remaining parameters are fixed as in Figure 6.11.

From Figure 6.13a, it can be seen that, when α = 0.5, the BH/BH-RS network provides average message delays that are closer to the BH network than does the BH/BH-SI network. The difference in the average message delays between the two fault-tolerant BH/BH networks increases as the network size increases. However, at α = 0.8, the corresponding differences between the three networks is only marginal.

When α = 0.5, the BH/BH-RS network is uniformly better than the BH/BH-SI network over the range of network sizes considered. Because the BH/BH-RS network link cost increases with increasing network size, the difference in *LR* ratios decreases as the network size increases. When α = 0.8, the BH/BH-SI network provides marginally better cost-benefit ratio. This is mainly due to the fact that there are fewer inter-cluster messages and the benefit of obtaining decreased message delays is small (see Figure 6.13a). Again, this difference in *LR* ratios increases with increasing network size because of the penalty associated with the BH/BH-RS network in terms of increased link cost without substantially decreasing the average message delay.

6.5.3.3. Sensitivity to Message Generation Rate

In message-passing systems, the computation-communication ratio is an important characteristic of an application [LINT 81]. If an application is computationally intensive, it tends to generate fewer messages (and hence lower network message load). Here we can model this fact by smaller λ values. On the other hand, a communication-intensive application should be modelled with higher λ values. Furthermore, applications may also vary in their degree of communication locality (in our model, varying values of α). If the overall system workload is of mixed

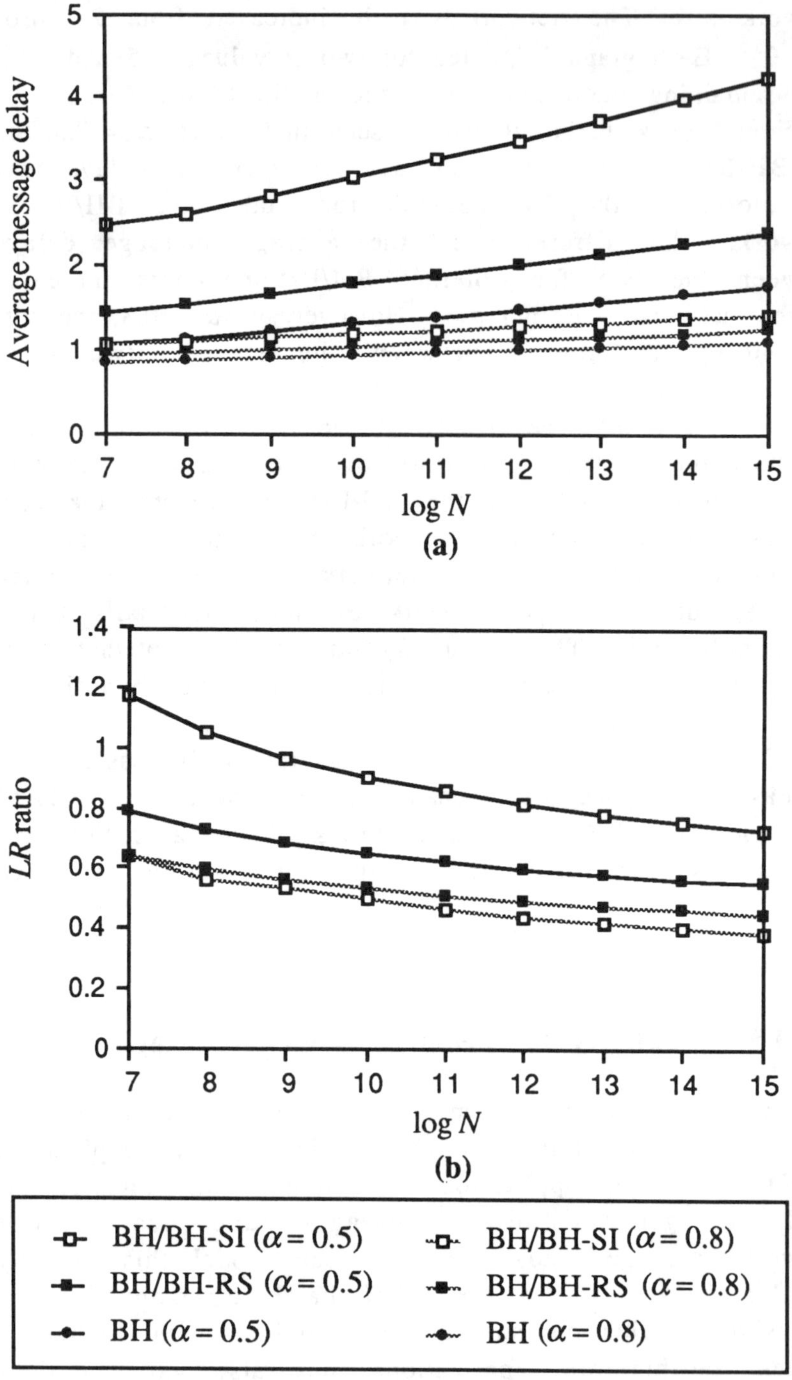

Figure 6.13 Average message delivery time and the corresponding *LR* ratio as a function of network size

type, the interconnection network should gracefully handle different types of workload.

To assess the capability of these three networks to handle various workloads, we use the saturation message generation rate λ_{sat} supported by each network. Figure 6.14a shows the λ_{sat} values for the three networks when a cluster size of 8 is used. All other parameters are the same as those used in Figure 6.11 At α = 1, all three networks are equivalent, and therefore support the same saturation message generation rate. For other α values, the BH/BH-RS network supports λ_{sat} values that are intermediate between those supported by the BH network and the BH/BH-SI network. In particular, for $0.5 \leq \alpha \leq 0.6$, the BH/BH-RS network supports a message generation rate that is twice that supported by the BH/BH-SI network. This is because at these α values and for the parameters considered here, non-cluster links saturate before cluster links do (This can be verified from $\lambda_{link,CL}$ and $\lambda_{link,NCL}$ equations in Section 6.5.1). For higher values of α, it is the cluster links that determine the value of λ_{sat}. (This is the reason why the curves associated with the BH/BH-RS and BH/BH-SI networks show two distinct slopes.)

Figure 6.14b shows the sensitivity of λ_{sat} to α when the cluster size is changed to 4. The impact of cluster size on λ_{sat} can be seen by comparing Figures 6.14a and 6.14b. Since there are more non-cluster links when the cluster size is smaller, λ_{sat} is now essentially determined by when the cluster links saturate. With smaller cluster size, the BH/BH-RS network tends to support λ_{sat} values that are closer to those supported by the BH network.

With increasing cluster size, the BH/BH-SI network supports comparatively smaller λ_{sat} values than the BH/BH-RS network. This is because, as the cluster size increases, there are more and more inter-cluster messages (for a fixed α value) flooding the cluster links closer to the interface node (Figure 6.15). The situation is comparatively better in the BH/BH-RS network because this message load is distributed between the two interface nodes as shown in Figure 6.15.

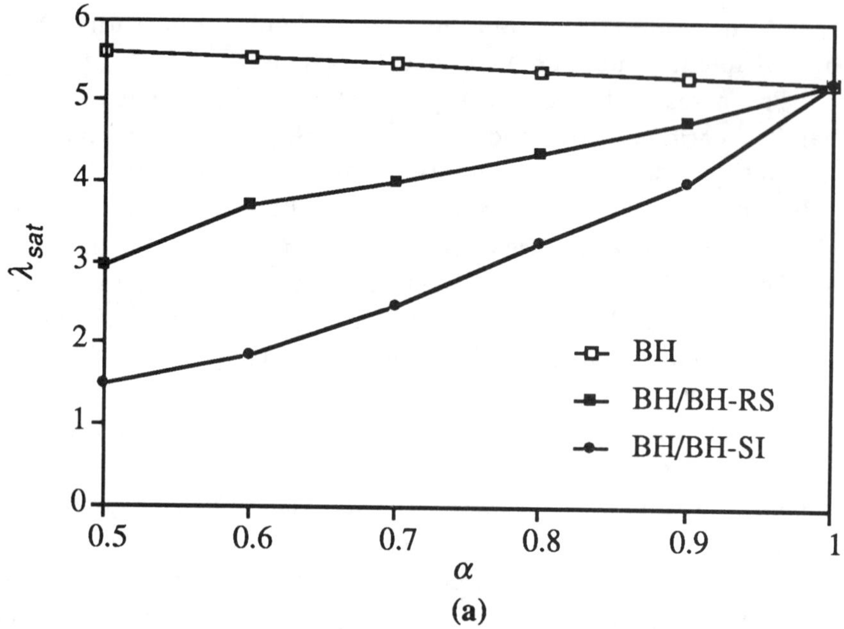

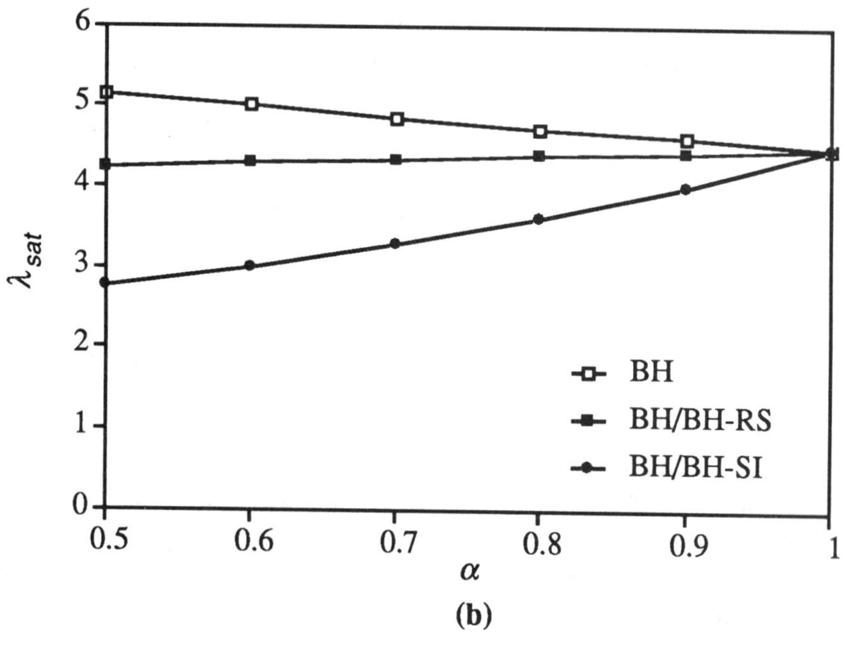

Figure 6.14 Saturation message generation rate supported by the three networks as a function of α (a) cluster size is 8; (b) cluster size is 4

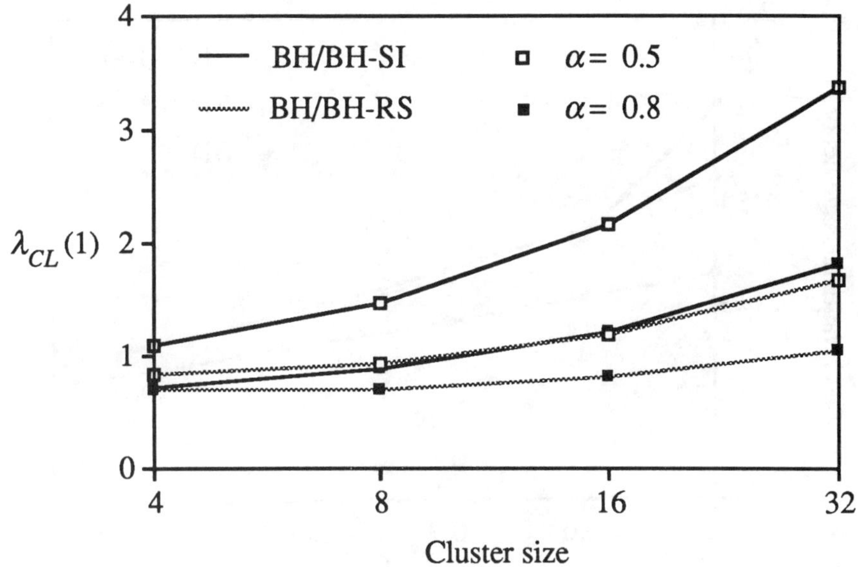

Figure 6.15 Effective message arrival rate seen by the cluster links connected to the interface nodes when $\lambda = 1$

6.5.3.4. Performance under Constant Network Cost

This section discusses the relative performance of the two fault-tolerant BH/BH networks under the constraint that they both use the same number of physical links. As stated earlier, in this case, the BH/BH-SI network maps each logical link in the level 2 network to two physical links. We model this by making $\mu_{NCL} = 2\mu_{CL}$. The BH/BH-RS network essentially redistributes these level 2 network (physical) links of the BH/BH-SI network (therefore we use $\mu_{CL} = \mu_{NCL}$ for the BH/BH-RS network).

Figure 6.16a shows the average message delay as a function of α. The parameters are the same as those used in Figure 6.11 (except that the BH/BH-SI network uses $\mu_{NCL} = 6$). By increasing the message processing rate of the level 2 links, the BH/BH-SI network provides performance that is close to the BH/BH-RS except for α values less than 0.6. Thus, for this network size, these two BH/BH networks

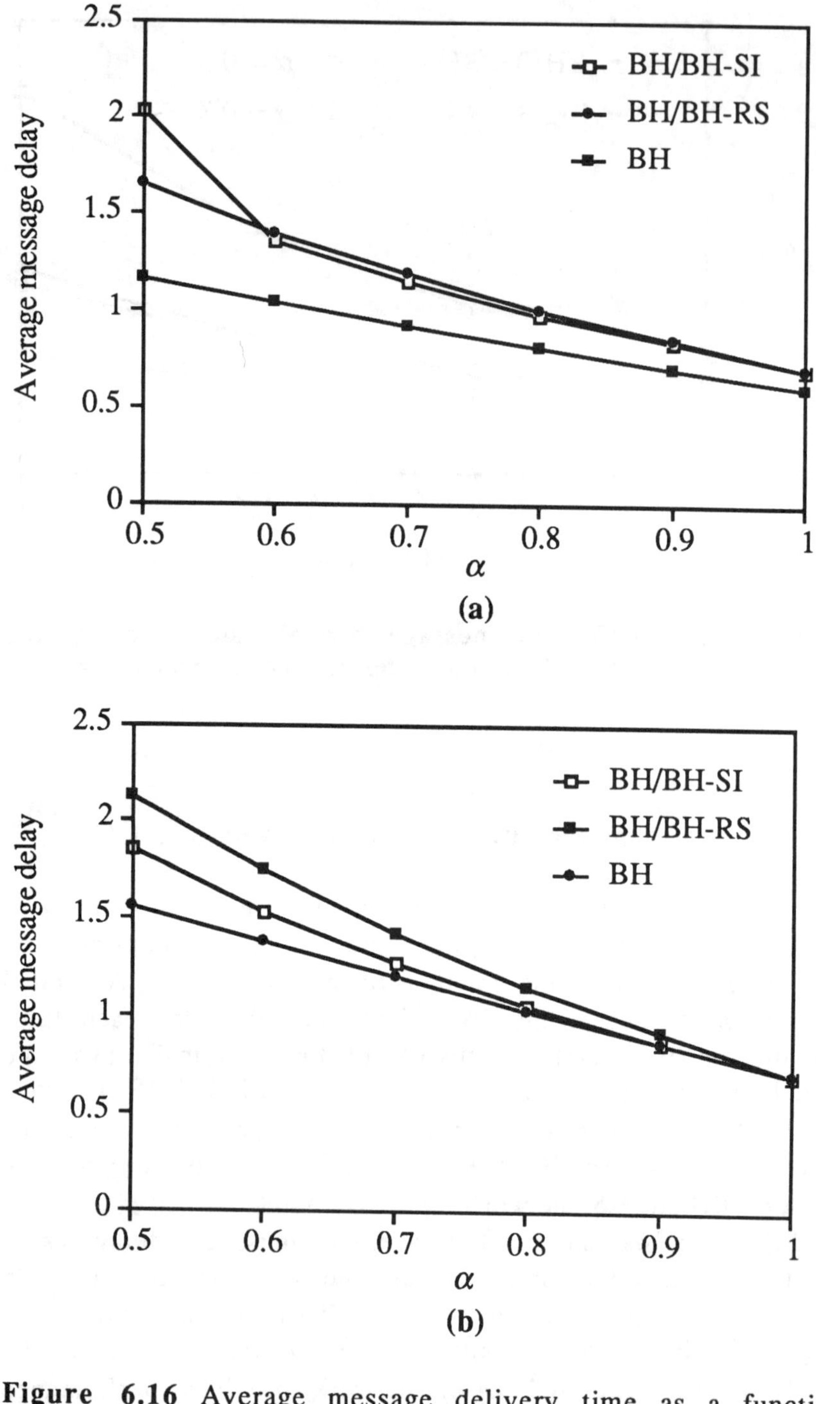

Figure 6.16 Average message delivery time as a function of α under constant network cost (*a*) network size is 512 ($D = 9$); (*b*) network size is 8192 ($D = 13$)

provide the same cost-benefit ratio as measured by the LR ratio. However, as the network size increases, the BH/BH-SI network provides better performance. As shown in Figure 6.16b, when $N = 2^{13}$, the BH/BH-SI network gives message delays that are intermediate between the BH/BH-RS network and the BH network.

The impact of increasing the network size is further demonstrated by Figure 6.17, which gives the average message delays as a function of network size N for $\alpha = 0.5$ and $\alpha = 0.8$. These graphs show that the major component

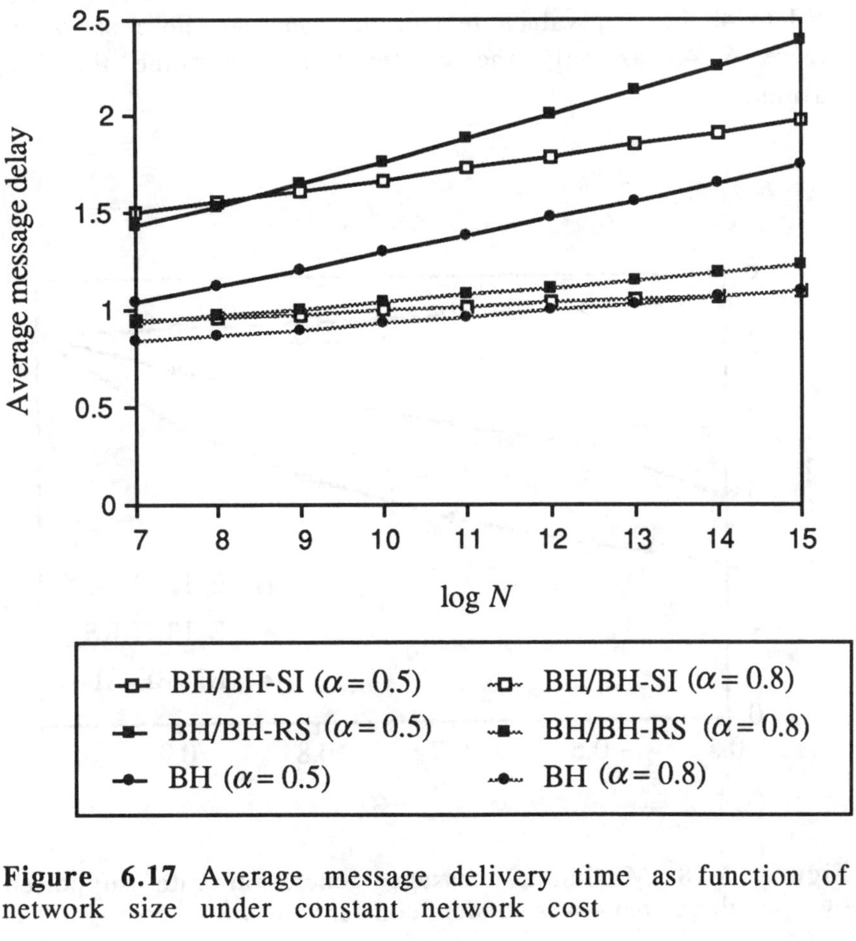

Figure 6.17 Average message delivery time as function of network size under constant network cost

of the delay in message transmission is contributed by the non-cluster links in Figure 6.11a. However, if the parameters were chosen such that the major component of the delay was contributed by the cluster links, then such improvement in performance could not be associated with the BH/BH-SI network. This is clear from the saturation message generation rate λ_{sat} supported by these networks as shown in Figure 6.18. Comparing Figures 6.14a and 6.18, it can be seen that the improvement in λ_{sat} due to increased λ_{NCL} value is marginal. This is mainly due to the fact that the λ_{sat} values are now determined, for the whole range of α values, by when the cluster links saturate. (Note that, in Figure 6.14a, for $0.5 \leq \alpha \leq 0.7$, λ_{sat} is determined by when the non-cluster links saturate.) When the cluster size is reduced to 4, the λ_{sat} values remain the same as those shown in Figure 6.14b as only the cluster links determine the λ_{sat} values.

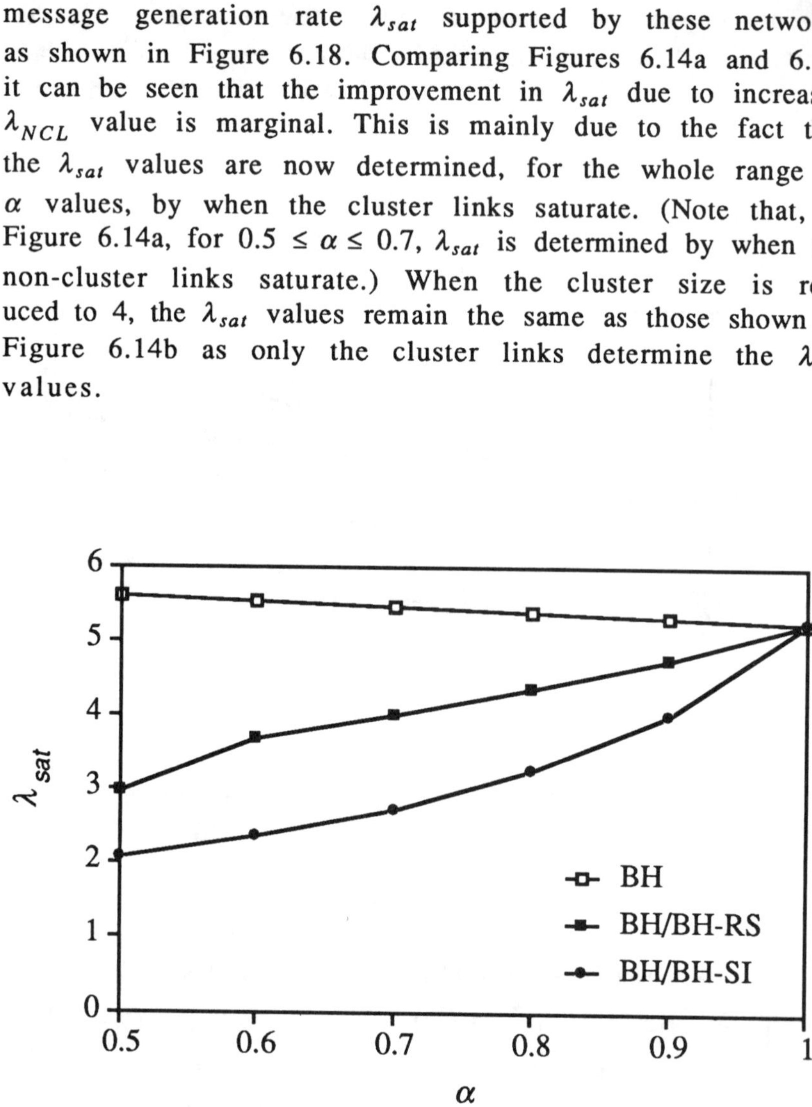

Figure 6.18 Maximum message generation rate supported by the three networks under constant network cost

6.6. Summary

We have provided task-based reliability evaluation of binary hypercube-based hierarchical interconnection networks. By means of simulation, we have shown that these HINs provide reliabilities that are intermediate between the reliabilities of the bidirectional ring network and the binary hypercube network (which provides reliability as good as that of the complete connection network).

We have presented two fault-tolerance improvement schemes for the HINs. Both these schemes use hardware redundancy. In one, a standby spare interface node is provided to reduce the impact of interface node failures on network reliability; in the other, the level 2 network is duplicated. Both these schemes provide similar improvements in reliability of the HINs. Typically, these fault-tolerant HINs provide reliabilities which are intermediate between the original HIN and the BH network.

However, from a performance point of view, neither of the two networks dominates the other for all parameter values and system characteristics. If the network supports applications that have varying degrees of communication locality and/or different computation-communication ratios, the BH/BH-RS network is to be recommended. On the other hand, when applications that exhibit high degrees of communication locality and high computation-communication ratios, the BH/BH-SI network provides marginally better performance. It should, however, be noted that as the cluster size increases, the BH/BH-RS network tends to improve its performance over the BH/BH-SI network.

A weakness of the BH/BH-RS and BH/BH-SI networks is that their reliability is uniformly poorer than the BH network. This drawback can be remedied by adding standby-spare interface nodes to the BH/BH-RS network (the BH/BH-RS&SI network). This, of course, increases the network cost but this increase is a one-time design cost and can easily be amortized without significantly affecting the overall system cost. Thus, from an overall system design point of view, the penalty associated with the BH/BH-RS&SI

network may not be significant. This, however, improves overall network reliability substantially as shown in Figure 6.3. Its reliability is comparable to that of the BH network. The performance of this network, however, remains the same as that of the BH/BH-RS network. The BH/BH-RS&SI network, therefore, may be attractive in high reliability applications providing reliability as good as that of the BH and the complete connection networks.

Further Reading

We have presented simulation-based reliability evaluation of hypercube networks. Kim *et al.* [KIM 89] present an approximate analytical model to derive task-based reliability of the standard hypercube network. Fault-tolerance issues in multicomputer systems have also been discussed in [ABRA 88], and [KUHL 86]. Reliability comparison of various link-oriented multicomputer networks (including the HINs) is given in [DAND 90b]. [DAS 90] gives a tutorial on dependability and performance-related dependability models for multiprocessors.

Acknowledgement

Material presented in this chapter is partly based on [DAND 89] and [DAND 90a].

References

[ABRA 88] S. Abraham and K. Padmanabhan, "Reliability of the Hypercube," *Proc. 1988 Int. Conf. Parallel Processing*, 1988, Vol. I, pp. 90-94.

[ADAM 87] G. B. Adams III, D. P. Agrawal, and H. J. Siegel, "A Survey and Comparison of Fault-Tolerant Multistage Interconnection Networks," *Computer*, Vol. 20, No. 6, June 1987, pp. 14-27.

[BHUY 86] L. N. Bhuyan and C. R. Das, "Dependability Evaluation of Multicomputer Networks," *Proc. 1986 Int. Conf. Parallel Processing*, 1986, pp. 576-583.

[DAND 89] S. P. Dandamudi, "Reliability of Hierarchical Hypercube Multicomputer Networks," Research Note, School of Computer Science, Carleton University, Ottawa, Ontario K1S 5B6, Canada, 1989..

[DAND 90a] S. P. Dandamudi, "Performance Analysis of Fault-Tolerant Hierarchical Hypercube Multicomputer Networks," Research Note, School of Computer Science, Carleton University, Ottawa, Ontario K1S 5B6, Canada, 1990.

[DAND 90b] S. P. Dandamudi, "A Comparison of Link-Oriented Multicomputer Networks" Research Note, School of Computer Science, Carleton University, Ottawa, Ontario K1S 5B6, Canada, 1990.

[DAS 90] C. R. Das, J. T. Kreulen, M. J. Thazhuthaveetil, and L. N. Bhuyan, "Dependability Modeling for Multiprocessors," *Computer*, Vol. 23, No. 10, October 1990, pp. 7-19.

[DEO 74] N. Deo, *Graph Theory with Applications to Engineering and Computer Science*, Prentice-Hall Inc., 1974.

[HAYE 86] J. P. Hayes, T. N. Mudge, Q. F. Stout, S. Colley, and J. Palmer, "Architecture of a Hypercube Supercomputer," *Proc. 1986 Int. Conf. Parallel Processing*, 1986, pp. 653-660.

[HILL 85] W. D. Hillis, *The Connection Machine*, MIT Press, Cambridge, MA.,1985.

[INGL 77] A. D. Ingle and D. P. Seiwiorek, "Reliability Models for Multiprocessor Systems With and Without Periodic Maintenance," *Proc. 7th Annu. Int. Conf. Fault Tolerant Computing*, 1977, pp. 3-9.

[JOHN 89] B. W. Johnson, *Design and Analysis of Fault Tolerant Digital Systems*, Addison-Wesley, Reading, 1989.

[KIM 89] J. Kim, C. R. Das,W. Lin, and T. Feng, "Reliability Evaluation of Hypercube Multicomputers," *IEEE Trans. Reliability*, Vol. 38, No. 1, 1989, pp. 71-73.

[KLEI 76] L. Kleinrock, *Queueing Systems: Volume 2*, Wiley, New York, 1976.

[KUHL 86] J. G. Kuhl and S. M. Reddy, "Fault-Tolerance Considerations in Large, Multiple-Processor Systems," *Computer*, Vol. 19, No. 3, March 1986, pp. 56-67.

[LINT 81] B. Lint and T. Agerwala, "Communication Issues in the Design and Analysis of Parallel Algorithms," *IEEE Trans. Software Engineering*, Vol. SE-7, 1981, pp. 174-188.

[TANE 81] A. S. Tanenbaum, *Computer Networks*, Prentice-Hall Inc., 1981.

7

Routing Algorithms

This chapter considers routing algorithms for binary hypercube-based HINs. Four routing algorithms are considered: fixed, random, shortest queue, and retrograde routing. The first two algorithms are oblivious algorithms in that routing decisions are independent of the network state. The last two are adaptive algorithms that make routing decisions dependent on the network state. Further, only the first three algorithms use shortest path routing. These algorithms are described in Section 7.1. We derive bounds on message delay and saturation message generation rate and compare the performance of these routing algorithms in achieving these bounds. The locality and workload models used in this performance evaluation are given in Section 7.2. Section 7.3 presents the analysis of bounds on message delay and saturation message generation rate for the BH/BH network discussed in Chapter 3. A performance comparison of the four routing algorithms is given for this network in Section 7.4. Section 7.5 considers the impact of these routing algorithms on the fault-tolerant HIN – the BH/BH-RS network – discussed in the last chapter. Section 7.6 concludes the chapter by summarizing the results of this chapter.

7.1. Introduction

The purpose of this chapter is to provide a performance comparison of routing algorithms for binary hypercube-based HINs (see Figure 3.3). Our goal is to compare the performance of distributed routing algorithms; in particular our interest is in comparing *adaptive* routing schemes versus *oblivious* routing schemes (which disregard the state of the network in making their routing decisions).

We consider four routing algorithms: fixed, random, shortest queue, and retrograde routing algorithms. Note that the first two routing algorithms belong to the oblivious group; the remaining two are adaptive algorithms. The adaptive routing algorithms require only the local state information available at a node. Also note that the first three routing algorithms use only the shortest paths to route messages from the source node to the destination node.

(a) *Fixed Routing:* In binary hypercubes, routing information can be computed from the source and destination node addresses. The routing code is computed as the *exclusive-or* (**xor**) of the source and destination addresses (expressed in binary form). This code indicates the dimensions that the message must traverse to reach its destination. In the fixed routing scheme, the routing code is always scanned from lower to higher (we assume here that this corresponds to a left to right scan) dimension until a dimension that the message must traverse is found (i.e., until a '1' bit is found). This process is illustrated in Figure 7.1. It should be noted that all commercially available hypercube multicomputer systems use this routing scheme. This scheme has the advantage of avoiding deadlocks when there is finite number of buffers available at each node.

(b) *Random Routing*: This scheme is similar to the fixed routing scheme described above except that the dimension that the message should follow next is selected randomly from the routing code. Random routing is often assumed for mathematical convenience (we have used this routing algorithm in previous chapters). Furthermore, it tends to distribute the message load uniformly over *all the shortest paths* between any pair of nodes in the network.

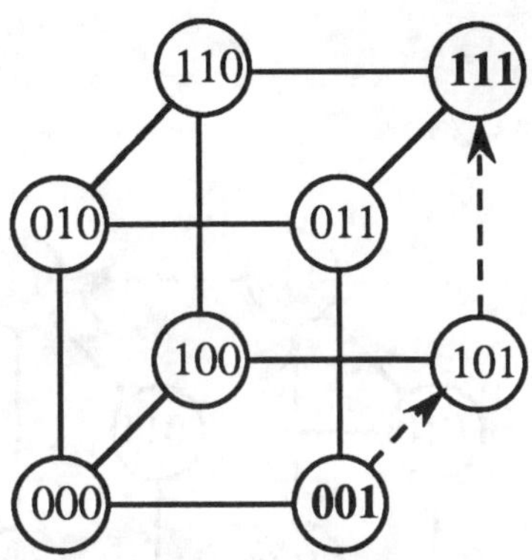

Routing code: 001 xor 111 = 110 -> 010 -> 000

Figure 7.1 Shortest path routing of a message in a 3-cube

(c) *Shortest Queue Routing*: In this adaptive routing scheme, at each node, if a message can take one of l links (l is equal to the number of 1's in the routing code computed at that node) the message will be routed to that link which has the shortest queue length. Note that the message still follows the shortest path; since there are several shortest paths in hypercubes, it tends to select a path that minimizes the message delay. Furthermore, all the information it needs is available locally at each node.

(d) *Retrograde Routing:* The three routing schemes described above route messages over a shortest path.

However, it is quite possible that the overall message delay could potentially be reduced if we relaxed this restriction by allowing messages to follow a longer path that uses links that are lightly loaded than those on any of the shortest paths. This process is illustrated in Figure 7.2. In this figure, it is assumed that the links connected to nodes 101 and 011 are the most heavily utilized links. Thus, when node 001 sends a message to node 111, it is routed around these links by following a longer path.

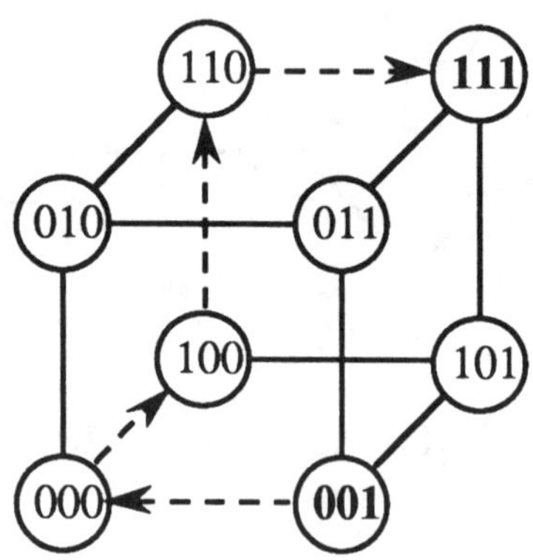

Routing code: 001 xor 111 = 110 -> 111 -> 011 -> 001 -> 000

Figure 7.2 Retrograde routing of a message in a 3-cube

This type of unbalanced link utilization exists in HINs because the links that are closer to the interface nodes are heavily loaded than the links that are farther away. While inter-cluster messages will have no choice but to use these links to reach the interface node, intra-cluster messages have alternative paths around these links. Thus, if intra-cluster messages can undergo retrograde motion by avoiding these heavily loaded links, the overall message delay may be reduced.

It has been shown that such a routing scheme is effective in reducing overall delay in synchronous hypercubes[1] [MCCR 86].

It is then quite possible for a message to infinitely loop around by repeatedly undergoing retrograde motion without ever reaching its destination node. Therefore, it is necessary to impose a limit on the number of retrograde steps a message can take. If a message reaches this limit, it simply follows a shortest path from that point onwards. In this chapter, we investigate whether such a routing scheme would be effective in asynchronous hypercubes, in particular in HINs.

7.2. The Locality and Workload Models

This section describes the communication locality and workload models used in evaluating the performance of the routing schemes described in Section 7.1. As in previous chapters, we refer to the level 1 network links as cluster (CL) links and the level 2 network links as non-cluster (NCL) links.

Each node is assumed to generate messages at rate λ and the inter-message times are exponentially distributed. The node message generation processes are assumed to be independent of each other. Message service times are exponentially distributed; each cluster link processes these messages at rate μ_{CL} and each non-cluster link processes at rate μ_{NCL}. Each node is assumed to have unbounded buffering capacity. Packet-switching is used for message transmission.

Locality in communication is characterized by a single parameter α as discussed in Chapter 3. Briefly, let α be the probability of both source and destination nodes of a message being in the same cluster (i.e., intra-cluster commu-

---

[1] In synchronous hypercubes, routing is done by all the nodes in lock-step. These networks are typically used in SIMD systems (see Chapter 1) such as the Connection Machine [HILL 85].

nication). Therefore $(1-\alpha)$ represents the probability of inter-cluster communication. It is assumed that:

- Intra-cluster communication is uniformly random (i.e., a source node sends messages to each node within its cluster with equal probability).

- Inter-cluster communication is uniformly random (i.e., a source node sends an inter-cluster message to each other cluster with equal probability, and to each node within the destination cluster with equal probability).

7.3. Analysis of Bounds on Performance

This section, which considers the BH/BH network shown in Figure 3.3, derives a bound on the average message delay and also presents the network saturation analysis giving an upper bound on the maximum message generation rate (at each node) supported by the network. These values can then be used as an yardstick to measure the performance of various routing algorithms.

7.3.1. A Bound on Average Message Delay

A characteristic of HINs is that the interface node acts as an 'hot-spot' and the cluster links closer to the interface nodes handle higher message traffic than the links that are farther away. While inter-cluster messages will have no choice but to use these links, intra-cluster messages can be routed around these heavily utilized links. We would like to derive a bound value on the average message delay that measures the ability of a routing scheme to divert intra-cluster messages as mentioned above. This bound is computed by assuming that the message load is uniformly distributed across all links within each cluster and also within the level 2 network. Note that, if the message load were uniformly distributed, then adaptive routing schemes would give average message delays better than this bound.

Acting against this is the imbalance of the message traffic that exists among the cluster links.

Each network link is assumed to be full-duplex. In our analysis, we conceptually replace each full-duplex link by two simplex links, each of which is modelled as a queueing centre. As in previous chapters, we use Kleinrock's independence assumption [KLEI 76] to facilitate the analysis. This assumption states that each time a message arrives at a link, a new service time is generated for this message from the exponential service time distribution (i.e., there is no "memory" of message lengths from hop to hop). This assumption is often used in the delay analysis of communication networks [GOPA 81]. The results of the simulation experiments presented in Chapters 3, 5, and 6 indicate that this assumption is reasonable. This allows each (simplex) link to be modelled as an M/M/1 queueing centre [KLEI 75].

This analysis follows closely that given in Section 3.5.2. Consider a source cluster in a BH/BH network with $N = 2^D$ nodes and a cluster size of $n = 2^d$ nodes. Let λ denote the message generation rate at each node. Following the locality model, the intra-cluster messages are generated at $\alpha\lambda$ rate and inter-cluster messages at $(1-\alpha)\lambda$ rate. Therefore, message load due to intra-cluster messages is give by

$$2^d \alpha\lambda \left(\frac{d\ 2^{d-1}}{2^d - 1} \right) \tag{7.1}$$

because the messages are generated at $2^d\alpha\lambda$ rate and each such message travels, on average, $(d\ 2^{d-1})/(2^d-1)$ cluster links. Similarly, inter-cluster messages originated in the source cluster travel $d/2$ cluster links to reach the interface node and these messages are generated at $2^d(1-\alpha)\lambda$ rate. Therefore, message load due to out-going inter-cluster messages is given by

$$2^d (1-\alpha)\lambda \left(\frac{d}{2} \right) \tag{7.2}$$

Finally, we have inter-cluster messages whose destination nodes are within the source cluster under consideration.

This group of messages contribute a message load equal to that given by Eq. (7.2). Therefore, the effective arrival rate seen by a cluster link is given by

$$\lambda_{CL} = \lambda\left[\alpha\left(\frac{2^{d-1}}{2^d - 1}\right) + (1-\alpha)\right] \tag{7.3}$$

Note that if we assume that a node can send messages to itself or if $2^d \gg 1$, the above equation reduces to $\lambda_{CL} = \lambda\left(1 - \frac{\alpha}{2}\right)$.

To compute λ_{NCL}, we note that each cluster generates these messages at $2^d(1-\alpha)\lambda$ rate and these messages traverse, on average, $\left[\frac{(D-d)\,2^{D-d-1}}{2^{D-d} - 1}\right]$ non-cluster links. Therefore,

$$\lambda_{NCL} = \frac{2^{D-1}\,\lambda\,(1-\alpha)}{2^{D-d} - 1} \tag{7.4}$$

If $2^{D-d} \gg 1$, this simplifies to $\lambda_{NCL} = 2^{d-1}\,\lambda\,(1-\alpha)$.

It is then straightforward to compute the average message delay bound R_B. It is given by

$$R_B = \alpha\left[\frac{d\,2^{d-1}}{2^d - 1}\right]\Delta_{CL} + (1-\alpha)\left[d\,\Delta_{CL} + \left\{\frac{(D-d)2^{D-d-1}}{2^{D-d} - 1}\right\}\Delta_{NCL}\right] \tag{7.5}$$

where

Δ_{CL} = average message delay experienced on a cluster link,

$$= \frac{1}{\mu_{CL} - \lambda_{CL}}$$

and

Δ_{NCL}= average message delay experienced on a non-cluster link,

$$= \frac{1}{\mu_{NCL} - \lambda_{NCL}}$$

7.3.2. Saturation Analysis

We present an upper bound on message generation rate at individual nodes λ_{sat} that results in network saturation. While the value of λ_{sat} is a function of various network parameters such as the message processing rates of various links and the structure of the network, our interest here is mainly to study the impact of various routing algorithms on λ_{sat}. Since there are two types of links in the BH/BH network, we can express λ_{sat} as

$$\lambda_{sat} = \min\left(\lambda_{sat_{CL}}, \lambda_{sat_{NCL}}\right) \tag{7.6}$$

An upper bound on λ_{sat} can be obtained from the bound analysis of the previous section. It is straightforward to derive the following from Eqs. (7.3) and (7.4).

$$\lambda_{sat_{CL}} = \frac{\mu_{CL}}{\alpha\left(\frac{2^{d-1}}{2^d - 1}\right) + 1 - \alpha} \tag{7.7}$$

Note that if we assume that a node can send messages to itself or if $2^d \gg 1$, the above equation reduces to $\lambda_{sat_{CL}} = \frac{\mu_{CL}}{1 - \frac{\alpha}{2}}$.

$$\lambda_{sat_{NCL}} = \frac{\mu_{NCL}\left(2^{D-d} - 1\right)}{2^{D-1}(1 - \alpha)} \tag{7.8}$$

When $2^{D-d} \gg 1$, this reduces to $\lambda_{sat_{NCL}} = \dfrac{\mu_{NCL}}{2^{d-1}(1-\alpha)}$.

Eqs. (7.7) and (7.8) can be used in Eq. (7.6) to obtain an upper bound on λ_{sat} for the BH/BH network.

7.4. Performance of Routing Algorithms

The results for the random routing algorithm were obtained analytically (see Chapter 3). We have conducted simulation experiments for the remaining three routing schemes. We found that the retrograde routing scheme is not useful in asynchronous hypercube networks. Therefore, the remaining three routing algorithms are compared in the following sections. The performance of the retrograde routing is briefly discussed in Section 7.4.5.

7.4.1. Principal Comparison

Figure 7.3 depicts the average message delay associated with the three routing algorithms for the BH/BH network with the following parameters: $\lambda = 1$, $\mu_{CL} = 1.5$, $\mu_{NCL} = 3$, $d = 3$ (i.e., cluster size = 8), and $D = 6$ (i.e., network size $N = 64$). The value of α is varied from 0.5 to 1 in steps of 0.1. Since HINs are cost-effective when there is communication locality, we do not consider α values less than 0.5 (see Chapter 3). Figure 7.4 shows the average message delay as a function of message generation rate at each node λ for $\alpha = 0.7$ (all other parameters are the same as in Figure 7.3).

It can be seen from Figure 7.3 that fixed routing results in extreme sensitivity to locality in communication α. For smaller α values, fixed routing gives unacceptable performance even when compared with random routing. The reason for this performance difference is that random routing tends to distribute message load uniformly on *all the shortest paths* between a pair of nodes whereas the fixed routing tends to favour *one particular shortest path*.

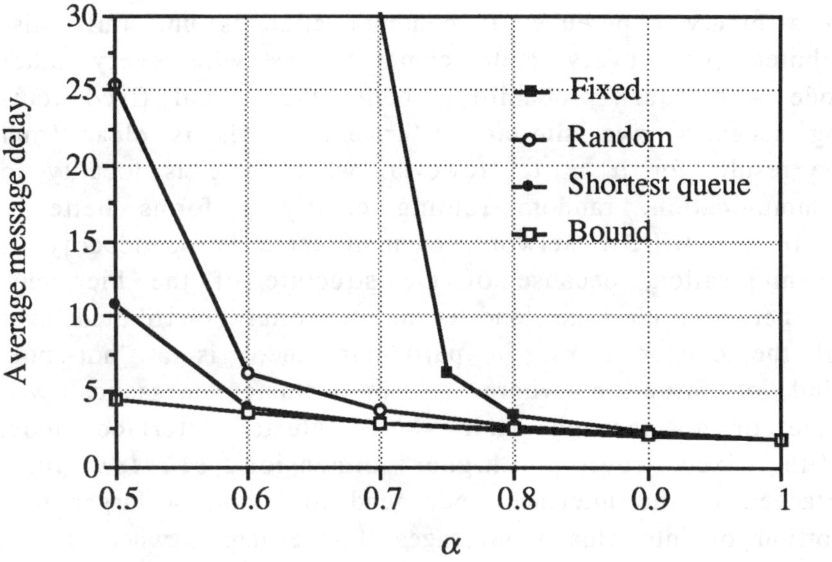

Figure 7.3 Average message delay as a function of communication locality (D = 6, d = 3, λ=1, μ_{CL}=1.5, μ_{NCL}=3)

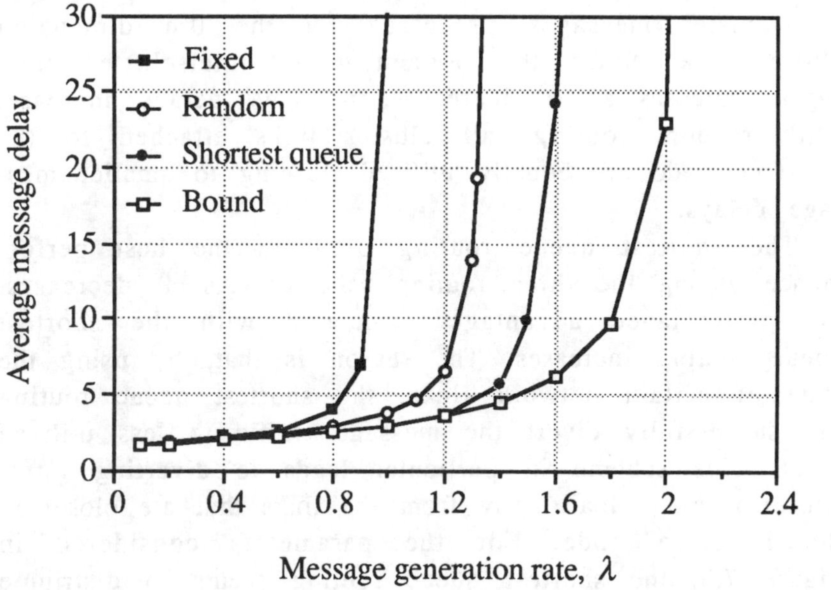

Figure 7.4 Average message delay as a function of message generation rate at each node (D = 6, d = 3, α= 0.7, μ_{CL}= 1.5, μ_{NCL}= 3)

In a binary hypercube, if communication is uniformly distributed (i.e., every node communicates with every other node with equal probability), both random and fixed routing schemes give similar performance. This is clear from the results for $\alpha = 1$. However, when there is locality in communication, random routing clearly performs better.

In the BH/BH network, even if there is no locality in communication, because of the structure of the hierarchical network, message load is not uniformly distributed over all the cluster links. In particular, there is a "hot-spot" kind of situation where all inter-cluster messages will have to go through their source cluster interface node. With fixed routing, higher dimension *cluster* links attached to the interface node tend to handle a larger proportion of inter-cluster messages. For example, when $d = 3$, the number of inter-cluster messages processed by the dimension 1 cluster link is twice the corresponding number for the dimension 0 link; the dimension 2 cluster link processes four times as many messages. In general, the ith dimension cluster link processes 2^i times the number of inter-cluster messages processed by the 0th dimension cluster link. Since the percentage of inter-cluster messages increases as α decreases, message delays increase. With random routing, all cluster links attached to the interface node are equally utilized, leading to smaller message delays.

The shortest queue routing produces the best performance among the three routing schemes. As α decreases, the performance advantage associated with the shortest queue routing increases. The reason is that, by using the state of certain network links, the shortest queue routing can successfully divert the message traffic to less utilized links. This scheme in particular leads to diverting intra-cluster message load away from the links that are closer to the interface node. For the parameters considered in Figure 7.3, the shortest queue routing seems to distribute message load more or less uniformly for $\alpha \geq 0.6$. It can be seen from Figure 7.4 that the shortest queue routing improves performance substantially when compared with random and fixed routing schemes. The network saturation message generation rate increases from 0.9 with fixed routing to 1.3 with random routing to 1.6 with shortest queue routing.

7.4.2. Impact of Network Size

Figure 7.5 shows the average message delay as a function of network size. (The results for fixed routing are not shown in Figure 7.5 but it exhibits similar behaviour and its message delay values vary around 30.) The network size is varied from 32 nodes to 256 nodes by keeping the cluster size fixed at 8. The results show that, as long as the cluster size is fixed, the results are scalable to larger systems. Intuitively, we can see that increasing the system size by adding more clusters will not affect link utilizations of either cluster links or non-cluster links. This is because, for binary hypercubes, if each node generates messages at rate λ and with uniform communication pattern, the effective rate at which links service these messages is given by $\lambda/2$, which is independent of the hypercube dimension. The impact of changing the cluster size is discussed in the next section.

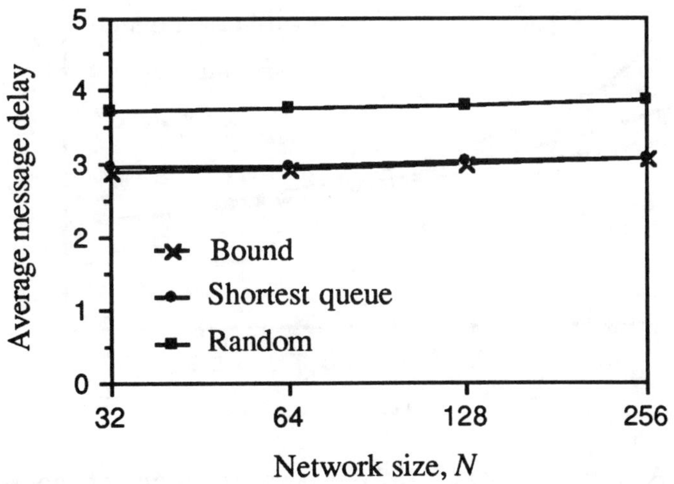

Figure 7.5 Average message delay as a function of system size ($d = 3$, $\alpha = 0.7$, $\lambda = 1$, $\mu_{CL} = 1.5$, $\mu_{NCL} = 3$)

7.4.3. Effect of Cluster Size

The impact of reducing the cluster size can be seen by comparing Figures 7.6 and 7.7 with Figures 7.3 and 7.4, respectively. The results given in Figures 7.6 and 7.7 are obtained with a cluster size of 4. All other parameters are fixed as in Figures 7.3 and 7.4. In particular, note that the network size remains the same (at N = 64). The results show that increasing the cluster size leads to more pronounced differences in performance among the routing algorithms. This is because, as the cluster size increases, the imbalance in message load within a cluster increases as there will be more inter-cluster messages destined for the interface node. Since the performance difference among the various routing schemes increases with increasing message load imbalance, the routing schemes exhibit greater sensitivity to the cluster size variation.

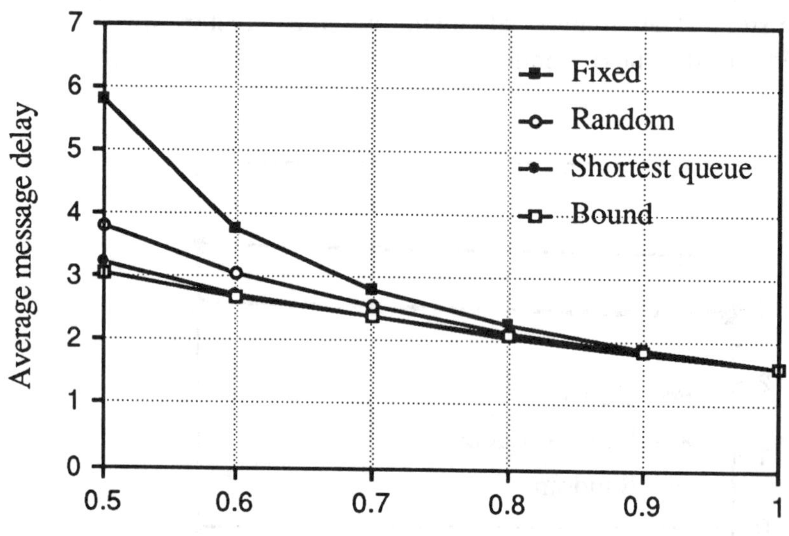

Figure 7.6 Average message delay as a function of communication locality (D = 6, d = 2, λ=1, μ_{CL}=1.5, μ_{NCL}=3)

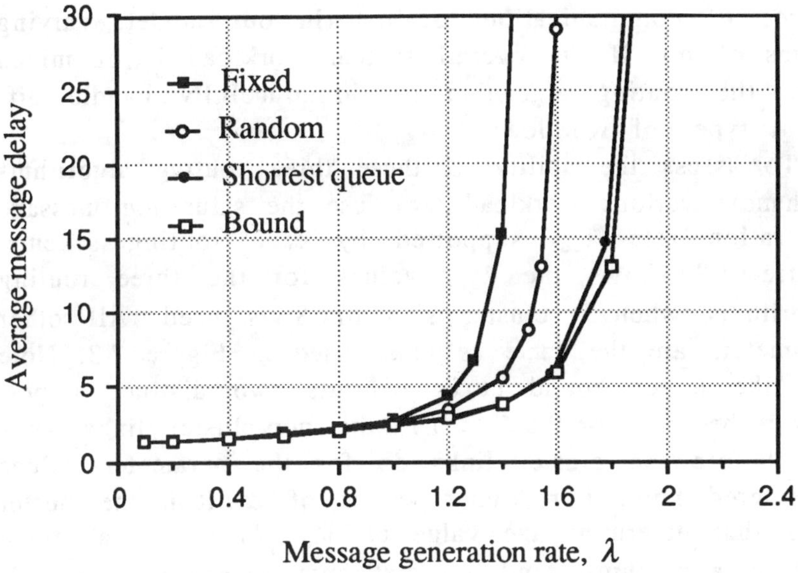

Figure 7.7 Average message delay as a function of message generation rate at each node (D = 6, d = 2, α = 0.7, μ_{CL} = 1.5, μ_{NCL} = 3)

For the parameters given in Figures 7.6 and 7.7, the shortest queue routing provides performance close to the bound values. This suggests that, unless cluster sizes are large and communication locality is weak, there is little to gain by using more complex routing schemes that use global rather than the local network state information.

7.4.4. Saturation Message Generation Rate

In message-passing systems, the computation-communication ratio is an important characteristic of an application [LINT 81]. If an application is computationally intensive, it tends to generate fewer messages (and hence lower network message load). Here, we can model this fact by smaller λ values. On the other hand, a communication-intensive application should be modelled with higher λ values. Furthermore, applications may also vary in their degree of communication locality (in our model, varying values of α). If the overall system workload is of mixed type, the routing algorithm should gracefully handle different types of workload.

To assess the ability of these three routing algorithms to handle various workloads, we use the saturation message generation rate λ_{sat} supported by each routing scheme. Figure 7.8 shows the λ_{sat} values for the three routing algorithms when a cluster size of 8 is used. All other parameters are the same as those used in Figure 7.3. Note that the upper bound curve exhibits two distinct slopes. This is because, for $0.5 \leq \alpha \leq 0.7$, the non-cluster links saturate before the cluster links do for the parameter values considered here. For higher values of α, it is the cluster links that determine the value of λ_{sat}. At $\alpha = 1$, all three routing algorithms tend to distribute message load uniformly over the cluster links, and therefore support the same saturation message generation rate. For other α values, the random routing scheme supports λ_{sat} values that are intermediate between those supported by the fixed routing and the shortest queue routing. In particular, for $0.5 \leq \alpha \leq 0.8$, the fixed routing supports a message generation rate that is approximately half of the corresponding bound value.

Figure 7.9 shows the sensitivity of λ_{sat} to α when the cluster size is changed to 4. The impact of cluster size on λ_{sat} can be seen by comparing Figures 7.8 and 7.9. Since there are more non-cluster links when the cluster size is smaller (for the same system size), λ_{sat} is now essentially determined by when the cluster links saturate. With smaller cluster size, the shortest queue routing tends to support λ_{sat} values that are close to the bound values.

7.4.5. Performance of Retrograde Routing

The structure of the BH/BH network creates an imbalance in cluster link utilization. In particular, the cluster links closer to the interface nodes tend to process more messages

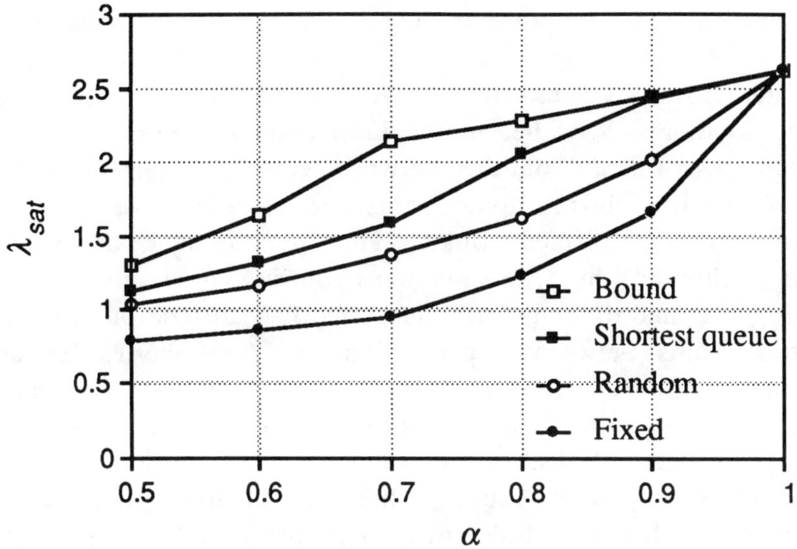

Figure 7.8 Saturation message generation rate as a function of communication locality (D = 6, d = 3, μ_{CL} = 1.5, μ_{NCL} = 3)

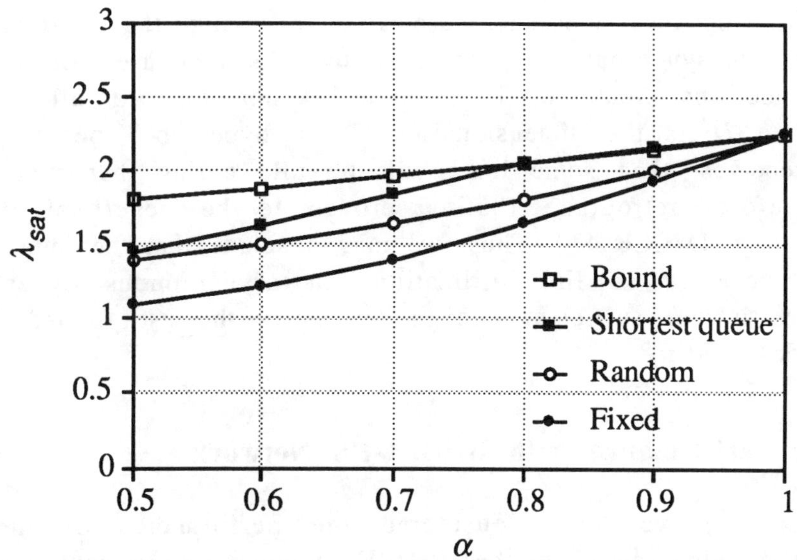

Figure 7.9 Saturation message generation rate as a function of communication locality (D = 6, d = 2, μ_{CL} = 1.5, μ_{NCL} = 3)

than those that are farther away. This tendency increases with decreasing degree of locality in communication (i.e., for decreasing values of α) and increasing cluster size because there will be more inter-cluster messages. The overall performance of the network could be improved by diverting the intra-cluster message traffic away from these heavily utilized links. The performance improvement achieved by the random routing over the fixed routing is mainly due to the effective utilization of all shortest paths between a pair of nodes. The shortest queue routing improves the performance further by basically diverting the intra-cluster message traffic away from the heavily utilized links.

With retrograding routing there is greater potential to balance the network link utilization further. However, this potential advantage has an associated cost - an increase in message path lengths. We have conducted simulation experiments with various parameter values to see if these advantages outweigh the associated costs. In every case, the resulting message delay is much greater than that obtained with the shortest queue routing. The reason is that the network will have to handle increased message traffic because messages are not following the shortest path. In synchronous hypercubes, such as that used in the Connections Machine, if a node cannot forward all D (where D is the dimensionality of the hypercube) messages it receives, then some links will be idle during that cycle. Therefore, retrograde routing proves to be beneficial in this case [MCCR 86]. Thus, we may conclude that the imbalance created in link utilizations in asynchronous hypercubes is not sufficient enough to justify the use of retrograde routing.

7.5. Performance with BH/BH-RS Network

Thus far, we have considered the performance of the routing algorithms in the BH/BH network. Note that the previous discussion also applies to the fault-tolerant HIN with standby-spare nodes, the BH/BH-SI network. In this section, we consider performance implications of these routing algorithms in the other fault-tolerant HIN, the BH/BH-RS network.

As with the BH/BH network, we first present the analysis of bounds on performance (Section 7.5.1) and then discuss the performance of the three routing algorithms (Section 7.5.2).

7.5.1. Analysis of Bounds on Performance

In this section, we derive a bound on the average message delay and an upper bound on the saturation message generation rate (at each node) supported by the BH/BH-RS network.

7.5.1.1. A Bound on Message Delay

Consider a source cluster in the BH/BH-RS network with $N = 2^D$ nodes and a cluster size $n = 2^d$ nodes. In this network, when a node generates an inter-cluster message, it is forwarded to the closest of the two interface nodes. If both the interface nodes are at the same distance, which is the case when d is even, one is selected at random. Note that the behaviour of intra-cluster messages remains the same as that in the BH/BH network. Therefore, the message load due to intra-cluster messages is given by Eq. (7.1).

Let P_s and P_d be the average internode distance traversed by inter-cluster messages within a source cluster and destination cluster, respectively. Then,

$$P_s = \begin{cases} \dfrac{1}{2^d}\left[2\displaystyle\sum_{i=0}^{\frac{d}{2}-1} i\binom{d}{i} + \dfrac{d}{2}\binom{d}{d/2}\right] & \text{if } d \text{ is even} \\[2ex] \dfrac{1}{2^{d-1}}\left[\displaystyle\sum_{i=0}^{\frac{d-1}{2}} i\binom{d}{i}\right] & \text{if } d \text{ is odd} \end{cases}$$

and

$$P_d = \frac{d}{2}$$

The message load due to out-going inter-cluster messages in a source cluster is $2^d(1-\alpha)\lambda P_s$ and that due to incoming inter-cluster messages (i.e., inter-cluster messages whose destination nodes are in the cluster under consideration) is $2^d(1-\alpha)\lambda P_d$.

Therefore,

$$\lambda_{CL} = \alpha\lambda\left(\frac{2^{d-1}}{2^d - 1}\right) + \frac{(1-\alpha)\lambda}{d}\left[P_s + P_d\right]$$

λ_{NCL} is given by Eq. (6.1). Then, R_B^{RS} is given by

$$R_B^{RS} = \alpha\left(\frac{d\,2^{d-1}}{2^d - 1}\right)\Delta_{CL} + (1-\alpha) \times$$
$$\left[\left(P_s + P_d\right)\Delta_{CL} + \left(\frac{(D-d)2^{D-d-1}}{2^{D-d} - 1}\right)\Delta_{NCL}\right]$$

where

$$\Delta_{CL} = \frac{1}{\mu_{CL} - \lambda_{CL}}$$

$$\Delta_{NCL} = \frac{1}{\mu_{NCL} - \lambda_{NCL}}$$

7.5.1.2. Saturation Analysis

As in Section 7.3.2, we can express λ_{sat} by Eq. (7.6). An upper bound on λ_{sat} can be obtained from the analysis of the previous section. It is straightforward to derive the following.

$$\lambda_{sat_{CL}} = \frac{\mu_{CL}}{\alpha\left(\dfrac{2^{d-1}}{2^{d}-1}\right) + \dfrac{(1-\alpha)}{d}\left[P_s + P_d\right]}$$

$$\lambda_{sat_{NCL}} = \frac{\mu_{NCL}\left(2^{D-d}-1\right)}{2^{D-2}(1-\alpha)}$$

7.5.2. Performance Comparison

The performance results for the random routing algorithm were obtained analytically (see Chapter 6). Simulation was used to obtain performance of the remaining two routing algorithms.

7.5.2.1. Principal Comparison

Figure 7.10 depicts the average message delay associated with the three routing algorithms for a network with the following parameters: $\lambda = 1$, $\mu_{CL} = 1.5$, $\mu_{NCL} = 3$, $d = 3$, and $D = 6$ (i.e., network size $N = 64$). The value of α is varied from 0.5 to 1 in steps of 0.1. Note that the parameter values are the same as those used in Figure 7.3. Figure 7.11 shows the average message delay as a function of message generation rate at each node λ for $\alpha = 0.7$ (all other parameters remain the same as in Figure 7.4).

It can be seen from Figures 7.3 and 7.10 that, for the BH/BH-RS network, the difference in performance between the fixed and random routing is substantially less because the message traffic is better balanced in this network. For the BH/BH-RS network, the shortest queue routing provides average message delays better than the bound. This improvement, as discussed in Section 7.3.1, is due to the fact that the bound value was obtained by assuming a random routing algorithm. Since the message load imbalance is not as high as that in the BH/BH (or BH/BH-SI) network, the use of shortest queue routing algorithm results in smaller delays.

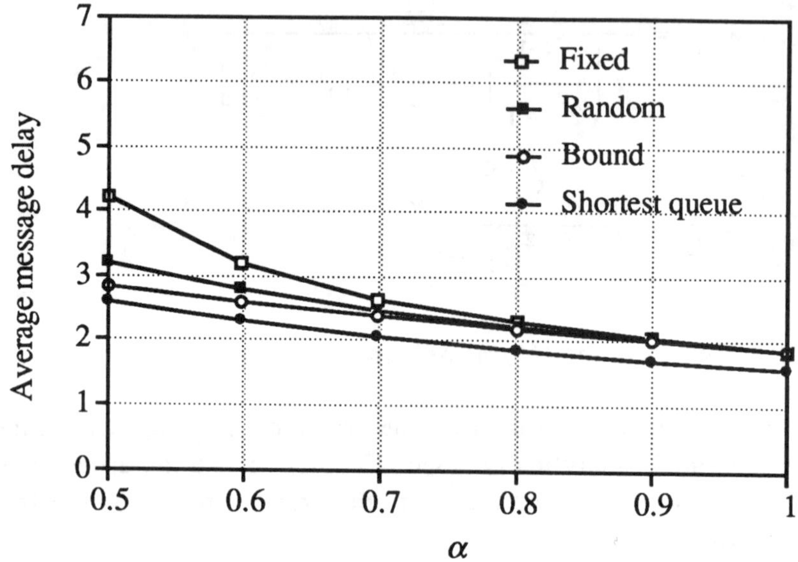

Figure 7.10 Average message delay in the BH/BH-RS network as a function of communication locality (D = 6, d = 3, μ_{CL} = 1.5, μ_{NCL} = 3)

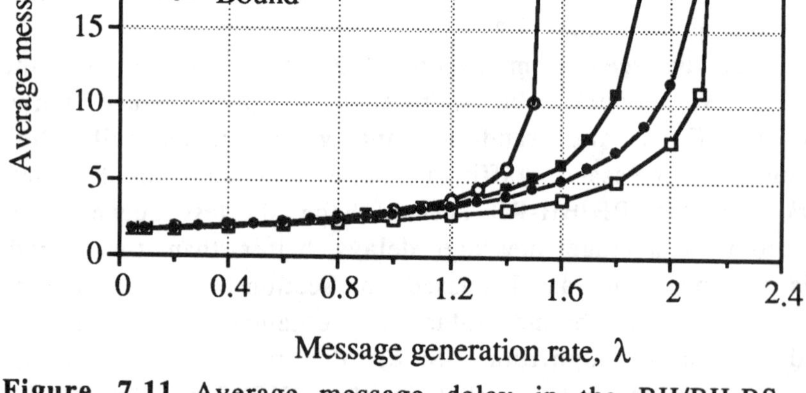

Figure 7.11 Average message delay in the BH/BH-RS network as a function of message generation rate (D = 6, d = 3, μ_{CL} = 1.5, μ_{NCL} = 3)

7.5.2.2. Saturation Message Generation Rate

As in Section 7.4.4, we use λ_{sat} to assess the ability of these three routing algorithms to handle various workloads. Figure 7.12 shows the λ_{sat} values for the three routing algorithms when a cluster size of 8 is used. All other parameters are the same as those used in Figure 7.8. Note that the upper bound curve, in Figure 7.8, for the BH/BH-SI network exhibits two distinct slopes. This is because, for $0.5 \leq \alpha \leq 0.7$, the non-cluster links saturate before the cluster links. This is not the case for the BH/BH-RS network. For higher values of α, it is the cluster links that determine the value of λ_{sat}. At $\alpha = 1$, all three routing algorithms tend to distribute message load uniformly over the cluster links, and therefore support the same saturation message generation rate. For other α values, the random routing scheme supports λ_{sat} values that are closer to those supported by the shortest queue routing. For the BH/BH-RS network, the shortest queue routing provides λ_{sat} values close to the upper limit. These results suggest that a more sophisticated routing scheme that utilizes global rather than the local state information provides only marginal improvement in performance and may not be worthwhile.

7.5.2.3. Performance under Constant Network Cost

Figures 7.13-7.15 show the performance of the three routing schemes under constant network cost (i.e., both the BH/BH and the BH/BH-RS networks use the same number of physical links - see Section 6.5.3.4). The average message delay as a function of communication locality is shown in Figure 7.13. Compared with the performance of the BH/BH network (shown in Figure 7.3), the BH/BH-RS network provides substantial performance improvements, particularly at low α values. These results are similar to those shown in Figure 7.10. Similar observations can be made about the results in Figure 7.14, which gives the average message delay as a function of message generation rate λ.

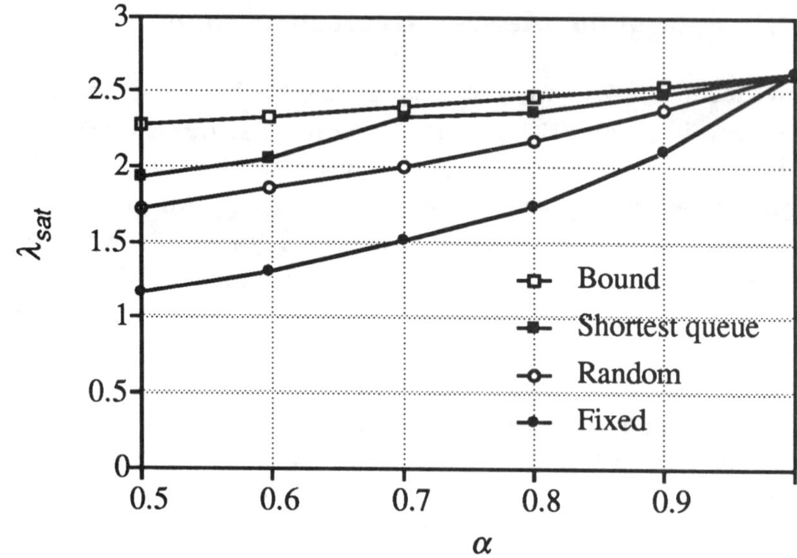

Figure 7.12 Saturation message generation rate supported by the BH/BH-RS network as a function of message generation rate (D = 6, d = 3, μ_{CL} = 1.5, μ_{NCL} = 3)

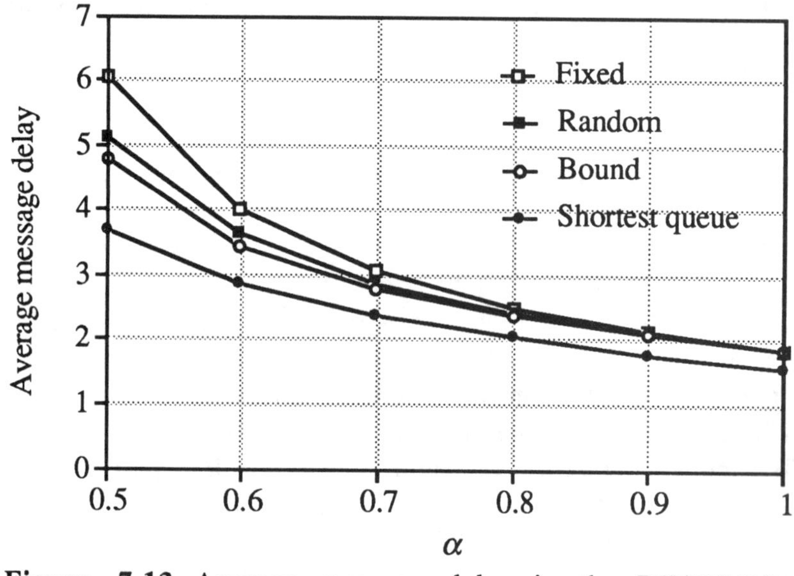

Figure 7.13 Average message delay in the BH/BH-RS network as a function of communication locality (D = 6, d = 3, μ_{CL} = 1.5, μ_{NCL} = 1.5)

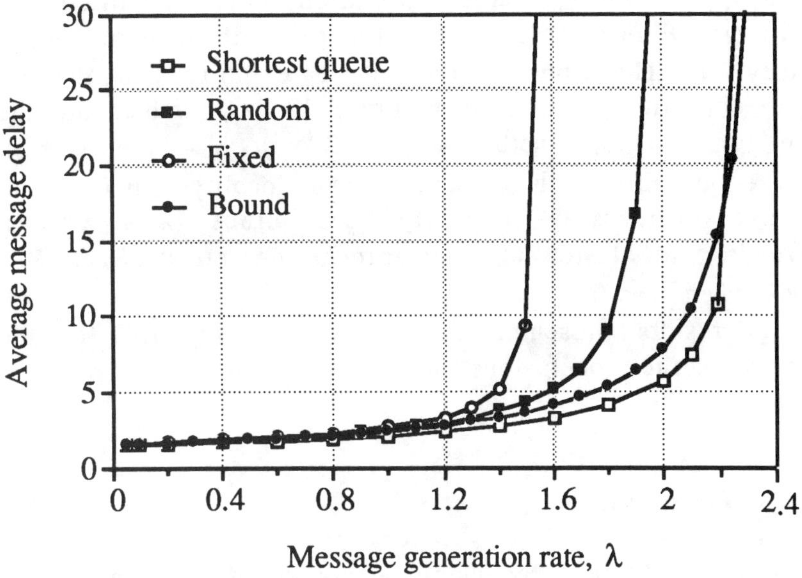

Figure 7.14 Average message delay in the BH/BH-RS network as a function of message generation rate (D = 6, d = 3, μ_{CL} = 1.5, μ_{NCL} = 1.5)

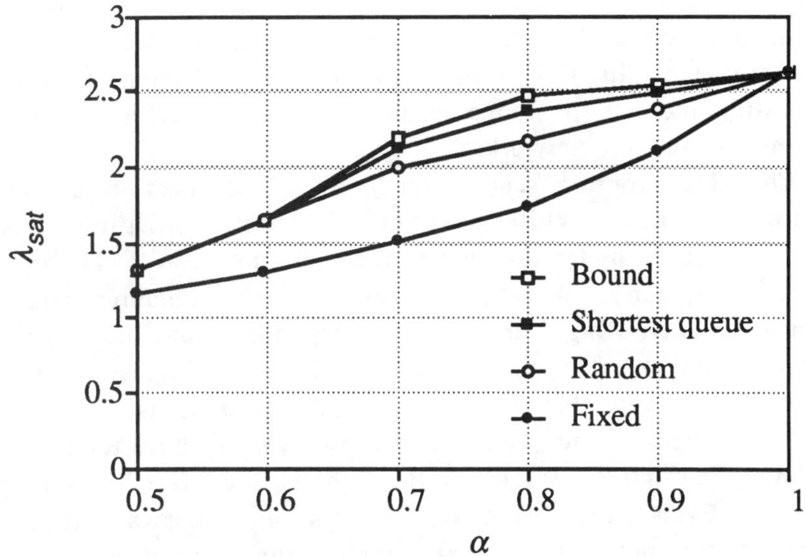

Figure 7.15 Saturation message generation rate supported by the BH/BH-RS network as a function of message generation rate (D = 6, d = 3, μ_{CL} = 1.5, μ_{NCL} = 1.5)

The saturation message generation rates supported are shown in Figure 7.15 as a function of communication locality α. The upper bound curve exhibits two distinct slopes compared to that in Figure 7.12. λ_{sat} values are the same for $\alpha \geq 0.8$, whether μ_{NCL} = 3 or μ_{NCL} = 1.5. This is because, at this high communication locality, cluster link message processing capacity determines λ_{sat} values. However, non-cluster message processing rates affect λ_{sat} values when $\alpha < 0.8$.

The results presented in this section support, for the most part, the conclusions arrived at in the last two sections.

7.6. Conclusions

We have compared, by using a combination of analytical and simulation models, the performance of four routing schemes for hypercube-based hierarchical networks: fixed, random, shortest queue, and retrograde routing. The retrograde routing scheme, which was shown to be effective in synchronous hypercubes, is not found to be useful in asynchronous hypercube networks. The reason is that the imbalance in link utilizations is not sufficient enough to justify the use of longer paths to send messages between the nodes in the network.

The fixed routing scheme tends to utilize links in a non-uniform fashion. While this uneven link utilization may not exist in a hypercube when there is no locality in communication, any deviation from uniform communication results in favouring certain links depending on the source and destination node addresses. This leads to increased message delays and decreased saturation throughputs.

In contrast, the random routing algorithm tends to balance message traffic better than the fixed routing scheme. Even though the random routing takes no knowledge of the network state in making the routing decisions, it provides considerable improvement over the fixed routing scheme. In terms of saturation throughput, the random routing provides substantial improvement over the fixed routing unless there is strong locality in communication.

The shortest queue routing scheme provides the best performance among the routing schemes considered in this study. It provides performance close to the bound values when there is moderate to strong locality in communication. The results show that any improvement obtainable by using a more complex routing scheme that uses global rather than the local network state information should be marginal and may not be worthwhile.

The BH/BH-RS network is much less sensitive to the routing algorithm because this network is a better balanced network than the BH/BH network (and the BH/BH-SI network).

Further Reading

Communication issues in multicomputer networks are discussed in detail in [REED 87]. The discussion in this chapter assumed a store-and-forward protocol, in which message transmission time is proportional to the product of path length and message length. As discussed in Chapter 2, there are other methods that are more efficient; these methods, in some way, can be considered as a cross between packet switching and circuit switching. Such methods include staged circuit switching [ARAN 85, BADR 86] and wormhole routing [DALL 86b, DALL 90a]. See also [DALL 90b] for a different approach.

The discussion in this chapter assumed unbounded number of buffers at each node. However, when the number of buffers is finite, there is a possibility of deadlock in multicomputer networks. There are several ways in which this problem can solved. In Chapter 5 we have employed a deadlock avoidance technique proposed by Merlin and Schweitzer [MERL 80]. Other references include [DALL 86a], [GELE 81], and [GOPA 85].

Since reducing communication overhead is important in improving performance of multicomputer systems, there have been efforts for efficient support of message routing in hardware. The reader is referred to the following for further information: [HSU 90], [RAMA 90], [NUGE 88].

Acknowledgement

Material presented in this chapter is partly based on [DAND 90a] and [DAND 90b].

References

[ARAN 85] M. Arango, H. G. Badr, and D. Gelernter, "Staged Circuit Switching," *IEEE Trans. Computers*, Vol. C-34, No. 2, February 1985, pp. 174-180.

[BADR 86] H. G. Badr, D. Gelernter, and S. Podar, "An Adaptive Communications Protocol for Network Computers," *Performance Evaluation*, Vol. 6, March 1986, pp. 35-51.

[DALL 86a] W. J. Dally and C. L. Seitz, "Deadlock-free Message Routing in Multiprocessor Interconnection Networks," *IEEE Trans. Computers*, Vol. C-36, No. 5, May 1987, pp. 547-553.

[DALL 86b] W. J. Dally and C. L. Seitz, "The Torus Routing Chip," *J. Distributed Computing*, Vol. 1, No. 3, 1986, pp. 187-196.

[DALL 90a] W. J. Dally, "Performance Analysis of *k*-ary *n*-cube Interconnection Networks," *IEEE Trans. Computers*, Vol. C-39, No. 6, June 1990, pp. 775-785.

[DALL 90b] W. J. Dally, "Virtual-Channel Flow Control," *Proc. 17th Int. Symp. Computer Architecture*, June 1990, Seattle, Washington, pp. 60-68.

[DAND 90a] S. P. Dandamudi, "A Performance Comparison of Routing Algorithms for Hierarchical Hypercube Multicomputer Networks," *Proc. 1990 Int. Conf. Parallel Processing*, 1990, Vol. 1, pp. 281-285.

[DAND 90b] S. P. Dandamudi, "Performance Analysis of Fault-Tolerant Hierarchical Hypercube Multicomputer Networks," Research Note, School of Computer Science,

Carleton University, Ottawa, Ontario K1S 5B6, Canada, 1990.

[GELE 81] D. Gelernter, "A DAG-Based Algorithm for Prevention of Store-and-Forward Deadlock in Packet Networks," *IEEE Trans. Computers*, Vol. C-30, No. 10, October 1981, pp. 709-715.

[GOPA 81] G. Gopal and J. W. Wong, "Prevention of Store-and-Forward Deadlock in Computer Networks," *IEEE Trans. Communications*, Vol. COM-33, No. 12, December 1981, pp. 1258-1264.

[GOPA 85] I. S. Gopal, "Delay Analysis of Broadcast Routing in Packet-Switching Networks," *IEEE Trans. Computers*, Vol. C-30, 1981, pp. 915-922.

[HILL 85] W. D. Hillis, The Connection Machine, MIT Press, Cambridge, MA.,1985.

[HSU 90] J. M. Hsu and P. Banerjee, "Hardware Support for Message Routing in a Distributed Memory Multi-computer" *Proc. 1990 Int. Conf. Parallel Processing*, 1990, Vol. 1, pp. 508-515.

[KLEI 75] L. Kleinrock, *Queueing Systems:* Volume 1, Wiley, New York, 1975.

[KLEI 76] L. Kleinrock, *Queueing Systems:* Volume 2, Wiley, New York, 1976.

[LINT 81] B. Lint and T. Agerwala, "Communication Issues in the Design and Analysis of Parallel Algorithms," *IEEE Trans. Software Engineering*, Vol. SE-7, 1981, pp. 174-188.

[MCCR 86] C. D. McCrosky, "Message Passing in Synchronous Hypercubes," Tech. Rep. 86-4, Department of Computational Science, University of Saskatchewan, Saskatoon, 1986 (to appear in *Computer System Science and Engineering*).

[MERL 80] P. M. Merlin and P. J. Schweitzer, "Deadlock Avoidance in Store-and-Forward Networks – I: Store-and-Forward Deadlock," *IEEE Trans. Communications*, Vol. COM-28, No. 3, March 1980, pp. 345-354.

[NUGE 88] S. F. Nugent, "The iPSC/2 Direct-Connect Communications Technology," *Proc. Third Conf. Hypercube Concurrent Computers and Applications*, January 1988, Pasadena, California, Vol. I, pp. 51-60.

[RAMA 90] U. Ramachandran, M. Solomon, and M. K. Vernon, "Hardware Support for Interprocess Communication," *IEEE Trans. Parallel and Distributed Processing*, Vol. 1, No. 3, July 1990, pp. 318-329.

[REED 87] D. A. Reed and R. M. Fujimoto, *Multicomputer Networks: Message-Based Parallel Processing*, MIT Press, Cambridge, MA., 1987.

8

Summary and Conclusions

8.1 Summary

The interconnection network is an important component of a parallel processing system. As the system size increases, the interconnection network becomes the dominant component in terms of both system cost and overall system performance. Therefore, designing a cost-effective interconnection network is of paramount importance in designing large-scale parallel systems.

In previous chapters we have seen the effectiveness of a hierarchical organization in designing interconnection networks for large multicomputer systems. As shown in Chapter 3, a well-designed hierarchical interconnection network tends to decrease link cost substantially while moderately increasing the average message delays. It should, however, be noted that hierarchical interconnection networks are useful only when there is communication locality. We have also seen that hierarchical interconnection networks allow different network topologies to be integrated so that computations exhibiting different communication patterns can be mapped to the appropriate subnetwork. This is an important asset in designing general purpose multicomputer systems, which are expected to efficiently support a wide range of applications.

In designing a hierarchical interconnection network, there are two important design issues: the number of levels in the hierarchy and the optimum cluster size. Clearly, the resolution of these issues depends on the characteristics of the workload that the hierarchical interconnection network is going to support. In Chapter 4 we have shown that, for hypercube-based networks, the optimum cluster size is either 4 or 8 when a two-level hierarchy is used. This is true for a wide range of system sizes and a variety of communication locality characteristics. Note, however, that these conclusions are based on a cost-benefit ratio that uses the number of links as the cost measure and the average internode distance as the performance measure. The results have shown that the impact of various locality characterizations is relatively minor compared to the impact of number of links in the network. If our goal were to minimize the link cost of a two-level hierarchical interconnection network, we essentially derive the same conclusions (i.e., optimum cluster size values of 4 or 8).

Performance in the presence of hot-spots has been studied in Chapter 5 for hypercube-based networks. This study indicates that, just like the standard binary hypercube, hierarchical interconnection networks exhibit extreme sensitivity to hot-spot traffic. Note that the actual saturation throughputs supported by hierarchical interconnection networks are smaller than those supported by the hypercube network owing to reduced number of links in the network. However, we have shown that both hardware combining and software combining schemes are effective in reducing the adverse effects of hot-spot contention on system performance. This has been shown to be the case even when the number of buffers is finite. Also, it appears that, when there are multiple paths, the routing algorithm plays an important role in improving system performance. In particular, the use of adaptive routing algorithms results in substantial performance improvements.

Fault-tolerance and reliability issues are important for large-scale multicomputer systems. These issues for binary hypercube-based hierarchical interconnection networks are considered in Chapter 6. It has been shown, by means of simulation, that the reliabilities of binary hypercube-based hierarchical interconnection networks are intermediate between the two extremes provided by the bidirectional ring and complete connection networks. However, it has been shown that hierarchical network reliability can be improved by employing the standard fault-tolerance techniques.

Routing algorithms for binary hypercube-based hierarchical interconnection networks are considered in Chapter 7. Four routing algorithms have been considered: fixed, random, shortest queue, and retrograde routing. The first two algorithms are oblivious algorithms in that routing decisions are independent of the network state. The last two are adaptive algorithms that make routing decisions dependent on the network state. Further, only the first three algorithms use shortest path routing. (Note that a store-and-forward protocol has been assumed in this comparison.)

The retrograde routing, which has been shown to be effective in synchronous hypercubes, is not found to be useful for asynchronous hypercube networks. The reason is that the imbalance in link utilizations is not sufficient enough to justify the use of longer paths to send messages between the nodes in the network.

The fixed routing results in an unacceptable performance in most cases because of its tendency to favour certain links. The random routing provides substantially better performance than the fixed routing. This is mainly due to the fact that this routing scheme eliminates the non-uniform utilization of links by the fixed routing scheme. The shortest queue routing, owing to its adaptive nature, provides performance that is close to the maximum attainable.

8.2. Further Research

We have established the efficacy of the hierarchical interconnection networks for interconnecting large numbers of processors in a multicomputer system. The work presented in this monograph can be extended in several directions. Here we list a few of them.

Problem decomposition and mapping is an important aspect of parallel processing that can seriously impact the overall "observed" performance. For example, a bad mapping could actually result in decreased speedups. Several researchers have considered this problem in the context of binary hypercubes. However, these strategies are not directly applicable to hypercube-based hierarchical interconnection networks because two nodes that appear as neighbours in the hypercube may not be neighbours in the corresponding hierarchical network. While some problems such as finding the minimum of a set of elements can be easily mapped without incurring extra message passing steps, much work needs to be done in this area.

The use of circuit switching or wormhole routing could improve the performance of hierarchical interconnection networks because longer message path lengths may not have as serious an impact on performance as is the case with the packet switching protocol. Even when wormhole routing is employed, communication locality will still be important to minimize circuit blocking. The performance implications of these routing protocols need further investigations.

Another application of the hierarchical organization used here is to combine the shared-memory and distributed-memory architectures to construct a hybrid system. For example, each cluster of, say, 16 processors can be implemented as a shared-memory system. Such hybrid systems can potentially exploit the advantages associated with shared-memory and message-passing architectures. An implication is that the limitations on system expansion associated with shared-memory systems can be removed.

8.3. Concluding Remarks

We believe that future parallel processing systems will essentially be hybrid systems such as the one mentioned here. Hierarchical organizations play an important role in building these hybrid systems.

Increasingly, we will also see exploitation of dataflow techniques in implementing large-scale parallel systems. In essence it will be increasingly difficult to classify future parallel systems as multicomputers, multiprocessors etc.

Experience in designing and using parallel systems has essentially given us a list of things that we should avoid in future system designs. As a result we can expect future parallel systems to be much more efficient and useful.

INDEX

ELLIS HORWOOD SERIES IN COMPUTERS AND THEIR APPLICATIONS

Series Editor: IAN CHIVERS, Senior Analyst, The Computer Centre, King's College, London, and formerly Senior Programmer and Analyst, Imperial College of Science and Technology, University of London

Lucas, R.	DATABASE APPLICATIONS USING PROLOG
Lucas, A.	DESKTOP PUBLISHING
Maddix, F.	HUMAN–COMPUTER INTERACTION: Theory and Practice
Maddix, F. & Morgan, G.	SYSTEMS SOFTWARE
Matthews, J.J.	FORTH
Michalewicz, Z.	STATISTICAL AND SCIENTIFIC DATABASES
Millington, D.	SYSTEMS ANALYSIS AND DESIGN FOR COMPUTER APPLICATIONS
Moseley, L.G., Sharp, J.A. & Salenieks, P.	PASCAL IN PRACTICE
Moylan, P.	ASSEMBLY LANGUAGE FOR ENGINEERS
Narayanan, A. & Sharkey, N.E.	AN INTRODUCTION TO LISP
Parrington, N. & Roper, M.	UNDERSTANDING SOFTWARE TESTING
Paterson, A.	OFFICE SYSTEMS
Phillips, C. & Cornelius, B.J.	COMPUTATIONAL NUMERICAL METHODS
Rahtz, S.P.Q.	INFORMATION TECHNOLOGY IN THE HUMANITIES
Ramsden, E.	MICROCOMPUTERS IN EDUCATION 2
Rubin, T.	USER INTERFACE DESIGN FOR COMPUTER SYSTEMS
Rudd, A.S.	PRACTICAL USAGE OF ISPF DIALOG MANAGER
Rudd, A.S.	PRACTICAL USAGE OF REXX
Rudd, A.S.	IMPLEMENTING PRACTICAL DB2 APPLICATIONS
de Saram, H.	PROGRAMMING IN MICRO-PROLOG
Savic, D.	OBJECT-ORIENTED PROGRAMMING WITH SMALLTALK/V
Schirmer, C.	PROGRAMMING IN C FOR UNIX
Schofield, C.F.	OPTIMIZING FORTRAN PROGRAMS
Semmens, L. & Allen, P.	Z FOR SOFTWARE ENGINEERS
Sharp, J.A.	DATA FLOW COMPUTING
Sherif, M.A.	DATABASE PROJECTS
Smith, D. & Sage, M.	EDUCATION AND THE INFORMATION SOCIETY
Smith, J.M & Stutely, R.	SGML
Späth, H.	CLUSTER ANALYSIS ALGORITHMS
Späth, H.	CLUSTER DISSECTION AND ANALYSIS
Stratford-Collins, P.	ADA
Teunissen, W.J. & van den Bos, J.	3D INTERACTIVE COMPUTER GRAPHICS
Tizzard, K.	C FOR PROFESSIONAL PROGRAMMERS
Turner, S.J.	AN INTRODUCTION TO COMPILER DESIGN
Tsuji, T.	OPTIMIZING SCHEMES FOR STRUCTURED PROGRAMMING LANGUAGE PROCESSORS
Wexler, J.	CONCURRENT PROGRAMMING IN OCCAM 2
Whiddett, R.J.	CONCURRENT PROGRAMMING FOR SOFTWARE ENGINEERS
Whiddett, R.J., Berry, R.E., Blair, G.S., Hurley, P.N., Nicol, P.J. & Muir, S.J.	UNIX
Xu, Duan-Zheng	COMPUTER ANALYSIS OF SEQUENTIAL MEDICAL TRIALS
Yannakoudakis, E.J. & Hutton, P.J.	SPEECH SYNTHESIS AND RECOGNITION SYSTEMS
Zech, R.	FORTH FOR THE PROFESSIONAL

Computer Communications and Networking

Currie, W.S.	LANS EXPLAINED
Deasington, R.J.	A PRACTICAL GUIDE TO COMPUTER COMMUNICATIONS AND NETWORKING, 2nd Edition
Deasington, R.J.	X.25 EXPLAINED, 2nd Edition
Henshall, J. & Shaw, S.	OSI EXPLAINED, 2nd Edition
Kauffels, F.-J.	PRACTICAL LANS ANALYSED
Kauffels, F.-J.	PRACTICAL NETWORKS ANALYSED
Kauffels, F.-J.	UNDERSTANDING DATA COMMUNICATIONS
Muftic, S.	SECURITY MECHANISMS FOR COMPUTER NETWORKS